JAMES LANE ALLEN

James Lane Allen

JAMES LANE ALLEN

AND

THE GENTEEL TRADITION

BY

GRANT C. KNIGHT *cochran* 1893-

ASSOCIATE PROFESSOR OF ENGLISH
UNIVERSITY OF KENTUCKY

Chapel Hill
THE UNIVERSITY OF NORTH CAROLINA PRESS
1935

PRINTED IN THE UNITED STATES OF AMERICA BY THE SEEMAN PRINTERY
DURHAM, N. C., AND BOUND BY L. H. JENKINS, INC., RICHMOND, VA.

To

GEORGE FOLSOM GRANBERRY

PREFACE

I AM NOT one of those who believe that dead authors should be disinterred. Literary graveyards deserve respect as well as do other burial grounds, and once a writer and his books have completely and rightfully passed into oblivion they should for the sake of decency be permitted to remain there. But it sometimes happens that headstones are placed over authors who have prematurely been laid away, authors who because of some shift in taste or spread of prejudice have been buried under epitaphs more or less kind and then unjustly forgotten. To resurrect such authors and to attempt to confer upon them that bit of immortality which they claim becomes not the duty of a pedant, therefore, but the pleasure of the student of literature who, not carried away by the high wind of contemporary opinion, wishes to assess calmly and independently the values of the men who have created our letters. In doing so he often discovers that second and even third-rate authors are not only good reading but also of lasting importance for anyone who wishes to trace the development of our national culture.

James Lane Allen was accustomed to say that if his biography were written he preferred that it should be done by one who was neither his friend nor his foe. In that respect I am well qualified to set forth the story of his career. I never saw Mr. Allen, had no personal relation with him, had read but one of his novels before beginning my investigation of his worth, and came from a state several hundred miles distant from the Bluegrass region of Kentucky. If I had any feeling at all about him it was one approaching condescension, for I had been disappointed in *The Choir Invisible* and had been taught that he was sentimental to the point of sweetness and romantic to the border of unreality. As I proceeded in my reading, however, I found that I must revise my first impression, that Allen was, because of his place in the literature of his time and because of his ability, a figure of considerable significance, and because of his character, a gentleman whom I could admire. It became apparent that he had been, for years, ranked by the representative critics of an epoch as second to Hawthorne among our novelists; and although that judgment will never be voiced again, an understanding of why it was once prevalent is of use to American scholarship. It became apparent, too, that he had been a popular success, but not merely that: he had also served to introduce certain aspects of European realism to American fiction; he had written the first good southern defense of Darwinism in the history of the novel; he had employed anthropology in a striking symbolical novel which had horrified part of his public and puzzled the remainder; he had given us a few imperishable short stories; he had been the last champion of the Genteel Tradition. When that is said I must add that I nurse no delusions as to his greatness. As a writer he was never of the first class. But the question of why he was once elevated to that class and why he was later removed from the seats of the elect is one, it seems to me, which asks a full and fair answer.

As a man Allen illustrated the best traits of that American "rugged individualism" which has too often been the cloak for everything but righteousness: he stood stalwartly, almost fanatically, upon his own feet, treading the way from poverty and obscurity to fame and moderate wealth with but a minimum of aid from others, taking from no one what he could not feel that he had earned and giving to no one what he could not honorably part with; seeking no special favors, no expedient friends; refusing to roll logs for the influential; embodying that conservatism which gives the South its social tone—a conservatism sometimes supported by too much violence and too much bigotry but a force, nevertheless, which more than one impartial observer believes indispensable to the working out of the American experiment. In admiration I resolved that Allen should have the kind of biography he would have wished, one candid, unbiased, and, as far as I could make it, sensible. Not that I should surrender my critical standards to his: many of the opinions expressed in this book would have hurt him deeply. But rather, that his dignity and courage called for a volume which would not follow the fashion too common for the past ten years—the fashion which demanded that the chief purpose should be not to reveal the subject but to demonstrate what a clever iconoclast the biographer was, how he could prove that all black is white and all white black, that all swans are geese, and that Freud had said the last word on the comprehension of human personality. Such a fashion could tailor no clothes to fit James Lane Allen. One can no more honestly invent a melodramatic theory to explain him and his writings than one can honestly invent a melodramatic episode to make his record colorful.

Finally, let me declare plainly that although I have sought to define and to defend the Genteel Tradition I by no means uphold it or long for its return as a paramount influence upon our literature. I have intended only to assert that the Tradition had and has its good uses and that the genteel writers were not so silly and so futile as rebellious critics of the Coolidge era proclaimed. The genteel writers were extremists and therefore liable to the verdict which history always passes upon their kind: that they were blind to certain facets of truth and beauty against which no artist should close his eyes. But American literature has not lacked extremists in each decade, and it is less than reasonable to reserve our bitterest mockery for those of a particular generation. I am impatient for the time to come when criticism will treat such diverse writers as Allen and Howells, Bodenheim and Hecht with an even hand. So essential is good taste to the preservation of civilization that I am confident the genteel writers— and their Tradition was founded upon good taste—will some day have a larger measure of appreciation. Among them, with all his imperfections, will be James Lane Allen.

Since this is the first full-length biography of James Lane Allen it was necessary to go often to primary sources which the general reader cannot consult; some, indeed, can no longer be consulted. I used chiefly: (1) Allen's fragmentary attempts to write an autobiography; (2) his few printed autobiographical statements, the principal ones being found in prefaces to *Flute and Violin* (1900 edition in the United States and in subsequent editions), to *A Kentucky Cardinal and Aftermath* (1900 edition), and to *The Landmark*, and in the essay on Henry Mills Alden (see Bibliography for 1919); (3) his letters; (4) reference articles, doubtless based upon information supplied by Allen, in such works as *Who's Who in America*, cyclopedias, anthologies, and textbooks; (5) magazine articles about him, inasmuch as many critics responded to the public wish to know more of a popular author's life; (6) the notes, letters, journals, souvenirs, and odds and ends found in two of his trunks, now the property of the city of Lexington, Kentucky; (7) his books and friends, especially important in view of Allen's reticence about himself and therefore studied for some seven years; (8) statements by relatives and associates. The main authorities consulted have been listed more specifically by chapters under the heading of "Notes on Sources."

In the years spent in gathering material for this biography I have met only with kindness and interest from those to whom I had to go for information, and to those acquaintances and associates and relatives of Allen I owe a debt which no printed statement can repay. Especially am I grateful for the help given me by George Folsom Granberry, Allen's closest friend and literary executor; by Mrs. Frank Gentry, Allen's last surviving niece; by Superintendent M. A. Cassidy of the Lexington public schools; by John Wilson Townsend, who generously turned over to me material which he had collected and who was ever ready with encouragement; and by Professor R. L. Rusk of Columbia University, who read parts of the manuscript and made valuable suggestions. Others to whom I must give my thanks are Miss Florence Dillard, Mrs. W. T. Lafferty, and W. H. Townsend, of Lexington, Kentucky; Henry van Dyke, Sir Edmund Gosse, Isaac F. Marcosson, Mrs. Sue Porter Heatwole, Dr. Charles Parkhurst, T. S. Jones, Jr., Dr. William B. Smith, Ellen Glasgow, Professors Fred Lewis Pattee, Arthur Hobson Quinn, and John Herbert Nelson; Walter K. Patterson, Arthur Bartlett Maurice, James H. Stover, Joseph B. Gilder, Cale Young Rice, Alice Hegan Rice, Richard Burton, Dr. Rolfe Floyd, Francis H. Bangs, Orson Lowell, George Fox, and R. Dalverny, of Le Havre, France. I note with sorrow that it is too late for several of those whose names I have listed to read this acknowledgment of my debt to them.

GRANT C. KNIGHT

Lake Junaluska, North Carolina
August, 1934

TABLE OF CONTENTS

JAMES LANE ALLEN

The progress of an artist is a continual self-sacrifice, a continual extinction of personality.

—T. S. Eliot, *The Sacred Wood.*

CHAPTER I
PRELIMINARY YEARS

In 1849 it would not have been much of an exaggeration to have said that all good Kentuckians hoped to go to the Bluegrass region of their native state when they died. That broad central plateau in Kentucky was to them literally, as it had been to their pioneer fathers, a promised land upon which their hearts were set with an affection that admitted no change. To be born anywhere in Kentucky was a privilege, but to be born in the Bluegrass was to be especially favored of providence, and though destiny might arrange one's birth in another section of the dark and bloody ground yet it could not prevent one from dreaming of the time when he might own acres of the chosen rich soil or retire to live amid the blessings of the Bluegrass capital, Lexington. Dwellers on this plateau believed their country was God's very footstool and said so in those exact words, nor could a traveler from abroad or a visitor from any other part of the state persuade them to any opinion which would deny that the Bluegrass was the most beautiful part of the whole world.

An outsider on his first entrance into this region might for a time have been at a loss to account for this unusual sectional pride, which has by no means vanished from the speech of the present generation of Kentuckians. The landscape offers no spectacular attractions. The mountain ranges which bestow loveliness and majesty upon the sister states of North Carolina, Tennessee, Virginia, and Maryland do not penetrate the Bluegrass; its average elevation is between nine hundred and a thousand feet, and it has no hills or waterfalls worthy of special mention. The Kentucky River, it is true, cuts its circuitous way through a gorge whose cliffs parade a pageant of beauty in spring and autumn, but the river was, with the exception of its appeal to hunting instincts, little in the mind of the Kentuckian of 1849. It was upon the rolling pastures that his eyes liked to rest; it was down the fine pikes, fragrant with honeysuckle, colorful with redbud, trumpet-vine, and dogwood, shaded by elms and locusts and oaks that he liked to ride at a slow canter, while his thoughts swelled with the realization that this was his own, his native land. For him it needed no peaks, no lakes, no valleys; he was content with its soft contours, its blue sky, its golden haze. The man of this section loved those swells and falls of land covered with luxuriant grass trampled by his sheep and cows and, above all, by his horses. Everything was quiet, serene, and plentiful so far as Mother Nature was concerned. The limestone soil nourished abundant crops as well as the grass which gave the country its name, and to the agricultural society it supported want in its sharp sense was almost unknown.

This land of unbroken verdure, of forests, lawns, lanes, turnpikes, fields of grain and hemp, brooks and creeks and ponds, flocks and herds and paddocks, this land of natural repose, of material ease, of tranquil beauty, exerted a peculiar charm upon its inhabitants. Certainly their immediate ancestors had been roving enough in character, but once settled in the Bluegrass the Anglo-Saxon stock put down tenacious roots and grew from the soil like a plant. The characteristics of the landscape came, in time, almost to dominate the characteristics of its population; its meadows and tilled fields were so English in detail that the American seemed to revert to his English type, to cling to English social customs, to revive that passion for the land which was so marked a trait of the English country squire. Kentucky, too, had its country gentry, living in Georgian houses, entertaining with a hospitality sometimes too lavish, devoted to sport, tory in politics but democratic in behavior, fiercely assertive of individual rights, and covetous of privacy. The Kentucky gentleman took life much more easily than did his Yankee relative. Whereas New England or Pennsylvania children had been taught for two centuries that idleness was a vice, the Kentucky boy of family was instructed to live elegantly, to remember that a gentleman delegated as much work as possible to subordinates; the girl was reminded that her supreme virtues were goodness and beauty, and it was not infrequently the boast of a Kentucky belle before the Civil War that she never walked outside her garden—there was always a carriage with a slave to drive for her.

The man who owned little land may have looked with envy upon the well-to-do landowner, but he did not allow that envy to come too near the surface. Since the population of the Bluegrass in the forties and fifties was, as a whole, mid-western rather than southern in its manners and in the matter of social distinctions, the small landowner made it a point to hold his head as high as that of his richer neighbor. And he could do so, especially if he were allied to the ever-important "good family." He did not, because of any need to do manual labor, lose caste; he certainly lost the coveted leisure of the gentleman, but in a section where the pioneer ideology was actual and the genuinely southern feeling (that is, the feeling of a Virginian or a Carolinian) was present mainly as a wish, he might still think of himself as belonging to the aristocracy and as being only temporarily shut off from some of the higher privileges. Economics triumphed over any attempt to establish an artificial class system, so that manual labor was quite consistent with membership in one of the better families. Birth, not fortune, determined the extent of the aristocracy. To be sure, people who gave their minds to reflection upon gentility were not likely to overwork with hands and arms, even when there was good reason for their doing so. But they were a vital people, all the more so, perhaps, because of their refusal to develop a harsh competitive system of any kind, by their unwillingness to work themselves to death for someone else even if well-paid for so doing. Life was made an occasion for living. These people, rich or poor, were bent upon enjoyment of their earth, of all that they could put into it and get out of it, and not greatly troubled whether in doing so they went to Heaven or went to Hell. Religion was, to be sure, the cause of public debates, or bitter schisms, of baptisms in creeks and ponds, of decorous worship, but it did not greatly interfere with a free plunge into all the red-blooded pleasures within reach, pleasures most keen when shared with friends. Spring races (much slower in 1849 than today), summer barbecues, autumnal fairs, picnics in the greenwoods to the music of fiddles, venison suppers, court days, Christmas festivities when the entire land was blue with the smoke from smokehouses, duels, shootings, stabbings, frank drunkenness and frank profanity—these embroidered the texture of an agrarian society essentially romantic and peaceful but dangerous when aroused to combat, a society whose men were by actual measurement taller and broader than those of any other state save Tennessee and whose women have always been looked at admiringly.

The traditions of these people were chiefly those of provincial England of the eighteenth century, and in these traditions family prestige bulked large. To belong to one of the best families was to have a distinction that could arrive through no other circumstance. Achievement counted for less than birth, although achievement might lay the foundation for a good family and certainly a good family might make a name for itself in ways other than the social usages. As in England, the preferred career was that of service to the state; the ambitious Kentucky gentleman read law, entered politics, and practised oratory in the hope of going to Congress. Painting, literature, science, music were neglected, almost scorned by the many. The Waverley novels were read, it is true, and so was the poetry of Byron, because they ministered to a taste for chivalry and tempestuous expression respectively, but the Bluegrass youth of antebellum days who attempted to write novels or verse was likely to be discouraged if not shunned. The landowner might name his daughter after one of Sir Walter's heroines or send his architect abroad to copy the plan of Newstead Abbey, but he turned his own urge for expression into the channel of political speech-making and apprenticed his son to Blackstone. Generally speaking, the art of the Bluegrass found its outlet in the building of houses that fitted the scene; science was made useful in stock-breeding and in farming; literature was converted into shelved books to be read occasionally; and music was left to blacks who sang while they toiled and who danced behind many a small log cabin after the sun had gone down.

The heart of the Bluegrass region was Lexington, called by its citizens "the Athens of the West." It had some claim to that appellation. Founded in 1775 and named for the Massachusetts town in which minute-men had died, the Kentucky Lexington had grown rapidly for thirty years after the Revolution; then the development of steamboat traffic on the Ohio River had carried commercial supremacy to Cincinnati; but the coming of railroads in the middle of the nineteenth century had restored some of its lost prosperity. In 1849 its population was about nine thousand, of which approximately one half were Negroes. To its markets farmers brought horses, mules, cattle, hogs, and sheep for sale or exchange, while the many fields of hemp supported fifteen establishments in which that commodity was prepared for eastern factories. It was not in its commercial activities, however, or in its eleven well-built churches or in its two daily newspapers that Lexington took the greatest satisfaction. It reflected most complacently about its cultural past, the galaxy of notable men who had once moved through its streets, its former leadership in the theatre and in the appreciation of literature—literature always being defined as something written by a Greek, a Roman, or an Englishman. It boasted of the fact that the fascinating Aaron Burr, revolving schemes for a western empire of which Kentucky might have been a province, had stopped at Postlethwaite's Tavern; so had Lafayette during his visit in 1825. In Lexington Matthew Jouett, a pupil of Gilbert Stuart, had painted portraits of local gentlefolk; Joel Hart had produced his sculptures; Constantin Rafinesque had taught botany; Edward West had navigated on the Town Branch the first steamboat. From Lexington John Breckinridge had gone to Washington to be Jefferson's attorney-general. Henry Clay, pride of American Whiggism, lived just outside Lexington and often visited its courthouse when Congress was not in session; now he was brooding over his late defeat for the presidency of the United States. In Lexington a newspaper had been published as early as 1787; a magazine, in 1803; a college was founded in 1798; a theater was built at the opening of the nineteenth century. With its place in history thus assured and with proof of its wealth apparent in handsome residences and well-dressed citizens, Lexington felt pretty well pleased with itself. Louisville might surpass it in size and St. Louis in contemporary culture, but they could not filch from the Bluegrass city its memory of the time when it had been the metropolis of the West.[1]

In this stronghold of agrarianism, this land in which simplicity and passion, evangelicalism and hedonism mingled in strange combinations, James Lane Allen was born backward and near midnight on the twenty-first of December, 1849, the shortest day in the year. The Allen house, a small

[1] Those interested in the sources of this study will find them listed, by chapters, beginning on p. 279 below.

frame structure surrounded by trees that shut off a view of the Versailles Pike, stood near a lane now called the Parker's Mill Road. Opposite the house and across the road was a country school-building; nearly five miles away to the east the spire of St. Peter's and the reflection of the oil street lamps of Lexington would have been visible if the bosky swells of land so characteristic of the Bluegrass could have been leveled. Several days before the birth of this, his seventh child, the father had, like a true country squire, gone fox-hunting along the Kentucky River, some twenty miles away. This seeming indifference to the advent of his third son had one consequence which that son, grown to manhood, charged solemnly against his father's account. It seems that while the father was absent the mother was aroused one night by footsteps on the porch outside her room. Her natural alarm aggravated by her nervous condition, the mother listened breathlessly within, not daring to strike a light or call out. To this fright James Lane Allen attributed that fear of the dark which haunted his childhood and remained with him until college days, when a walk or ride home through pitch blackness made necessary a bolder front. As further argument for his belief in prenatal influences Allen pointed out that his sister Sally had a harelip; she was the only one of the Allen children to be disfigured from birth, and this disfigurement Allen believed to have been caused by his mother's having been disagreeably aware, during pregnancy, of the harelip of a visitor the father brought home.

The Allens in 1849 lacked money but they had two possessions more valuable in the Bluegrass: a Virginian ancestry and good family connections. For three generations they had been gentlemen farmers in Kentucky; before that they had come from the Old Dominion; before that, their traditions said, they had been landowners in England. On the twenty-ninth of April, 1790, a James Lane had made his will in

Loudoun County, Virginia. This Lane (1718-1790) had
married a Lydia Hardage (1723-1793), and one of their children was Ann (1753-1822), who married Henry Payne
(1753-?). This Payne was the son of Edward Payne (1726-
1806) and Ann Holland Conyers (1728-?), also Virginians.
In the spring of 1786 Henry Payne and his wife migrated
with a group of fellow-churchmen (among whom were a
Richard Allen and his wife, Ann Wisdom Allen), to Kentucky, where their daughter Lydia was born July 19, 1791.
Lydia Payne married John Allen (1787-1849), son of the
Richard Allen, above mentioned, and it was their son Richard (1811-1872) who went fox-hunting in that third week
in December, 1849, just before the birth of his last child.

On the distaff side much less is known of James Lane
Allen's ancestry. His mother was, before her marriage,
Helen Jane Foster, daughter of a John Foster, planter of
Jefferson County, Mississippi; this Foster's wife was a Mary
Brooks of Virginia; his father, Daniel Foster, had been killed
in Pennsylvania during the Revolutionary War. Left an or-
phan, Helen Foster came north to Lexington, where she was
reared by the Megowans and where she met, no one knows
how or when, Richard Allen. With them it was again an
affair of opposites' exerting a mutual attraction; Allen was
high-spirited, jovial, fond of society and sport; Helen Foster was retiring, religious, too grave for her years. The man
saw in the southern girl a maidenly sweetness not apparent to
everyone; perhaps, too, he felt instinctively that she had a
certain matter-of-fact competence which he lacked and which
would not come amiss in the management of a household; she
had received, moreover, an inheritance which made it possible to speak of her as an "heiress." The girl doubtless saw
in Richard Allen not only a handsome young suitor but also
something of the liberality of spirit, the largeness of living,
which reminded her of plantation scenes in Mississippi and of

her father. Whether the courtship was long or short we do not know, but the ages of the couple suggest that they did not lose much time in making up their minds. They were married in Lexington on the twenty-seventh of May, 1833, by the Reverend R. T. Dillard, a Baptist minister. Since Helen Foster had been born on the sixteenth of September, 1816, she had not quite reached her seventeenth birthday when she became a bride.

From the very beginning of his life, his mother was the dominating influence in the career of James Lane Allen. He believed that she had stamped upon his nervous system something of her fear before his birth. Much more important than that mythical prenatal endowment, however, was the strong affection which bound the mother and her little son together. He was her youngest child and so entitled to especial tenderness; then, too, his brothers and sisters—Lydia, May, Sally, John, Henry, and Annie—were, with the exception of the last, so much older than he that he was obliged most of the time to play by himself, and this loneliness called for added interest on the mother's part. Doubtless she was grateful for this new love, which she could hold tightly, almost secretly, to her heart, for however fond of her husband she may have been, she must, in the course of sixteen years, have lost some of her illusions concerning him. His good nature could not atone for the fact that he was not the man to be entrusted with property, either in real estate or in cash; his instincts were those of a country gentleman rather than of a farmer who must make his living in the sweat of his brow, and even when he did work hard, things did not prosper. She had brought him some money but it gradually disappeared through the unwise generosity and inexpertness of her husband. In some ways, too, he was forever a stranger to her—he and his kin and his region. Solitary and uncommunicative by nature, she made friends with difficulty, found it impossible to show her deepest feelings even to the man who stood nearest her. He was so masculine in his acceptance of and enjoyment of life, she so feminine in spiritual secretiveness, in the final devotion to trivia. How could she ask him, unimaginative as he was, to share her delight in the flame of a grosbeak's wing, her mystic response to an evergreen cedar, her wonder at the eternal procession of the seasons?

Her other children, too, were in some respects alien to her. Like her husband they were robust animals, bright of eye, ready to laugh, forthright in expression. But little Laney—he had been named directly for an uncle, Reverend James Lane Allen of Danville, Kentucky—seemed to be more like herself; he was shy and quiet, with an apparent lack of vitality; a docile little fellow contented with his few toys and learning to turn more and more to the mother, who set in front of him a blue mug full of fresh milk—that mug which was in those days the rightful inheritance of every freeborn American child. It was she who one day carried him across the pike to the schoolhouse, where he might have his introduction to American educational methods by watching and listening to recitations on Friday afternoon; it was she who taught him to toddle to the pump when he wished a drink; it was she who looked after all those indefinite and definite aches and terrors which beset a growing baby. He recognized her gentleness, her concealed warmth; he learned that of all the adults who moved titanically in his vision she alone would surrender her own concerns at once in order to make him comfortable and happy.

The attachment between mother and son became stronger as the years passed and the boy learned to evaluate the other members of the household. When Laney was in his fifth year the Allens, not prospering on his birthplace, moved a couple of miles across country to another house, situated on what was then called the Cold Spring Pike. The new dwelling had five rooms. It had been bequeathed to the Allen children by their paternal grandfather "so that they might have a roof over their heads till grown," and it was in this brick house that Laney Allen grew to young manhood under the tutelage of his mother. As Kentucky houses went this was a fairly old one, dating back toward pioneer times in the wilderness, but in Laney's childhood it stood in the midst of fruits and flowers; in front of it was a lawn that merged into a garden, sloping down to a spring from which the boy could, after taking a cool drink, look out over a small orchard, a smaller vineyard, and, farther off, the fields of hemp and the typical Kentucky woodland pastures. Here was a spot almost ideally suited for the fair-haired, blue-eyed, rather delicate child whom the mother watched tenderly without allowing her tenderness to become officious. All about was tranquillity, broken by no harsher sound than the voice of the sower or the cry of a bird or an animal; all about was space, in which the lad, like a newly planted sapling, could grow to full height and strength. The near-by Harrodsburg Pike was still too far away to offer any disturbing sounds of travel, and Lexington, only four and a half miles distant, might as well have been forty miles off so far as its distractions and clamor were concerned.

The mother soon saw that her youngest son needed especial attention and was worthy of it. His loneliness, his shyness, his seriousness found compensation in a mind that early showed itself quick to absorb whatever she could teach him. From her he learned to read and thus to add a world of experience to the narrow area of his goings and comings. He learned from her also things not found in books: it was her finger that beckoned him to the windows early on a winter morning to see a design etched by Jack Frost; it was she who called his attention to the rose just opened; it was she

who asked him to admire the first snowfall and to watch
and listen to the redbird sitting in one of the cedars that
marched at right angles to the wide porch. Laney rested
in her lap on long afternoons and followed her leafing
through the big Bible, bound in red morocco and made fascinating by numerous illustrations, of which the one rep-
resenting the Garden of Eden proved most memorable.
He pondered the ethical precepts and the eloquence of the
King James version of the Scriptures, and he heard that truth
and honor and purity were the qualities that revealed genuine manhood. There were other books, too, and his blood
stirred at mention of the names of Arthur and Lancelot and
Merlin and all the shining ones of the Table Round. Were
there knights nowadays like those of long ago? he must have
asked. Yes, his mother could assure him, there were; men
like Daniel Boone. She didn't know very much about Boone,
but she was sure he had braved monsters as fierce as those in
medieval romances, and he had always protected women and
children and the weak and had led the whites in their settlement of Kentucky. There were dauntless women, too, in
Kentucky's history, and so she would recite the story of the
pioneer wives and sisters and daughters who at Bryan Station
faced Indians and renegades fearlessly in order to carry buck-
ets of water to the menfolk who were defending the fort.
Bravery in men and women was a gallant thing, the thing
that distinguished good blood, blood like that of the Allens,
from common stock. But bravery should be tempered with
wisdom, and so she may have recalled to the boy the exploit
of the reckless McGary at Blue Licks and of how his
derring-do led to tragic disaster. Yes, noble men and women
exist in every age—the noble few who contrast with the many.
His own family, Laney was told, could be proud of its men;
in its various ramifications it boasted connection with the Mad-
isons, the Paynes, the Johnstons, the Lanes, and these were

high names in the history of the ante-bellum South. One of his ancestors, a Colonel William Payne, though small of stature had in an altercation struck no less a personage than George Washington and knocked him down, and the Father of his Country had apologized the next day for having been in the wrong—an anecdote that the boy James Lane Allen never forgot and which he alluded to in his second book. Then there was Laney's great-grandfather, that sturdy old Richard Allen who had migrated from Virginia in search of religious freedom and who, upon settling down.in Kentucky, had been chagrinned to find his coadjutors turning bigots and so had founded an independent church for worshipers of all creeds, had even erected from his own funds a building which he named the Republican Church. A hero he, certainly, as manly in his day, in his fashion, as the Bayards of the Middle Ages, and Laney was going to remember him and put him into a novel one day. As the boy's mind matured he read selections from Milton and Wordsworth, Coleridge and Thomson, and came to know that favorite romancer in the Old South, Walter Scott. But he was not encouraged to read fiction; southern Puritanism frowned upon fiction even so late as the mid-Victorian era, and Allen, like Robert E. Lee and George W. Cable and a host of other young people, grew up with the feeling that reading novels was not only a frivolous waste of time but also an indulgence in something that was pretty close to immorality. It was poetry which won Laney Allen and claimed him for years; did not, indeed, ever release him from its hold. Given much to daydreaming and conscious of a disparity between what the Allens were and what they should have been, the lad cherished an ambition, carefully concealed for years, to become a poet and thus in a measure to redeem the family fortunes.

Meanwhile, there was always the outdoor world calling to him, calling irresistibly. For he was neither a bookworm nor an indoor boy, in spite of his early lack of robustness. At leisure from his chores, he seemed to have the whole world to wander in—a world of fruit trees, cultivated and wild, of berries, of flowers, of bees, birds, and insects; he must name them all, study their habits; must perforce as a farm boy come to understand what Shakespeare meant by "country matters." His mother kept him from school on the plea that he should not be required to walk so far alone, but he was ever going to school to nature, which is likely to be a kindly pedagogue to a sensitive boy; and gradually on his walks through field and wood, nourishing his boyish philosophy, searching always for the truth which his mother valued so highly, he learned to see man as merely one of the products of a lifeforce which is universal in its application and not as a being just a little lower than the angels. Such reflection did not occupy his mind for long and was probably less a speculation than it was the storing up of impressions, but it is worth remembering that those impressions did filch from man some of his divinity and that in after years Allen's evolutionary beliefs were to make him many enemies, especially in Kentucky. For the most part, he did and thought those things common to the boys of his countryside. He made a cornstalk fiddle and tried to play a hymn tune on it. By the necromancy peculiar to childhood he transformed alder sticks into horses and tied them to fences with halters of green hemp; he strung horsehair across a windowpane and thus manufactured for windy days a rude æolian harp. The day set aside for butchering was a gala one not only for the adults but also for him; and after all the excitement attendant upon slaughter and the preparation of meat had calmed, he took as his own booty the hog-bladders, which he blew up with goose-quills, hung in the smokehouse to dry, and used as explosives at Christmastime, for when jumped upon they made a loud report. He squeezed the red juice of pokeberries on the

plumage of white roosters and curiously watched the resulting battle, being neither then nor later a pacifist. One evening his elder brothers approached him mysteriously. Would
he like to see the Devil he had heard so much about? The
fiend was in the neighborhood and might be observed if one
were cautious. To spy upon such an infernal presence required some courage, but Laney was not going to be laughed
at by his family, and so he followed the older boys around
the corner of the house and saw glowing eyes and nose and
jagged teeth—a carved and lighted pumpkin, which was
spectral enough in the mist of a rainy night.

Unfortunately, he did not often have the companionship of these brothers. They had been born in a prior decade and were unable to share his sports and imaginings to
any considerable extent, even had they found many opportunities to forget their work and their plans to leave the farm
in order to make their own way elsewhere. Age and temperament fixed a barrier between them, which was eventually
to become insuperable and which even then was not to be
jumped too easily. If he found a playmate among the members of his own family, it was sure to be Annie, who was only
three years older than he; but Annie was kept pretty busy
at the domestic tasks of sweeping and dusting and cooking,
and her brother was usually obliged to take his rambles alone.
When she did play with him, the games were less energetic
and more conventional than those he invented, for the girl,
already aware that she was pretty and that feminine graces
were not at all those of a man, did not care to be tumbled
about. She did help him contrive picture frames by gluing
acorns and pine-cones to boards and covering them with a
coat of varnish, but she also counted seeds of apples in order
to divine her destiny—an incantation which, happily, did not
reveal the tragic affliction and the sad dull years that lay
ahead of her. And she taught him to blow the seeds off

dandelion tops and by the residue tell how many years remain before marriage, and then to slit the stems and throw
them into the tiny brook that ran in front of the house and
under the road, a fast-flowing streamlet that converted the
pieces of stem into the ringlets of a water spirit. Buttercups,
she showed him, were not only ornamental but also useful
because they could be held under chins and thus demonstrate
who likes and who does not like good butter.

But only a part of the day could be set aside for such
amusements; there was work to be done, for the father, whatever his own faults, was convinced that evil lay in wait for
idle hands and therefore undertook to discipline his smallest
son by directing that he did not spend all his time poring over
books or mooning under the cedars. In the battle for a
livelihood another pair of masculine hands was not to be
neglected, and so Laney was schooled in the duties as well as
the pleasures that went with the ownership of land. He
learned the names of the fruits, what they were used for,
how to store and cook them; he learned from his father the
names of shrubs, of grasses; how to sow and to cut hemp.
He was sent to chase and round up turkeys that persisted in
running every way but the right one. He planted corn, assisted in shocking it, rode along with the men to see it ground
at the mill. He helped harvest wheat and oats. He pruned
the vines, gathered the grapes, and liked the taste of wine,
for the discipline of his parents was not entirely puritanic
and the Allens placed no taboos upon either homemade wine
or Bourbon whisky used moderately. He pulled weeds until
he almost hated the sight of vegetables. He wondered
whether it was right to take from the bees their golden sweet,
but he watched the process and he retained throughout his
life a fondness for Kentucky honey—a jar sent to him in his
last years would always elicit a grateful letter and the desire
for more. He cut wood, carried water from the spring, bent

his back sometimes over rows of potatoes, ran errands to the neighbors' houses, fed the stock.

In that wise Laney Allen grew up, a pensive boy, never hard-worked but accepting his share of responsibilities for household and outdoor chores. It is not probable that he had any greater partiality for these tasks, which take a boy from his own business, than a normal boy is likely to have; what he did realize after a time was that it is a wise policy to go at one's work vigorously, get it over with, and then have time for play or reading. Work as work had for him little charm then or later. His parents believed he should have his duties and should perform them, but they also let him feel that an Allen, that a gentleman, after all, was one who engaged in manual toil only from necessity.

The continuity of this idyllic life was soon to be broken. By the time Laney was nine or ten he could sense an increasing tenseness in the table discussions of what was going on in Lexington and in distant communities which were only names to the boy. There were, it seemed, meddlesome people who were agitating against the selling and keeping of Negro slaves —abolitionists, who could not understand that the economy of the southern states was rooted in the institution of chattel slavery and who failed to appreciate the culture, the aristocratic society which rested upon that economy. Madcaps and fools they were, damyankees most of them, although too many "nigger lovers" lived right here in the Bluegrass, headed by that monster with an honorable name which he disgraced—Cassius Clay. Richard Allen was decidedly proslavery; he owned no Negroes, but his sympathy for the South sprang from the sectional pride which nurtured a chivalry as romantic as that displayed in the Waverley novels; and the fact that he had no selfish interest in the preservation of slavery did not lessen his championship of the slaveholder's rights. Presently emerged from the discussions

the homely name of Abe Lincoln, a man who was, the newspaper stated, as homely as his name, an uncouth rail-splitter
who had declared that the Union could not exist part free,
part slave territory. This Lincoln had married Mary Todd,
a Lexington girl, who might have been expected to lead him
away from the abolitionists; but if she had tried to do so she
had not wholly succeeded, for he was now a candidate for
the presidency of the United States. If he were elected, dire
things were certain to follow, for the southerners were not
going to let Abe Lincoln free the slaves even if he were president. They had Bible and law and justice to uphold their
claims to their Negroes, and rather than let them go free—
which would only turn the ignorant creatures out to starve—
the people of the South would leave the Union, peacefully
if they could; if not, then by force.

The tension increased until it found relief in the violence
of a war that divided many Bluegrass families, setting neighbor against neighbor and not infrequently father against son
or brother against brother. Laney Allen knew little if anything of the raids, the seizing of arsenals, the wild talk, the
bloodshed in pitched battles; nor, perhaps, did he understand
that Kentucky announced itself neutral and attempted to
maintain the letter of that avowal. But while the commonwealth was officially indecisive, Kentuckians were not, and
thousands of them donned blue or gray, thus offering their
lives as guarantees of their convictions or enthusiasms. One
night Mr. Allen did not return home for supper, and when
the youngest son had gone to bed the father was still absent.
The boy went to sleep and knew no more until he felt himself shaken gently by the shoulder.

"Don't waken him," a voice cautioned.

"Yes, we must wake him; I must tell him good-by," another voice insisted. Laney was shaken again and gently
pulled over on his back. Then he rubbed his sleepy eyes

and saw his father and brothers, with their riding-boots on, gazing gravely at him. Not until the next morning did he fully comprehend what had happened: Mr. Allen and Henry were off to New Orleans, where the daughter Sally was living with her husband, John Harrison, and John Allen was joining Morgan's cavalry. The war, therefore, meant to James Lane Allen at that time nothing more than the cause of the scattering of his family and the further interruption of his schooling, for he was now left the only male on the Allen place and for a time could not be spared from it.

But the day soon came when his more formal education could not be longer postponed without danger of making the postponement indefinite. Mrs. Allen was not wanting in the resolution of other southern women of that era, and so in 1864, with husband and grown sons away and with the war beating now and then almost against the walls of her house, she determined that her favorite son must have training more formal than he could obtain from her or from a few haphazard weeks in a country school. Laney was ready for the change. These fifteen years of wholesome toil and play, of equally wholesome food and drink, had developed the delicate child into a hardy stripling whose body was almost fit to assume the dignities of manhood. There was no longer any hope that the Allens could prosper through agriculture, and if this boy should become a preacher or a noted scholar, that might be some compensation for the mother's years of devotion and genteel poverty. For a few weeks in the autumn of 1864, accordingly, he was sent to the Dudley School in Lexington. The principal, William W. Crutchfield, took a fancy to the shy, overgrown pupil who afterward wrote of him as "an endlessly long rattling man." This schooling, for a reason which we do not know but which doubtless was connected with the troublous times, lasted but a short part of a term, and the only hearsay related to it is that the Allen boy did not care to play with the other boys, that he preferred to stand first on one bare leg, then on the other, while he watched them in their sports, and that his trousers were held up by a single button—this last detail more than a little dubious but in all likelihood suggested by the tradition of the Allens' poverty.

The next year Laney Allen returned to Lexington for tuition, to the preparatory school of Kentucky University this time, the school kept by the brothers Patterson: James K., remembered for his inspiring knowledge of the world's literatures, and Walter, unforgotten because of his "Scotch thoroughness in caning." In 1929 Professor Walter Patterson could recall clearly the coming of this new student. The school consisted of seventy or eighty boys who sat on wooden benches in a building whose site is now occupied by the Lexington Clinic. Young Allen entered late in the fall; it was thought that his father was in the Confederate army and so his late entry was excused on the ground that the boy had to do most of the working of the farm in order to prepare for the winter. He was a well-built lad, fair-haired, fair-skinned, light and large of eye; a typical Anglo-Saxon in appearance, with courtly manners, which were almost effeminate and which betrayed his slight acquaintance with boys of his own age. Presently the school was moved into the "kitchen," so called because it had once served as kitchen for Kentucky University; and in this building, now standing as a memorial in Gratz Park, Allen learned his *hic, haec, hoc* from Walter Patterson, completed his preparatory work in English, mathematics, and ancient languages, and recited one Friday afternoon Hamlet's most famous soliloquy. Only two members of the class that matriculated in 1865 in the "kitchen" now survive, and of those two Mr. James H. Stover, an attorney of Milwaukee, furnished an account of some aspects of his classmate's behavior:

When I boarded two years with Mr. William Van Pelt on a street running toward Nicholsville, "Laney" rode to town every morning on horseback from his father's farm and put the horse in Mr. Van Pelt's barn. He came up to my room every morning and together we looked over the hard parts of our lessons and then walked across the city to Morrison Chapel.

I never saw his parents but a few times [sic] and they impressed me as being in straitened circumstances. I never knew any of the other members of the family.

A peculiarity of his dress was that he put on clean white socks every morning and he also kept his pants from creeping up by straps under his shoe soles.

In 1867 a revival was held in the Main Street Christian Church by Moses E. Lard and many students joined. One morning I suggested to "Laney" that he should join as all his folks were members. He said that he would not have anything to do with religion, but the next night the first one to walk down the aisle was "Laney."

He was tall, perhaps five feet, eleven inches; of slim body and good features; he wore well-fitting clothes and low-cut shoes. I do not remember of his ever having had an overcoat, but he rode with clock-like regularity from the farm, which was about six or more miles southwest from Lexington.

I never heard him use an indelicate word nor tell an indelicate story. In all our years I never heard of his escorting a young lady anywhere.

When I left college in 1869 . . . he was at the train bidding me good-by and that is the last communication that I ever had from him. I wrote him a few letters which he never answered. After I read the "Kentucky Cardinal" I wrote him and complimented him on his production and he never answered my letter. Later when I was in New York City, and called on Dave Armstrong, a prominent lawyer in New York City, and Dr. Virgil P. Gibney, one of the most eminent physicians and surgeons in the United States (both were fellow-students of ours), they told me that it would be unpleasant to meet him so I did not call on him.

Several statements in these paragraphs call for comment. It is to be noted that James Lane Allen's father had returned to Lexington at the conclusion of the war; the son, Henry, remained in business in New Orleans and afterward moved to New York City; the other son, John, who had ridden off to join Morgan never returned and was doubtless one of the "unknown" victims of the civil strife. The fact that Laney Allen wore a shawl instead of an overcoat has sometimes been alleged as another proof of the family's lack of means, but a little reflection reminds us that a shawl was a proper, indeed a fashionable bit of apparel for the young man of the sixties. More serious is the implied charge that Allen was quick to forget his friends and that in the years of his success he had no desire to renew the acquaintances of his youth. There is, as will appear chapter by chapter, much to support these charges, but with respect to one of them let it be said that when the author had become famous and well-to-do, he was often annoyed by the visits of people who "had known him when"; that he was old enough to be skeptical of the wisdom of renewing a friendship which had subsisted a quarter of a century earlier; and that his vanity shrank from exposing the fact that he had grown older, had lost the appearance of youth along with most of his hair. Vanity, as we shall see, was one of the strongest of the Allen traits.

In 1868 James Lane Allen entered Kentucky University, now Transylvania College, as candidate for the degree of Bachelor of Arts. Three years after the close of the Civil War that proud institution had, under the leadership of John Bryan Bowman and despite the threats of the struggle just ended, advanced to a position where it was one of the largest and best universities in the South. Seven hundred sixty-seven students matriculated in its six colleges in 1868. The school was partly sectarian; one of its major purposes was to train ministers for the Church of Christ; and since its colleges were under the joint authority of that denomination and of the state, quarrels over policy were inevitable. Prospective students were required (at least according to the catalogue) to present certificates of character and to sign pledges of conduct, some of which illuminate the activities of the young men of that period. They were allowed to attend "no exhibition of immoral tendency; no race-field, theater, circus, billiard-saloon, barroom, or tippling house." A boy might "neither keep in his possession nor use fire-arms, a dirk, a bowie-knife, nor any other kind of deadly weapon." Especially indicative of the relations between the authorities and the students, and suggestive of the Kentuckian's inborn love of politics, was the regulation that no young man might sign a "petition or other paper to the Board or Executive Committee in regard to the government of the University, or to the appointment or dismissal of Professors or Officers; and that he do not attend or give countenance to any meeting to criticise the government of the University." The religious attitude was emphasized strongly. Even in the academy the boys were required to study the Four Gospels under Professor McGarvey, a formidable theologian with whom Allen was to have a bitter dispute long after graduation; and in the university flattering care was given to theological students, and an effort was made to build up a genuinely religious atmosphere in all the colleges.

Often as a student in the academy Lane Allen had gazed at the scattered buildings of the university, had looked with a kind of reverence at the noble Doric columns of Morrison College, which were to him as a bugle call to a soldier. Within those walls, he felt, one came at last to hear and to identify the truth, to know the good life; one listened to men renowned for learning and experience; one associated with eager youths from many other states. And there had flared up in Allen a new passion: he would prove to outsiders that he, a Kentucky boy, was their equal in spirit, in persistence, in gentlemanliness. In those classrooms he would discover more about the great doctrines of which he already had some knowledge through the teachings of his mother, the sermons of country preachers, and the instruction in the academy. There he would be able to find content, to satisfy aroused longings for certainty about man and man's future, to come close to, if he did not actually come upon, that elusive reality which all ardent souls hope to find, that reality which he might share with a picked few like himself.

And so on the opening day of the fall term Lane Allen passed through the turnstile into the twenty-acre campus and stood, as he thought, before his future. Had he matriculated? some other lads asked him. He had not, and did not even know what the word "matriculated" meant, but rather than show ignorance he made a noncommittal answer. Presently he was given explicit advice, was told where to go to register, and was informed that it would be a good thing to see the professors at once. Bashful but determined not to appear timid, he strode into the office of administration and removed his straw hat. What was his name? "James Lane Allen, Junior," he replied, and it was so set down. The date of his birth was then added, and for some reason the year was written as 1850, an error which was copied in all subsequent registrations at the university. His certification was satisfactory: he had mastered, according to his credentials, English grammar and composition, ancient and modern geography, arithmetic and algebra, Arnold's *First Book of Greek*, Latin grammar, four books of Caesar, five orations of Cicero, Sallust, and had struggled with twenty examples of Latin prose composition. A bit regretfully he handed over thirty dollars for tuition, mindful of the wood he had chopped and sold, the vegetables tended and marketed before that sum had materialized. Luckily he had long since learned the lesson of earning his pieces of silver at a sacrifice of comfort and making them pay dividends in satisfaction, for when he was not yet in his teens he had husked corn on a neighbor's farm in order to buy for his mother's Christmas a silver thimble, a gift which he valiantly had kept a secret until the holiday arrived. But those thirty dollars for schooling represented almost a privation for the land-poor Allens, and long afterward the man for whom they were appropriated looked back upon the transaction with remorse, declaring that if he had fully appreciated his father's difficulties in 1868 he would, instead of going to college, have secured some kind of job and contributed his earnings to the family exchequer.

Lane Allen was not popular among his schoolfellows nor, on the other hand, was he disliked. Tall, slender, handsome, he was doubtless looked at with interest by many a young belle, but his lack of ready money, his seriousness, his four-and-a-half-mile trip from home to college and back kept him from social diversions. Not that he would have indulged in frolics and parties even had his pockets jingled with coin; the reserve which must have arisen partly from constitutional defect and partly from imitation of his mother opened a gulf between him and most young people of his age. Already he was setting himself apart from contact, holding society at arm's length, and adopting a rôle of detachment which made him only an onlooker at the spectacle of life. He was pleasant enough with greeting or smile, but he did not enter into the heart-to-heart talks and confessions which always make for intimacy among undergraduates. Already he was manifesting his singular inability to give of himself to a group, his preference for a very few companions of like ideals and aspirations, his uneasiness at anything coarse or too robust, his lack of animal spirits. Courtly in manner, almost imperious by this time in temper, he moved about with his blonde head in a rarefied region of classical literature, pure

mathematics, and metaphysical speculation. With sport he
had nothing to do, although this lapse was in no way remarkable, since sport had not by 1870 become a chief collegiate concern and since he had plenty of chance to exercise at
home. He did play croquet occasionally on President Milli-
gan's lawn and he did learn to play whist. In both of these
games he was said to excel, though not without an outbreak
of pettishness now and then, for gossip has it that he once
hurled a mallet through the lattice of a porch and that at another time he challenged a card player to a duel. His favorite outdoor recreation, then as later, was walking, and more
strenuous play he left to others.

Lane Allen had three fairly close college friends: William B. Smith, Charles Edgar, and Alexander Campbell.
Of those three Smith was closest to Allen, and Edgar, later
an editor, may have done most to point his comrade's capacities toward writing. Smith's mind was speculative rather
than creative, and for a time he and Allen were akin, made so
by a like curiosity to know the truth, to get at the bottom of
things, to wander in a haze of transcendentalism. And Allen was thankful—what intent youth has not been?—to find
in Smith the fervency of application that nicely suited with
his own temper; for if the scenes in *The Reign of Law* which
represent David's first days at Kentucky University are autobiographical, as they may well be in measure, then the country lad must have turned from banal chatter to welcome a
conversation as stimulating as Smith's, and there is no doubt
but that these two scholars often wrestled together with the
weighty problems of metaphysics and ethics that were as dear
to the student then as economics and politics are to his grand-
child today. Smith, involved in Bible criticism, gave most of
his reading to Darwin, Spencer, Huxley, and other evolution-
ists and to German exegeses of the Scriptures and of theology.
Allen inclined toward the classics of Greece and Rome and

eighteenth- and nineteenth-century England—always passing by *Tom Jones*, which he steadily refused to read—and when the two found battleground and joined issue, they were likely to forget all time and place. Smith had a habit which had puzzled English observers of American manners, that of whittling as he talked or ruminated, and once when he and Allen walked into the country on the road that led to the Allen home Smith, absorbed in their discussion, nearly cut off a finger with his knife. On another occasion Smith and Edgar went to their friend's house by invitation, a step which may have caused Allen some qualms because, in Smith's words, "the heavy cloud that settled over Laney's family and darkened the first half of his life was poverty, particularly oppressive and humiliating to such a high-born and almost haughty heart. I know naught of the details of the father's misfortune, never made the faintest inquiry." Yet this time the Allens desired to show that they had not forgotten how visitors should be served. Smith tells of the visit:

Laney's sister was an uncommonly charming and attractive young woman, with whom I met on some of her short stays in Lexington. Edgar and I spent one night with Laney at his country home, after the death of his father [1872], whom I never met. The sister directed the hospitalities with perfect skill and grace. Broiled chicken was the center of the evening repast, so deliciously prepared and served as I had never seen before and have never seen since. The mother was very grave, courtly, and dignified, a lady with whom I never became really acquainted.

One can imagine that the mother took pleasure in her son's well-bred friends but was nevertheless unable to unbend in cordiality. That invincible shyness or reticence or skepticism which lay deep within her nature could not be dissolved even for the men whom her son liked best.

Not all of the boys' talk was serious. One day as the four walked along Gratz Park on their way to the campus, it was

suggested that they have their photographs taken as four
fools. Smith thereupon proposed that Campbell should pose
as fool by birth, Edgar as fool by vocation, Allen as fool by
education. "And you?" they demanded. "A fool by association," was Smith's blithe return, which did not please, and
the absurdity was abandoned. Possibly it was Allen who de-
murred, his extreme sensitiveness already well developed and
ever on the alert, even in the face of friendship. Later he
was to break decisively with the two closest companions of
these college years.

At first blush it seems strange that Allen should have
made little impression at the time upon the college literati.
No contributions by him to *The Collegian of Kentucky University* are extant, nor does it appear that he was ever chosen
from his literary society, the Periclean, as a co-editor of the
magazine. Yet neglect of him is, upon second thought, easy
to explain. College offices then, like some honors which
come after college, were often awarded on the score of winning personality rather than of mere ability, and on that basis
Lane Allen might easily have been overlooked by his class-
mates. Moreover, the little time he had to spare from his
studies and his walks to and from home, walks on which he
stopped at stores to purchase food—"but not so often as I
wished"—meant that he could scarcely be intrusted with a
campus activity. Finally, Allen made no bid for the position.
He was not the kind of person to seek an honor; if it did not
come to him at once he averted his head until it did; if it
never came, its absence was accepted philosophically, albeit
the time came when he almost regretted his failure to woo
popularity and when his stoicism could not hinder his making
pathetically timid advances for praise. But that was much
later than 1870—1870 when he felt something like contempt
for a certain student much different in respect to views on
popularity; a young man who made known his craving for

distinction, who left Kentucky University because of the in-fraction of a rule, who went then to Bethany College, from which he wrote back in a pious vein, even composing poetry; a young man who became speaker of the national House of Representatives and whom Allen disliked (was it envy?) as candidate for the Democratic nomination for the presidency of the United States; a young man who "wanted all the prizes even then"—James Beauchamp Clark.

Perhaps the failure of his courses and of his professors to encourage writing may account in part for his slowness in learning to love the pen. The prescribed English courses in-cluded a study of the structure of language, rhetoric, elocu-tion, composition, and logic; in the second year English lit-erature was required. Original essays, orations, disputations were called for, and in such exercises Allen was at his best. Unfortunately, the professor of English literature and sacred history, Joseph D. Pickett, did not inspire Allen, and W. B. Smith is of the opinion that the future novelist derived al-most no literary stimulus from his college work.

Ambition and high idealism supplied the driving power for four years of increasing difficulty. As graduation time approached, Lane Allen remarked that his father, whose hair had turned prematurely gray, was losing some of his strength and handsome appearance; the doctors could not understand why he grew thinner before their eyes, until he resembled a skeleton rather than his former stalwart self. The son tried not to think too much about his parent's illness; but, deter-mined to make no complaint with regard to the extra re-sponsibilities thrown upon his shoulders, quietly took over more and more of the direction of the Allen farm. Neces-sarily he must do the work that lay closer to his hand, must study and read, discuss and muse, expend energy and borrow hope, and all with no clearly seen objective as yet. Grad-ually he lost respect for religious dogmas and doctrines and practices; yet he continued to combine scholarly exercise with Sabbatical duty by teaching a Sunday school class, before which he made liberal use of Greek, thus furnishing to his listeners a kind of free coaching in a required language. Of all subjects studied in college, mathematics seemed to him the worthiest; it was freest from ambiguities and vagueness and mere theorizing, and therefore seemed most nearly related to truth. There was certainty in numbers, and there was justice, infallible justice. A thing was either right or wrong, true or not true, and this exactness, upon which he could rest his mind, was so attractive to him that for a long while he toyed with the idea of graduate study in mathematics and a career devoted to that science. But his loyalty was divided. He found a genuine and lively delight in Horace, Aeschylus, and Sophocles; he found pleasure also in the German and French classics and in the acknowledged English masterpieces. But it came to pass that when James Lane Allen, Junior, delivered the salutatory address in Latin, June 13, 1872, making one correction at the instance of his friend Smith, he left the platform in Morrison College undecided as to what he should now do with his learning. Necessity mothered the next step. Since it was imperative that he earn money at once, he looked about for a school to teach and was lucky enough to find one about two miles from his birthplace, the Fort Spring School. Here after a summer spent at home he began teaching in the autumn of 1872.

Scarcely had he become familiar with the ins and outs of his new position when he was interrupted by a blow which was not unanticipated: his father died at eleven on the morning of Friday, the first of November. The next day the *Kentucky Gazette* spoke of the deceased Richard Allen, son of Elder John Allen, as one "of unusual amiability of character, as ready and willing to do a service or any act of kindness as any man who ever lived"—no mean epitaph for any of the sons of men. The funeral over, James Lane Allen went back to his desk and ferrule, a little more serious than before, because he was now on the threshhold of his twenty-third year and had become the breadwinner for his mother and his sister Annie. The death of his father did not leave him with a feeling of intolerable bereavement, for, after all, Richard Allen and he were no more to each other than father and son, held together by accidental bonds, by mutual friendship and mutual service. The passing of the father did not haunt him, did not besiege his memory. In all his discovered letters he mentioned that parent only once and then to regret, as already cited, that he had not understood the sacrifices that were being made to keep him in Kentucky University; in all his published writings he alluded to his father but once and then in a preface to the 1900 edition of *A Kentucky Cardinal and Aftermath;* and whereas of his first eight books he dedicated six to the memory of his mother, he allotted to his father only a shared dedication of the eighth volume, *The Reign of Law.* Of his father as of his brothers he was singularly silent, so silent that he almost gave the impression that he disapproved of them.

At seventeen Allen had read Pollock's interminable *Course of Time,* whose "gloom and dignity made me of a severe and melancholy turn of mind," and now as he returned to teaching, after having followed his father's body from the Elkhorn Church to its grave in the Lexington cemetery, he spent many hours of the winter evenings in reflection upon matters that were becoming less and less positive in his thinking. First of all, what of the God that he had been taught to worship, the God whose reality he had apprehended through conversion? Did He exist as personality? Did the "envious wrangling creeds," which had made his college days discordant, express the nature and commands of that God? Did the clerical bigots have genuine knowledge

of the Creator? Was there, indeed, a Creator? From boy-
hood he had been familiar with the processes of life and had
known what birth and death meant, had seen hemp seeds
sown, warmed by sun, watered by rain, forced by natural
magic to tall growth, which ended in decay and burial—was
man different in his fibre from the stalk of hemp or from the
animal that came with labor into the world, that grew to consummation and decline, and then became extinct? The cry
wrung from all questioning hearts came from him: If a man
die shall he live again? And how should he live before he
dies? What was morality, what was righteousness, what was
truth? One faith at least could not leave him, that the greatest wrong was wrong done to womanhood. Still, where did
gentility end and priggishness begin?

Well, these questions were not to be answered, and
meanwhile he must teach. The records of his instruction are
scant and in some respects contradictory. For one year he
walked back and forth to the Fort Spring School, being
cheered at the end of that probationary period by a brief
item appearing in *The Collegian of Kentucky University:*
" . . . from Laney Allen uniting, as he does, severe logical
power, accurate judgment, and delicate sensibility, the Literature of Science and Art may, in after years, expect some valuable contributions"—a prediction from his friend Edgar
that may have suggested a possible development of his talents.
Not much better off financially for his winter's teaching, Allen was glad to spend the summer of 1873 at his homestead. That fall he followed in the steps of many younger
sons of less successful Kentuckians by migrating to Missouri,
where he became an instructor of Greek and mathematics
in Richmond College, then being transformed into a public
school. At the end of one year in Richmond, he moved to
Lexington, Missouri, where he was master of a boys' school
in 1874-75. En route to Lexington by stage from Lexington

Junction he was held up, with the other passengers, by the James brothers and relieved of all his funds, this being the only known theatrical event in his life.

Whatever else his teaching may have done for him up to this time, it had established the fact that further study and the acquisition of an advanced degree, perhaps even the doctorate, would be advisable. Back to Lexington, Kentucky, he therefore went in 1875 to enroll at his alma mater as a candidate for the degree of Master of Arts, a plan which a piece of good fortune assisted him in carrying out. Mrs. Hannah Moore Whitney, who lived on a farm situated on the old Russell Road about ten miles from Lexington, asked him to tutor her son George, and Allen countered with the proposal that he be installed as teacher for all the children of the neighborhood. This was agreed upon, and in September of 1875 Allen opened the new school. During that winter he boarded with the Whitneys and at the home of A. R. Pritchett, a pupil, and every Saturday morning he went in to Lexington to visit his mother, who lived in lodgings at 196 East High Street. It was no easy thing to teach, to pursue graduate study, to write a dissertation, to see his mother living in a house not their own, but he struggled on, patiently explaining problems to the immature, putting the finishing touches to a paper on "The Survival of the Fittest," and receiving his degree, after some argument with the faculty over the length of his oration, in 1877.

Reward stepped upon the heels of effort, for in 1878 he was made principal of the Academy of Kentucky University, thus drawing on the shoes of his old masters, the Pattersons, whose reign in the "kitchen" he never forgot. Two years in this place, and then he received a gratifying call to the highest academic position he ever held. In June, 1880, Bethany College of Bethany, West Virginia, the institution founded by Thomas and Alexander Campbell, conferred

upon Allen an honorary degree of Master of Arts and on
the fourteenth of that month elected him to the professorship of Latin Language and Literature. The election was
largely a tribute to Allen's waxing reputation as scholar and
teacher, but the Bethany authorities also had in mind the
chance of increasing the enrollment of Kentucky students, already numbering about one-sixth of the whole. Allen was
expected to, and did, write letters urging young men of promise to come to Bethany. In West Virginia he found himself in scenery very unlike the peaceful Bluegrass landscapes
of his youth: the coach ride of seven miles from Wellsburg
took him over small wooded mountains and along the tum-
bling Buffalo Creek to an eminence crowned with a good-
sized building of mixed Tudor and Swiss chalet styles, from
whose verandas he had an exhilarating view of miles of hills
and valleys. At Bethany Professor Allen drilled his students
in Latin composition, Caesar, Virgil, Sallust, Horace, Tacitus,
and "a Latin play"; here, too, he took long walks by himself and found leisure for intensive reading and thinking.
But in 1883, before the expiration of the term, he resigned
his chair and returned to Lexington. Gossip has long had it
that he was removed in order to make way for a minister,
the story being repeated in one variation as recently as 1930,
when Nelson Antrim Crawford used it in an article published in *Plain Talk* for June. There is, however, no evidence that his resignation was forced or even requested;
the minutes of the Board of Trustees of Bethany College
contain no account of a charge against him but state that he
withdrew voluntarily; and for some years afterward he made
long visits (three weeks at a time, according to Cloyd Goodnight, president of Bethany) at the home of President W. K.
Pendleton. Two things gave color to the tale of his requested resignation: his successor, W. H. Woolery, was a
minister who later headed the institution, and Allen's *The*

Reign of Law did picture a clash between honest intellectual inquiry and the closed minds of college professors. It is true, too, that he never denied the rumor that he had been removed from the faculty in order to give place to a minister, and it is possible that in later years he may almost have thought of himself as a martyr to outspoken opinion. It would not have been his only *idée fixe*. Whatever the full cause for leaving his highest college position may have been, differences in religious attitudes undoubtedly were operating to contribute to that cause. By 1883 Allen, chafing under the monotonous round compelled by the teaching of unending classes, groping toward literature as the desire of his heart, could have had little in common with the five dogmatic, strictly orthodox, and zealously evangelical members who completed the roll of Bethany's faculty or with the kind of atmosphere they created. College teaching must suddenly have seemed to him unbearably futile and bigoted.

There is the merest chance that a girl may have had something to do with his leaving Bethany, but it should be viewed as nothing more than the slenderest romantic possibility. A persistent story asserts that he was in love there with the President's daughter, who bore the rather redoubtable name of Alexandria Campbellina Pendleton, a name derived, of course, from one of the founders of her church. In the year of the Franco-Prussian War she had been graduated in French and German from Bethany, and when Allen arrived she was teaching those languages in her alma mater; in 1884, the year after he left, she became a full professor. Charming in manner and lively in mind, she must have been a welcome colleague for the new arrival, somewhat homesick for Bluegrass pastures and unable to adjust himself to the points of view of other members of the faculty. Did he fall in love with her? Did she prefer a safe career to an uncertain lot as wife to a poor young idealist who would doubtless al-

ways be poor and idealistic even when no longer young?   Is
there any significance in the fact that he left in the middle of
a term before she was elected to a professorship?   If so, why
did he later return for visits?   Did she feel a stronger allegiance to the college and its purposes than she could feel
for him?

Unfortunately, none of these questions can be answered
with definiteness.   People then did not pay unusual attention to the solemn, bespectacled Professor Allen; they saw in
him only a shy and probably stiff Kentuckian who did not
seem to mind being left alone by most of his fellows; a
handsome enough and scholarly enough gentleman with no
earmarks of genius and with no advertisement of future fame
written upon his face, and so they did not set great store upon
their impressions of him.   As for the two principals, they left
no chronicle, written or spoken, of any offers or pledges of
affection.   That Allen could compel feminine glances there
is abundant testimony.   From a photograph he had taken in
St. Louis when he was about twenty-seven he looks out at
the world with eyes at once commanding and somber, and
this almost irresistible combination is heightened by a face
grave without being stern and by thick blonde mustaches over
a goatee trimmed in the true style of a Kentucky colonel.   It
is undeniably a handsome face, the face of a dreamer but of
one who would not waste his life in dreams only; the face of
one who might have turned his path toward the Holy Grail
but would not have hesitated to kill his foe who stood in the
path.   Mrs. Margaret Brent Atkins, who as a girl studied
under him in Kentucky and at Bethany College, described
his appearance at the time: "Mr. Allen had light hair, scant,
and light blue eyes which were defective, giving him much
trouble at times.   He wore glasses, was tall, slender, and distinguished looking, and dressed with punctilious care."   And
in *The Writer* for July, 1891, John Fox, Jr., who had also

been a pupil of Mr. Allen, had this to say of his teacher's effect upon others: " . . . there is something in his bearing that gives an irresistible impression of superiority; so that while I have seen a good many men of distinction, I can remember no one who, in splendid balance of varied powers, does not shrink a little by contrast with James Lane Allen." Many similar tributes could be, and some will be, listed as we go on.

No, it would not be a hard matter to prove that Allen could be loved by women, but it would take a shrewd argument to establish his love for any woman other than a relative; and the allegation that he suffered a broken heart through a refusal by Miss Pendleton or anyone else invites strong skepticism. Only a fanciful person would reconstruct a romance out of what may well have been Allen's admiration for or friendship with any of the young ladies he knew, for of course he admired at various times several young ladies, as is natural for a healthy and personable young man. There was a Bettie Arnold of Lexington, Missouri, to whom he inscribed a valentine; there was a Mary Moore of Lexington, Kentucky, whom he occasionally escorted; and in the latter city lived also Mary Bullitt, a librarian, with whom he shared bookish interests. At the time Allen was most attentive to Miss Bullitt he was under the obligation of supporting his mother and his sister Annie, while Miss Bullitt's mother depended upon her daughter's income. Under such circumstances, both Allen and Mary Bullitt lacking the freedom to marry, the acceptance of responsibility meant the surrender of whatever inclination there may have been toward romance, and the two drifted apart. When, after the new century had turned, Allen's niece, Mrs. Frank Gentry, informed him that Miss Bullitt was dangerously ill in a hospital in Lexington he made no reply, but when Mrs. Gentry sent him word of the death of his old friend he wrote back:

"I thank God that she has found the peace of unconscious-
ness." And on an anniversary of Miss Bullitt's death he requested Mrs. Gentry to buy for him and place on the grave
a wreath of such flowers as the dead woman once preferred,
all of them white, and to see to it that his name was not mentioned in connection with the purchase. That, seemingly,
was as near as Allen ever came to being in love.

In that connection one other name emerges. A short distance up the fields to the southwest of the Allen home in the
country, lived Juliet Martin, of whom it was said that her
brother had cut off one of her toes in childhood—an item of
which we shall hear more by and by. Rumor says that Miss
Martin was the original of Georgiana in *A Kentucky Cardinal*,
and the probability is that she had something to do with the
making of that heroine. Certainly Allen felt a warm friendship for Miss Martin; indeed, he seems to have been fond,
in a way, of not a few belles of the period, for as the inquirer
goes about the Bluegrass he hears of many girls who inspired
Allen with a tender passion, who served as the models for
Georgiana, and whose willfulness kept Allen a bachelor.
When that gentleman heard reports of such claims he was
accustomed to remark: "I hope she thinks she is telling the
truth!" The very number of such claimants is disconcerting
and doubt-provoking. Allen's heart was scarcely the kind to
rival George Sand's as a cemetery.

As a matter of fact, no proof of his being in love has ever
been found. His affectional history is feminine rather than
masculine; he had a kind of maternal kindness, deepening as
he aged, for children, especially strange children; and he
felt an almost sisterly attachment for a very few men whom
he frankly loved as men once loved in the days of big-hearted
Dick Steele. A psychoanalyst would have little hesitation in
holding that Allen succumbed to a mother-complex, that his
coolness toward his father arose from jealousy of that parent,

and that an incestuous tenderness for his mother prevented his securing a normal outlet for his libido. Joseph B. Gilder, editor of *The Critic,* to which Allen sent his first magazine contribution, understood that Allen, like John Gray in *The Choir Invisible,* had been in love with a married woman and that the inelastic code of the nineties was responsible for his not breaking that marriage. Less dramatic than these suggested causes for his bachelorhood, but more plausible, is one already pointed out, the economic motive. When money did come to Allen he was fifty years old; illusions had lost their mother-of-pearl tints, and he had become enamored of an exacting mistress, the pen. One of the several books he planned but left unfinished was entitled *The Novelist,* and Chapter One of Part One bore the heading "The Novelist as Egoist." The priority thus given to egoism is no ambigious confession: Allen was throughout the best part of his life much more devoted to himself and his writing than he could have been to any other person or any other thing. Of all American writers he concentrated most completely upon his craft, so far as excluding himself from general responsibilities and contacts is concerned; even Hawthorne, to whom he was often to be compared, married, became a father, and held an appointive office, thus linking himself with common humanity. From common humanity, its joys and sorrows, Allen was to remain as aloof as possible. He was to be almost an incarnation of Hawthorne's ambitious guest, and his inflexibility of purpose may reasonably have been the chief agency which separated him from accepting the love of womankind.

After leaving Bethany, Allen once more put on what he called "the masklike, antique manner of professors," this time for the opening of a boys' school in the Masonic Temple of Lexington. One year of this private school, and then he made up his mind that he was, for good or ill, through with teaching. At thirty-five he no longer cared to collar mischievous lads; there were other if not bigger things that he could do. It took courage to break away from an assured income, however small and however earned, especially as that income was for his mother as well as for himself. But although he viewed the step anxiously he did not falter. In 1884 he lived in a lodging house on North Upper Street; in 1887 he took his mother to live with him in the house of Mrs. Ellen Martin, mother of the Juliet Martin already spoken of. The Martins lived in a cottage on East High Street and Clay Avenue where now stands the Park Methodist Church; at that time it was literally out in the country and Allen could and did walk about under the trees, listen to his beloved songsters, and dream about the stories that were slowly taking shape in his mind. The future was more than dubious, but his first essay had been printed by a New York magazine in January of 1884 and he was going to risk everything upon his ability to win his way into that and other leading periodicals.

Testimony regarding his popularity as a teacher is, as one could expect, divided; some of his former pupils affirm that he was inspiring and helpful—"the only teacher I ever learned anything from"—and others remember him as distant and unpleasant. Allen owned that he had a bad temper when young, and it is certain that in the schoolroom he had excuses for letting it go; one of his students, now a Lexington druggist, says that he has always taken to himself some credit for starting Allen into authorship by behaving so badly in school. It is certain, too, that his personality was never one to charm his Kentucky contemporaries; he was too much wrapped up in reserve, too strict upon his own counsel, to appeal to his fellow southerners, loving as they did warm comradeship, hearty and not too refined. With the younger children he was patient and gentle; with the older ones he could not always conceal his dislike of the need for discipline and for displaying wares not always eagerly bargained for. He never did acquire the art of suffering fools gladly.

But if those who once sat under his instruction disagree as to the value of what they received, there is no indecisiveness about their schoolmaster's attitude toward the pedagogical profession. "The memory of school," he wrote in 1921 to Superintendent M. A. Cassidy of Lexington, "is pure horror—either as student or teacher . . . I don't like either being a driver of geese or being one of them." A figure of speech which antedated by less than a year Upton Sinclair's *The Goose-Step.* Yet those twelve years in the schoolroom were not barren of profit. Teaching the young to use their language is an excellent way of learning how to employ that language, and Allen's experience was fairly wide; he taught, as he once told an interviewer, everything in academic English from the first reader to lectures based upon Max Müller; he taught also mathematics, German, Greek, geology, and evidences of Christianity; and he added that during this period he had "read nothing that was trash or even mediocre." It is impossible to overlook the importance of this training as a molder of his outlook and his style. Twelve years as schoolmaster will incline anyone to the dogmatic and pedantic, and it is not surprising to find in practically everything Allen wrote, to an increasing extent as youth departed, the exercise of the habit of improving and chastening inferiors, the lecture upon the urgency of unselfish, aspiring conduct, the gentility which was imposed upon him by breeding and profession. Nor will even the superficial reader go far in Allen's early works without discovering an indebtedness to certain English classics. He will find there a chastity and dignity of diction borrowed from Addison and Steele, a warmth of color derived from such romantics as Keats and Shelley, a sentiment such as informs Dickens and Thackeray, a decorum that often makes George Eliot ponderous. Of Americans,

Irving and Hawthorne had most to do with forming Allen's manner, the local colorists most in delimiting his field of effort. To all of these he owed not a little, and all of these he had read because months of study and teaching had given him the proper leisure.

And so it is that the people who wrote books and the people who existed only in books had more to do with settling the character of Allen's stories than had the actual professors and pupils among whom he moved. He drew little material from the schoolhouse or the college. True, *The Kentucky Warbler* has a schoolboy for hero and is addressed to school children; true that teachers are to be found in four of his longer books; but the problems of his novels are such as lie outside the walls of a lecture hall, and even his professional protagonists have little to do with chalk and globe and ruler. Teaching had been for Allen merely the easiest method of making money. It became an unhappy episode relieved only by the opportunities it gave for wide and useful reading.

CHAPTER II
TOWARD AUTHORSHIP

In the early eighteen-eighties James Lane Allen resolved that it was time to take inventory of his capacities and to make some forecast as to what they might bring him; a dozen years of pedagogy had, as we have seen, yielded him little return in either fame or wealth and had held forth no promise of future improvement. Approaching what was then regarded as middle age, he realized that as yet he had arrived at no comfortable resting place and that the road he was traveling might only too soon lead into a cul-de-sac. To continue to instruct changeless generations of boys and girls for a meager pittance, to live obscurely in a lodging house and to be obliged to eat with all comers, to wear out in an inglorious squirrel-cage of duties—these things were not to his liking. He had had his chance, it is true, at collegiate ranking, but had been made uneasy by an orthodoxy in religion which set shackles upon his thinking and actions. Was there anything to look forward to in the teaching profession? There was the East with its great colleges and professors, but what likelihood had he, graduate of a reorganized southern institution, to be called to one of their chairs, especially since he lacked the degree which most commended one to such a position—a thought which he revealed when in *The Bride of the Mistletoe* he spoke of Professor Ousley as about to join "the slender file of Southern men who have been called to Northern universities"? For a time he contemplated accepting this challenge and going to the Johns Hopkins University for a doctorate, and years later he told Professor Fred Lewis Pattee and Professor Arthur Hobson Quinn, on distinct occasions, that he had gone to Baltimore with that purpose in mind;

Professor Pattee even states that Allen was the "first appli-
cant for the degree of doctor of philosophy at Johns Hopkins, though he never found opportunity for residence."
However, the registrar at the Maryland university can find
no record of Allen's application for admission to graduate
standing. Perhaps Allen went to Baltimore, looked over the
ground, even attended a few lectures, but finding that his
means were too limited to permit his remaining in attendance
went away in discouragement; the certainty is that he left
no official trace of residence there. It seems likely that
he pondered the matter of going to Germany for research in
comparative philology, Germany being then the Mecca for
American workers in that field. But the money for the accomplishment of these ends was not forthcoming and would
not be unless he might in some way add to the slender trickle
of his earnings. If he could not thus swell his income he had
best select some other and more lucrative career, pursue it
strenuously, and in good time achieve material success as well
as self-satisfaction.

But what career? There, to adapt the words he had once
recited in the "kitchen," was the rub. He had fitted himself
for but one profession and it was now too late to change to
another even had he been aware of any desire for law or
medicine or the ministry. Unless he undertook to exploit
some business—and his father's failure in practical affairs
may have been a warning against this course—there was but
one answer to the pertinent question: he could try writing.
He had not been born with a pen between his fingers and had
so far manifested no unusual urge for creative writing. The
item already quoted from *The Collegian of Kentucky University* had remarked of Laney Allen that "he has written
but little as yet, but like the Irishman's owl, is keeping up a
'prodigious thinking.' " Nor had he any great passion for
books. He enjoyed them as a stimulant to reflection and as

a communication with great minds, but he was no bibliophile; even in later years when he could have afforded to indulge a taste for rare volumes, handsome bindings, or even collections of ordinary value, he owned few books, preferring to rely upon public libraries and the library of Columbia University, where he is still remembered as having been "a most distinguished-looking gentleman." The Allens had never been bookish or literary. But they had nourished a tradition of aristocratic feeling, and their blood called for distinction of some kind in their descendant. If he could become a noted author that distinction would be achieved in a manner that would make the best use of his scholastic preparation, his dreams of usefulness, his love of truth, his mother's hopes.

In an old trunk full of papers, manuscripts, and clippings, Allen kept until death what was probably his first earnest attempt at a short story, penned in 1879 in the back pages of *Todd's Index Rerum* and entitled "David Galbraith and Dr. Felix." It purported to be told by a young professor and to concern his friend, a young doctor, professional men who anticipate the doctors and professors of his later novels. Both had attended a university and both lived in New York City, but before the situation could be clearly introduced the manuscript broke off and the two friends appear no more in Allen's pages, although it should be noted that he seemed to have a partiality for the name David. Fiction, however, did not claim an undivided fidelity; indeed, his inability to finish "David Galbraith and Dr. Felix" may have been owing to the fact that he was attempting to force an interest in the short story form, and even in his best subsequent years he found that to complete a novel or story demanded infinite patience and toil, which he lightened by excursions into the realm of poetic composition. Poetry and the essay came easier to him and invited him earlier. In 1880 he printed in Lexington and Louisville papers some uninspired verses of his own, one of them about a warbler, and some mediocre translations from Schiller, André de Chénier, and Uhland. There was an interval of quiet while he was at Bethany College, an interval in which he stored up and meditated upon material. Then in 1883 he broke into print with a short essay in an important periodical and thus began his literary climb.

If any period in our literature can be said to have offered better opportunities than another for a young, aspiring author, that period would be the early eighties, especially if the ambitious young writer were a southerner or familiar with the South. The literary supremacy of New England and New York seemed then about to pass, perhaps to the land south of the Mason and Dixon line. Hawthorne, a recognized giant in our letters, had died before the Civil War ended; Melville, an unrecognized Titan, was almost forgotten after *Pierre* shocked his contemporaries in 1852. The deaths of Longfellow and Emerson in 1882 removed the best-loved poet and the most highly regarded thinker in America of that era. Whittier, Holmes, and Lowell were to live to the closing years of the century but with waning powers of influence, for Whittier's fury subsided with the emancipation of the slaves, Holmes failed to reach literary maturity, and Lowell cloistered himself with his books at Elmwood and hid himself in a shell of conservatism. Walt Whitman, it is true, was emerging from obscurity to command the ranks of American poets; but American criticism, in the grip of New England refinement, still looked at him askance, and the public allowed the good gray poet to live meanly at Camden. Henry James and William Dean Howells, admittedly the novelists who established the criteria by which lesser figures might be judged, were slowly becoming vulnerable to the onslaught of a school of writers not instructed in Bostonian niceties and wearied by endless probings of consciousness;

Mark Twain had cheered such penmen by publishing *The Adventures of Tom Sawyer* in 1876, succeeded by *The Adventures of Huckleberry Finn,* in 1884, clear warnings of a shifting interest in American fiction which turned eyes from New York and Cambridge to the western provinces and which was emphasized by the flood of local-color stories that followed the publication of Bret Harte's "The Luck of Roaring Camp" in 1868. As Allen noted the outpouring of fiction concerned with little-known communities in Louisiana, Tennessee, Virginia, Maine, and the Middle West, he reflected that the mere weight, if not the merits, of these tales would disturb what had been the coherent and simple development of American romanticism. Literature, as he thought, was being abused in the name of geography and sociology. Nor was he alone in fearing that the more classic examples and manners might be forgotten, at least temporarily, for George Edward Woodberry complained in the *Fortnightly Review* for May, 1881, that "among us literature has no continuous tradition; where the torch fell, it was extinguished. Irving, it is true, had imitators who came to nothing; but our fiction does not seem to be different because Hawthorne lived; no poet has caught the music of Longfellow; no thinker carried forward the conclusions of Emerson. These men have left no lineage"—words which must have set Allen to thinking.

Whatever their faults may be, he said to himself, Cable and Harris, Page, and Kate Chopin are being read, and this fact carries with it an obvious lesson. Allen noticed, too, that *Harper's Magazine,* mirroring the cultivated taste of the time, was catering to the local-color school by setting aside many pages to accounts of life in the less-known states or regions: to the hot springs in Arkansas, the Jersey seacoast, gold-mining in Georgia, the Texas prairies, the mines of Colorado, the harvests of the Dakotas. Why, he asked himself, should not Kentucky, or at least the Bluegrass, so romantic to him in its history and so lovely in scene, be represented in this chorus of the states?

The chance for such participation came sooner than he dreamed, although it came by a devious route. On the fifth of January, 1881, a new magazine appealing to the world of books and bookmen made its bow to the American and British public. It was *The Critic*, edited by young Joseph B. Gilder with the help of his sister Jeannette. From the first it was a genteel periodical, committed to a belief in the soundness of the union of morality and art, a gallant champion of good taste and breeding, and a decrier of the vulgar and drab in literature. It viewed George Eliot, then at the peak of her popularity, with great respect; it agreed with the current romantic love for nature by publishing essays on Thoreau; it denounced Zola's *Pot-Bouille* as "a filthy book" and lined up with the supporters of Anthony Comstock. True, it accepted contributions from Walt Whitman, but it did so charily, mindful that these were the days of George William Curtis and E. P. Roe, whose *Barriers Burned Away* had been so eagerly read for ten years that in 1882 it sold to the tune of ninety thousand copies of a limited edition. Such a magazine had an instant attraction for Allen, who by instinct, training, and profession had learned to look to books for a criticism of life and a statement of how it should be lived; and it was quite fitting that his début in the society of literature should have come through the introduction given by this mid-Victorian publication.

The introduction came about in this fashion. Sometime toward the close of 1882, having read Henry James's *The Portrait of a Lady*, which had created a stir the year before, Allen was moved to express disapproval of the first pages of the Master's novel and to set forth means by which that page of narrative could be improved. He had never published a line of fiction, but that consideration in no wise inter-

fered with his belief that he could have opened the novel in
a manner more satisfactory, and afterward he explained his
audacity by writing that "if a man is a paid pedant and author-
ized egotist to others in his lectures, he will be that identical
pedant and essential egotist to himself in his library." So he
dispatched to *The Critic* an essay on "The First Page of *The
Portrait of a Lady*," in which he quibbled over unimportant
features of the first sentences of James's masterpiece and himself fell into the error of using "party" for "person," a mistake he never repeated. He accused the novelist of reiterating
too often the time of the day, complained of the way in which
a reader is misled into believing that several people are drinking tea, only to find that but one individual is so engaged,
and objected to the description of the shadows of an old man
sitting in a deep wicker-chair and of two young men strolling
before him, as being "straight and angular." In justification of his hair-splitting in this article, Allen averred that
even the smallest details "may not be disregarded by any one
who aims at perfect finish of literary workmanship"—a conscientious dictum which always controlled his own attitude toward his work. To his surprise *The Critic* took the paper
and paid for it. Gladdened by this first eastern recognition
of his talents, he cashed the check and boarded a train for
Cincinnati, there to give himself a holiday treat—for the
Christmas recess had just begun—by hearing *The Messiah*
sung in the Queen City's "vast, shadowy, sonorous hall." On
the slow-moving train he amused himself by conjuring up
visions of the consternation his attack would cause in the camp
of James, Howells, and their publishers and by reminding
himself that his Lexington friends would now be brought to
a realization that although teaching had won for him neither
great reputation nor a comfortable balance in the bank yet he
had intelligence sufficient to impress a New York editor. But
even in his elation he was bowed down by a quiet melan-

choly as he gazed out the car window upon the dead white-
ness of the snow and reflected upon the contrast between his
lot and that of a freezing bird whose "thorny toes" grasped
"the wire that runs around the world." To the accompaniment of rumbling wheels his thoughts assumed metrical
form; a few days later he wrote them down and mailed the
poem, ambitiously enough, to *Harper's Magazine*, which published it a year later as "Midwinter." The only remarkable
thing about "Midwinter" is that it should have been approved
by the editor of *Harper's*, for its unchecked sentiment would
seem to be more appropriate for *Godey's Lady's Book*.

Meanwhile, before this poem issued in type, Allen continued writing for *The Critic*. Since it was good strategy to
train his guns upon so prominent a figure as Henry James,
the essayist exercised his wits again upon the author of *The
Portrait of a Lady*, this time taking him to task for self-com-
placency and wearisome repetitions. James had printed in
The Century Magazine, two years old in 1883, an essay on
Alphonse Daudet and it was against this that Allen turned
his heaviest artillery. *The Critic* liked the cannonade and
called for more and, from 1883 on, James Lane Allen had
never to waste his powder. But although he had no trouble
getting into print the problem of an adequate income was still
far from solved, and Allen presently, as we shall see, was
obliged to cast about for a way in which to supplement his
earnings from pay-check and pen.

It would be tiresome to enumerate here in full detail
the essays by which Allen first gained a name as a "magazinist," and such a list will be given only in the bibliography,
but notice of the periodicals for which he wrote and of the
variety and extent of his subjects is justified. Most of these
early papers appeared in *The Critic;* others are to be found in
The Continent and *The Forum*. A poem, "The Rifled
Hive," playfully revealing the keen eye with which the lad

Laney Allen had watched the behavior of insects, and showing Poe's influence in its striving for lush melodic effects, is
in *Lippincott's Magazine* for September, 1884. Another,
"Beneath the Veil," evidence of the fascination which a nun's
life held for him at this time, and much the best verse he
had written to date, was in *The Atlantic Monthly* exactly one
year later. Allen's prose, however, is invariably to be preferred to his poetry, and it is to his prose that we must turn in
order to trace the evolution of his literary skill.

The best of his early magazine essays are still eminently
readable, and what might be called the worst—such as "Mary
Reynolds and *Archibald Malmaison*" and "Parturiunt
Montes," the latter a whimsical plea for "a lying-in hospital
for poor and virtuous authors, when about to be delivered of
their little children"—do not fall far below high journalistic
levels. One paper argued with Joel Chandler Harris as to
whether Negroes played banjos, for the Georgian had declared in *The Critic* that he had "never seen a banjo, a tam-
bourine, or a pair of bones in the hands of a plantation negro"; one described the gargantuan nature of Samuel Pepys'
appetite; another pointed out the prevalence of night shadows in the poems of Edgar Poe. Then he returned to the
bombardment of Henry James, charging that the novelist did
not justly represent American traits and making a confession
of faith with regard to what he thought the proper tone of
literature, a credo of great significance to anyone who wishes
to understand what Allen was trying to do in the first years
of his carer as author:

. . . life as a whole is neither agnostic nor pessimistic; shall the
novel that represents it be both agnostic and pessimistic? Life, as
a whole, is spiritual and religious; shall the novel of life be devoid
of spirituality and religiousness? Life, as a whole, presents a scene
of happiness and success; shall the novel of life present a spectacle
of wretchedness and failure? Life reveals character through ac-

tion; shall the novel of life reveal character through a minimum of action and a maximum of psychological analysis? Life is made up of finished lives; shall the novel of life begin to weave the tissue of lives, and then, suddenly dropping them, leave the threads with loose and dangling ends?

It is hard to believe that Allen at thirty-five could have been as naïve as these statements and questions suggest; yet his lack of experience of the world beyond his more or less idyllic country life and the seclusion of his schoolmaster's room might guarantee his sincerity; one suspects, however, that only prejudice or a desperate will to find fault could have dictated the strange opinion that "life is made up of finished lives." What is quite clear is that at this date Allen was not qualified to speak of reality, that he was surprisingly ignorant of the ways of the world, that he peeped at men and women through the dark glass of literature instead of seeing them face to face, and that he had definitely aligned himself with the idealists and romanticists, who were, in his opinion, the true realists.

Two other essays of the year 1884 are worthy of being resurrected: "Keats and His Critics" and "A Word About Heine," both in *The Critic*. In the first he examined dubiously the growing belief that harsh criticism had done little to aggravate Keats's illness and hasten his death; and in his criticism of the arguments of such commentators as Lord Houghton and Messrs. Speed and Stedman, he betrayed his own sensitiveness to hostile judgments. Heine, who had been advertised in America by Emma Lazarus's translation in 1881 but whom Allen had for years been reading in the German, received a eulogy reminiscent of Kentucky oratory in its most florid stages. In the final apostrophe Allen cried out that the Teutonic Jew was "brother to Aristophanes, Rabelais, Cervantes, Burns, Sterne, Richter, Swift, Voltaire, Byron, Béranger, Ariosto!"—a flourish of pedantry which may well have astonished his Kentucky neighbors, if any read it, and which may have made some wonder why its writer would read Sterne but look upon Fielding with absolute disfavor.

All this time Allen was wearing the pedagogue's harness, but, as already stated, he cut the traces in 1884 and with a feeling of holiday relief cantered off into literary pastures. Encouraged by the acceptances which had come so regularly, he closed to himself forever the door of the schoolroom and did what most young men who longed for literary renown did: he went to New York City. We do not know just what his resources were, but he was not equipped for a long campaign. In 1895 he told a friend that he arrived in the metropolis with a few dollars and a pencil in his pocket; two years later he mentioned to an interviewer the sum of one hundred dollars; in 1906 he told a correspondent that he had but fifty dollars; he told Isaac F. Marcosson that he lived in the proverbial hall bedroom and came as near starving as he ever came in his life. Nor was the lack of funds his only handicap, for he had no personal acquaintance with editors and publishers; indeed, it is not likely he would have availed himself of such acquaintance even had he possessed it, for an Allen must win his spurs with no favor shown. He did not even look up his brother Henry, then in business in Wall Street. When it came to making the rounds of editorial offices, he selected as the first man to visit Henry Mills Alden, who directed the destinies of *Harper's Magazine* and who had accepted and printed "Midwinter." To the offices in Franklin Square he accordingly went, and found Alden a man whom he admired at once. Like himself Alden was big of frame and also like himself Alden moved and worked and spoke quietly—"the American way," Allen called it. "Instantly noticeable," he wrote, "as issuing from such a massive, rough-hewn head and body was his voice: so low that you seemed not to be hearing, but to be overhearing, him speak to you." The combination of rugged strength and gentleman's manner charmed Allen, especially as the editor received "the blonde young giant" kindly, made him feel that he was accustomed to welcoming timid young writers, and promised to read some of his manuscripts. After looking over several of the papers Allen had contributed to New York periodicals Alden suggested that what the novice lacked was "the discovery of a definite field," something that would concentrate his efforts and help the public identify his name. Why not take advantage of the current fashion for stories about out-of-the-way places and interpret Kentucky to the Atlantic seaboard? asked Alden, adding that he would be willing to give every encouragement to such an undertaking. The advice to make a spiritual as well as an actual return to Kentucky suited well the feelings of the younger man, who, until he had attained manhood, had never seen a town of larger size than Lexington and who found the chief American city, even in those more placid days of hansom cabs and high silk hats, too jangling and heartless and wearying. He never did, even in his long subsequent residence in New York, develop an O. Henry-like affection for that city. One of his last-written manuscripts, left unfinished at his death, contains this suggestive comment: " . . . what human being in his senses harbored an emotion for New York? As well expect a man to feel patriotism for a ferry."

Back to Lexington he therefore went, to spend the next five years, "anxious, struggling, high-strung, ambitious, consecrated years," in that city and in Cincinnati. He brought with him one tangible result of his summer's stay in New York: a commission from the *New York Evening Post* to do an article about the Cumberland Mountains, and upon his return to Lexington he was surprised by a telegram from the editor of *Harper's Magazine* ordering two papers about the Bluegrass, an assignment which was more to his taste. This latter attention was the result of his chat with Mr. Alden and of the editor's reading of "Too Much Momentum," a story which *Harper's* published in April of the year following Allen's visit to New York. This, the first of Allen's fiction to appear in print, was a surprise story hinting that the author may have been reading Thomas Bailey Aldrich, but its machinery is so defective that at the end the reader is annoyed by a jolt rather than amused by a quick surprise. The thin plot concerns a professor of chemistry named Evers, who lives on a farm near Owensville, Kentucky, and is regarded by his neighbors as an eccentric. Mrs. Artemisia, a widow, courts this gentleman in a mildly humorous manner, a detail which some of Allen's friends, to his irritation, viewed as autobiographical. Allen protested then, and protested ever afterward, that he did not use his friends, his enemies, or himself in his characterizations, and while this is not strictly true, as we shall see, it is close enough to the truth to serve as a cautious generality. Proud of the fact that *Harper's* had published this first completed effort at the short story form, Allen sent a copy of it to his college friend, W. B. Smith, who, wishing only to give helpful criticism, replied that the tale showed the writer's genius to lie not in the creation of character or the invention of plot but in the writing of prose, perhaps of essays, in the fine old classical style. Instantly offended, Allen wrote back roughly that if Smith felt that way there was no use in continuing their correspondence, which ceased thereupon and was not renewed until many years later and then upon the novelist's initiative. Neither again mentioned to the other the cause of the interruption of their friendship.

Fully determined now to succeed as a writer, Allen proceeded to busy himself with redoubled energy in turning out copy. He at once saw that if he were to adopt the advice of Henry Mills Alden, if he were to accept the commissions to write about Kentucky, and if he wished to make money by writing a kind of fiction highly pleasing to the public, he must turn to a consideration of the popular local-color short story. But first he must travel southward to the Cumberland Mountains, "the great Appalachian up-lift on the south-eastern border of the state." From Lexington he went to Burnside by train, then by buckboard to Pineville, and from that little town, now one of the most attractive of the smaller Kentucky cities but in 1885 a place of "squalid hovels, its ragged armed men collected suspiciously in little groups, with angry distrustful faces, or peering out from behind the ambush of a window," he rode horseback over Cumberland Gap, the famous pass through which the first white settlers had come into Kentucky. It was an interesting if not thoroughly comfortable trip, not untouched with a bit of excitement, for a shooting in Pineville, a few days before Allen's arrival, had stirred up bitter feeling; a deadline had been drawn through the town, so that partisans living on either side crossed to the other at the risk of their lives, and "there was blue murder in the air." In writing of this trip Allen treated his own danger half-humorously, half-seriously.

I was a stranger; I was innocent; I was peaceful. But I was told that to be a stranger and innocent and peaceful did no good. Stopping to eat, I fain would have avoided, only it seemed best not to be murdered for refusing. All that I now remember of the dinner was a corn-bread that would have made a fine building stone, being of an attractive bluish tint, hardening rapidly upon exposure to the atmosphere, and being susceptible of a high polish. A block of this, freshly quarried, I took, and then was up and away.

Nor could he have been easy in the necessary interviewing of mountaineers, for those survivors of Anglo-Saxon immigrants, always close-mouthed with "furriners," were not very responsive to a man who was so evidently not one of them. But Allen liked them in his cool way, liked their clannishness, their physical hardihood, their essential courage and manliness, their minor strain of melancholy.

In Lexington once more with his pockets full of notes, which he began to arrange and build into an essay, Allen also took up the postponed matter of analyzing the nature of local-color stories, for in his usual conscientious way he prepared himself for his attempt at this kind of literature by thinking through to some conclusions as to its limits and character. These conclusions he published in one of the most enlightening and critical of essays dealing with that subject, an essay to be found in *The Critic* for January 9, 1886. He laid down four rules for the local-color short story and its writer: (1) It should withdraw attention from character, plot, incident, and motive and fix it upon skies, atmosphere, horizons, sites, monuments. (2) It must look upon descriptions of scenery as a means, not an end, and must not furnish the reader with miscellaneous information of flora, climate, and other scientific features. (3) The writer should be a scientist. (4) The writer must be a stylist, ready to eschew the use of dialect and the nice dissection of personality.

Closely associated with the thought of this essay is the content of a paper, "Realism and Romance," contributed half a year later over the signature "A" to the *New York Evening Post*. It contains no unusual statements but it does make two which are full of meaning because they are the expression of ideas which Allen never abandoned, although he did modify one of them, and which must be taken under advisement by whatever critic wishes to assess his career. In the first place, he objected to the practice of those writers who saw in the South only an unexplored field of the picturesque and odd and who exploited freakish people and customs for the benefit of a gaping world which took it for granted that these extraordinary items were typical of conditions in Dixie. Such writers as Cable and Miss Murfree and Joel Chandler Harris he therefore blamed particularly for pandering to the curiosity of a magazine public. These and other apostles of the method were exhibiting, he maintained, a false kind of romance when the reality would have been equally romantic in other directions and would have been less liable to the suspicion of commercialism. In the second place, he came out boldly for a romantic coloring of literature as being justified by life itself. "Will not the world say," he queried, 'The romantic *is* true of human nature—one of the deepest and truest things in it'?"

It was not only for the South in general that Allen held this brief; it was his native state that he kept constantly in mind. "Kentucky," he wrote to the same newspaper in the same month, "needs literary interpretation. . . . I should like to write you of the better phases of Kentucky—of the happy pastoral life that goes on prosperously and happily year after year in the blue-grass region." Obviously he had decided to take Alden's advice to adopt a "definite field," and for him there was nothing more "definite" than the Bluegrass and its citizenry. For thirty years he had been storing up pictures of its landscapes and for a score he had been studying its people as fellow-students, fellow-teachers, neighbors, and strangers. Near the end of his life he made several abortive attempts to write an autobiography, and in seeking influences governing his choice of literary subjects and style he correctly gave first place to the scenes and persons he had known during the first half of his life. "I had no conception," he wrote retrospectively, "no mental picture, no creative imagination for any other country or kind of country. . . . The whole effect of this land, the spirit of its architecture, has, I think, determined the architecture of all my work. No ruggedness, no wildness, no savagery." And of the inhabitants he wrote: "I knew them . . . altogether as a people who, with a population of not so many thousand, compressed the whole range of human life from spiritual dreamers and austere saints down to vagabonds, aristocratic vagabonds." To celebrate this country and these Kentuckians remained Allen's prime purpose for the rest of his life; no editor's advice was ever more literally or more flatteringly taken. Of his nineteen books fourteen are devoted almost exclusively to the Kentucky scene; of the remaining, three have heroes of Kentucky birth who live in New York City, one is a prose poem without characters, and one, the last, contains a long unfinished story, "The Landmark," which was intended to be part of an historical romance dealing with the Bluegrass State. No American novelist more zealously attempted to make one small section of the nation known to the rest of the world.

In February, 1886, *Harper's Magazine* published the first of his Kentucky travelogues, "The Blue-Grass Region of Kentucky," a wordy description of the grass itself, the landscape of central Kentucky, the fertility of its soil, the agricultural and domestic aspects of its life and inhabitants. The essay is frankly journalistic, but informed with an emotion which leads the author into verbal excesses in the pictorial passages. In June the same magazine printed "Through Cumberland Gap on Horseback," not so well done as the earlier one because Allen was out of his milieu and, as remarked before, a little ill at ease when trying to talk with mountaineers not always adaptable as subjects for fine writing. In fact, he sometimes substituted, and shamelessly, fine writing for interview and then perpetrated passages like this:

The utter silence and heart-oppressing repose of primeval nature was around us. The stark white and gray trunks of the immemorial forest dead linked us to an inviolable past. The air seemed to blow upon us from over regions illimitable and unexplored, and to be fraught with unutterable suggestions. The full-moon swung itself aloft over the sharp touchings of the green with spectral pallor; and the evening star stood lustrous on the western horizon in depths of blue as cold as a sky of Landseer, except where brushed by tremulous shadows of rose on the verge of the sunlit world.

In the midst of this writing of feature articles Allen turned his hand again to fiction, which *The Century Magazine* published in February, 1887, as "Part of an Old Story," a rather lifeless tale revolving about Cagliostro, never reprinted, and worthy of comment only as showing his inclination to the historical background. The spring of that year was darkened by an event which brought no little humiliation to the Allens. Annie, a real beauty, vivacious and a bit vain because much sought after, had, contrary to the wishes of her mother and brother, married a man who proved to be intolerable, and the fact that she found herself unable to live with him was a blow not only to her pride but also to that of the other members of her family. Some subtle touch of disgrace was then attached to a young woman who failed to make a success of her marriage, and Annie Reed felt this disgrace all the more quiveringly because she had wed against the advice of those closest to her and because she now had to come back to Lexington and live, no longer sought after, in the scene of her former popularity. Her brother accompanied her from Baltimore to Lexington, and there, in the house with his mother and himself, the house kept by Mrs. Martin, he provided a place for her. Of course she went into a kind of retirement dictated by vanity and the sense of failure, and Allen, brooding upon several stories now thronging his mind and still preparing his Kentucky essays for different magazines and newspapers, worried over her, wishing that she might have her normal share in life and yet comprehending her reluctance to face her friends. As for Annie, the lively playmate of his childhood, existence had practically closed upon her. From that day forward she steadily

lost identity, so that as the years slipped by she became pro-
gressively less Annie Allen Reed and more the sister of a
noted man, a sister whom almost no one saw, a woman
thought to be an invalid but actually suffering from mortified
pride and later from a cancerous growth which forever
marred the beauty of her face and dealt her the final cruel
stroke. From that time on she became—although Allen
never said so outright and would resent the statement now—
a burden upon him; not merely an added drain upon his income, for that drain was heavily felt for only a short time,
but more irritatingly a tax upon his time and patience, a
constant obstruction in the path of his sustained creative effort.
Annie, as we shall see, did her best to make herself useful to
her brother, and thereby added pathos as well as tragedy to
the situation. The ill-starred marriage and the long continued years of his sister's dependence upon him evoked no
spoken complaint from Allen, and only once did he unburden
his heart in a letter. That was when he was old and ill, and
what he said then—to be noted in a following chapter—was
gentle.

Whatever the domestic complications, he did not dare let
the ink dry on his pen. In his exploration of the "definite
field" he had by this time narrowed down some of his interest
to the description of Negro slavery in Kentucky before the
war. He read through dusty files of Lexington newspapers.
He visited houses in which lived people old enough to be
able to retail to him memories of the days when blacks had
labored for "old master." He kept his ears open for folk-
tales, for anecdotes illustrating Negro humor and Negro
faithfulness. One of the queerest "characters" of the Bluegrass of that era was Charles C. Moore, a moneyed gentleman who lived on a farm about eight miles from Lexington
and was thought by many of his compatriots to be insane because he did not believe in using tobacco and was known to

be a "free thinker." In February of 1899 he was sentenced
to a term of imprisonment in the Federal Prison in Columbus, Ohio, on a charge of having sent obscene matter through
the mails, for in his paper, *The Bluegrass Blade*, he had
championed atheism and free love and naturally had aroused
the ire of the Christian churches. While in the penitentiary
Moore wrote his autobiography, *Behind the Bars; 31498*,
an oddity, and yet, for all its incoherence and absurdity,
worthy of respect as being the memoir of a dauntless and simple heart. In the course of this narrative Mr. Moore related
how he had helped Allen collect data for one of his papers:

One day Mr. Allen came to our house, and during our long conversation, said he was thinking of changing his life from teaching
to writing. I told him at once, that he ought to do it. He asked
me what he ought to write about, and I said: "About the Negroes
in the South; that is a subject that is fast growing in interest." He
said he was not old enough to know about slavery from memory,
and asked me who could tell him about it. I said, "I can; almost
anybody can who recollects it." I then started and told him a
number of stories about slavery, showing the best sides and the
worst sides of it. Among others, I told him the rabbit story about
my Uncle.

Some months afterward, I went into the book-store of Morton and Greenway, in Lexington, and picked up the last issue of
Harper's Magazine. Turning the pages to look at the pictures in
the magazine, I saw a full-page picture that I immediately recognized as the rabbit story of my Uncle John, and, looking further,
I found other stories that I had told Mr. Allen, and found his
name there, at the end of the first of the many printed articles I
have seen from his pen. At that time I was a prosperous farmer,
to whom a poor young man, like Mr. Allen, came for advice.

In at least one particular Mr. Moore was in error. Allen's
article, "Mrs. Stowe's Uncle Tom at Home in Kentucky,"
with illustrations by E. W. Kemble, who had also made the
drawings for "Through Cumberland Gap on Horseback"

and was to enliven several others of Allen's contributions, was not in *Harper's* but in *The Century Magazine* for October, 1887. The rabbit story alluded to was one meant to give an impression of the kinder side of slavery, of a sort of bonhomie to be found in many of the slave-owners: on a certain occasion some Negroes dropped work to run after a rabbit the dogs had started, and when a passer-by indignantly reported the fact to the master the latter exclaimed, "Sir, I'd have whipped the last d——n rascal of 'em if they *hadn't* run 'im!" As Allen tells this story he seems to ascribe it to De Tocqueville; at any rate he did not give Mr. Moore any credit and the "prosperous farmer" felt, as other people were to feel, that Allen had used and then forgotten him. "Mrs. Stowe's Uncle Tom at Home in Kentucky," composed with one eye on the novel which derived some of its material from Allen's state, gives a very favorable account of the relations between blacks and whites; it would have us believe that there was often affection between the two races; that few black families were torn apart at the auction block; that master and mistress took pains to establish the physical, moral, and spiritual well-being of their black dependents; that the Negro was usually better off as a slave than as a freedman. There is a regret that the good old aristocracy of landed wealth had been broken down by the Civil War and the Emancipation Proclamation and that a culture based upon a useful institution permitting a leisured class had passed away. Thus deliberately did Allen ignore what history has to say of the less roseate hues of slavery, even of slavery as it could be seen in Lexington.

In November he renewed his warfare upon the James-Howells camp by attacking the author of *The Rise of Silas Lapham* in an essay, published in *The Forum*, called "Caterpillar Critics." "The man who cannot criticize Howells nowadays isn't respectable," he had proclaimed in "Realism and

Romance," alluding to the condemnation allotted Howells for trying to stimulate the growth of realism, and in this new essay Allen thoroughly riddled his target, setting up at the close a very important text:

. . . we submit that the old point of view is right, and that the abiding and final test of literature will be furnished in the questions: What is its relation to truth? What to art? What to morals? As long as men are men, in a life where truth, art, and morals are to be extended by endeavor, they will assail as "misdemeanors" books that are violations of these, nor think themselves absurd for doing so.

Never did Allen make a clearer pronouncement of his neo-classicism, the spirit that was to guide his writing closely throughout not only these first years of his literary life but also until, with his last weariness, he laid the pen aside.

By this time Allen had good reason to feel that his abandonment of the schoolroom had been justified; his contributions were appearing regularly in the outstanding American magazines; none of his work had been rejected (nor was it ever to be); and, best of all, he was his own man, free to do what he wished when he wished. He had in the last three years written hard and, for him, very rapidly; he had as yet nothing like a national reputation, but he was making himself felt in the journalistic world. In one respect these acceptances by New York magazines and papers did Allen harm, because they heightened his sense of aloofness, of differentness from his fellow-townsmen. He suffered from the loneliness which must come to any creative person living in a community whose traditions are overwhelmingly social; he longed for someone with whom to share enthusiasms and ambitions in conversation, longed for a little understanding and encouragement now and then. Once he told the poet T. S. Jones, Jr., that when he began to write "the village prophets did all they could to discourage him." It was this feeling that he was set apart from his environment which inspired him to compose the essay by which he first attracted English commendation. This was "Always Bussing His Friends," in which he displayed strikingly that mastery over mingled sentimentality and pathos which was for a time to be his most apparent characteristic, almost his trade-mark. Pointing out that the wearing down of the exuberance of the days of Addison and Steele had resulted in a widespread lack of warmth and sympathy between acquaintances, he lamented the fact that men no longer demonstrated their friendship as unashamedly as Dick Steele had done—Steele, whose love for humankind had bubbled over until he made no effort to check it, had seen nothing unmanly in putting his arms about his friends, of kissing them as a token of his good nature. Nowadays such a practice would create only suspicion, thought Allen, because the laws of change are all against simplicity, more's the pity. "Of what perfect worth," he asked, "is a better civilization to us, if it make us not more kind?" Yet the sequel shows that when friendly advances were made to Allen he repulsed them almost as decisively as Addison had snubbed Steele's tenders of affection. For over in London Edmund Gosse read the essay and wrote at once to Joseph Gilder.

7 WHITEHALL GARDENS, LONDON, S. W.
March 21, 1888.

DEAR MR. GILDER,

I am very anxious to know who wrote the article "Always Bussing his Friends" in the *Critic*. It is one of the very best things you ever published—beautifully written, exquisitely felt. If it is a new writer, I should recommend you to hang on to him; but it is not possible that he is new. It is a pen possessed of every accomplishment.

I was so charmed with it that I took it straight over to Austin Dobson, and read every word of it to him. We wept, positively

wept—two foolish, middle-aged creatures with no figure left—
we wept.

Please let me know the author's name. And publish more by
the same hand.

Ever yours truly,

EDMUND GOSSE

Here was approbation from a distinguished Englishman that
should have made Allen or any other American writer toss his
hat into the air. But when Gilder, hoping to give pleasure to
his pseudonymous contributor, sent a copy of this complimentary letter to the Kentuckian, the reply from the man
who had just voiced a desire for appreciation was stiff, almost forbidding. In three sentences it disposed of the whole
matter of Gilder's letter:

I thank you for your favor of the twenty-eight inst., for the enclosed cheque, and for your letter of less recent date, which I
should have acknowledged had not the use of my eyes been forbidden me [at the time he was convalescing from a light attack of
typhoid fever].

To Mr. Gosse and to Mr. Dobson each I owe many debts of
gratitude; and it is a very pleasant surprise to learn that anything
of mine has fallen under their eyes and merited their recognition.
It would be enough for me to know this and to remain myself unknown; but I can have no objection to your telling the authorship
of my pseudonymous papers when and to whom you may desire.

Now this is gracefully expressed, but the trouble is that it is
too gracefully expressed; it is, like all of Allen's letters,
chilling in its self-conscious aim to be literary, to be graceful.
In a way it symbolizes the paradox that lay at the heart of
Allen's personality, the paradox of a strong wish for appreciation coupled with an instinctive recoil from friendly advances. For some reason he leaped back from contact with
people as a crab leaps back from the touch of something it
regards as dangerous, but instead of blaming himself for not

overcoming this diffidence he preferred to take the world to task now and then for not overcoming the obstruction which he had set up. It is a paradox not uncommon to sensitive people afflicted with some kind of feeling of guilt or inferiority, a paradox especially common to the writers of the romantic era that had barely closed. Think of Hawthorne and Melville, Emerson and Thoreau, all of them separatists, all of them oppressed with some sense of inadequacy, all of them unable to come even to those who would have received them. Recall Melville's pathetic hope of becoming intimate with Hawthorne; Hawthorne's chronic loneliness; Emerson's frequent self-raillery because of a lack of animal spirits; Thoreau's secession from the commonwealth and self-exile to Walden. These attitudes did not create their art, but they do help to explain it.

Moreover, ever since Scott, there had been growing up a tradition that the writer should be a gentleman. Writers before the Wizard of the North had assumed no such obligation, but Sir Walter's widely praised heroism and purity of word and deed had made as strong an impression upon his time as had his novels, and the cult of gentility for authors rose phoenix-like from his ashes. The influence of Victoria Regina and the approval she gave Tennyson fostered the cult; literature and its makers became eminently respectable; popular opinion bulwarked the respectability, and all writers who intended being accepted by the public conformed to what George Moore stigmatized as lending-library morals or took the consequences. Everyone knows what happened to Oscar Wilde and Rossetti and Swinburne when they ran counter to Tennysonian purity. In America, which was still obeying British conventions, the cult of the gentleman was as potent as it was abroad, at least in polite and accepted literature. Howells was as fastidious personally as his novels were placid, and Henry James, freed from the necessity of earning his living, took up his abode in a tower of ivory and became gentility incarnate. Allen had been lessoned by all these men save Melville; he believed himself made of finer fibre than most of his contemporaries; he had been trained by home and school and church in the traditions of *noblesse oblige* and of Christian ethics; he was familiar with Plato's doctrine uniting art and morality; he felt a revulsion at all that was ugly and brutal and cruel; and these things motivated his adoption of the mantle of gentility. He could not push himself, could not advertise himself, could not make use of his friends to his own advantage because such tactics were base. And so he set up about himself a wall of fire through which only the most knightly might pass and then only after severe trial. The physical determined this point of view only slightly. He was a bit neurotic, as any man so frustrated is likely to be, and his neuroticism was manifested in a restless moving from place to place, in quarrels with acquaintances, in failure to dismiss trifles with good humor, and later in his concentration upon his own symptoms, in his passing morbid interest in sex, in his suspicion of those who would have been his friends. But in 1888 Allen had no reason to feel physically inferior to anyone, and all who knew him are agreed that he did not appear to feel mentally inferior. Poverty, to be sure, had embittered him somewhat and sorely hurt his vanity, but his attitudes must be explained largely as arising from his concept of a gentleman. A gentleman, it would seem, was somewhat stand-offish and superior. But he was also loyal, brave, magnanimous, and clean, without fear and without reproach.

Besides the unexpected praise from Edmund Gosse, the year 1888 brought other memorable events. Mrs. Allen, who had been ill for some time with cancer, saw her son recover from his fever but knew herself weakening, and the convalescent now watched his mother anxiously as he had once watched his father. His literary career went forward. *The Century Magazine* published two essays and a short story, and in the late fall Allen went to Louisville to look up a young poet who worked in a poolroom and who was one day to be spoken of as the greatest nature poet of his time. But if Allen had any hopes of finding in Madison Cawein the friend for whom he was looking, he was disappointed; the Louisville man was not impressive in appearance, and Allen liked men of heroic proportions; and the poet was a little too convivial for the older man's taste. Nothing much came of the meeting, therefore; the two remained nominal friends, and later Allen admired Cawein's attractive wife, but that was all. Neither troubled himself to publicize the other's writing, and Allen found himself believing that Kentucky men of letters were either pretentious amateurs or men of talent who in one way or another fell short of the mark of gentleman. If he could but go to New York, perhaps. . . .

The story published in *The Century* was the outcome of Allen's visit to the most picturesque spot in Kentucky, the Abbey of La Trappe at Gethsemane, near Bardstown. He went there in order to write "A Home of the Silent Brotherhood" for *The Century*, but the first sight of the Abbey's gleaming white spire rising high above the trees must have given him a thrill and an eagerness that could not find complete expression in the writing of a travel essay, and when he passed from among the trees and had his first full view of the three-story pile of yellowish-gray masonry, a bit of medieval France transplanted as by a djin's might to the interior of Kentucky, he must have known that a story was inevitable. He thus described the main building in the opening paragraph of "The White Cowl":

In a shadowy solitary valley of Southern Kentucky and beside a noiseless stream there stands to-day a great French abbey of white-cowled Trappist monks. It is the loneliest of human habitations. Though not a ruin, an atmosphere of gray antiquity hangs about and forever haunts it. The pale-gleaming cross on the spire looks as though it would fall to the earth, weary of its aged unchangeableness. The long Gothic windows; the rudely carven wooden crucifixes, suggesting the very infancy of holy art; the partly encompassing wall, seemingly built to resist a siege; the iron gate of the porter's lodge, locked against profane intrusion— all are the voiceless but eloquent emblems of a past that still enchains the memory by its associations as it once enthralled the reason by its power.

He was admitted to the abbey; he was courteously received by the abbot and allowed to examine and learn whatever he pleased. The edifice, the inhabitants, the customs of piety, the atmosphere of rigorous worship and rigorous self-denial even of the right of speech, laid train to his imagination. But what would be the theme, the plot? Bothersome questions, always especially bothersome to Allen. The most popular theme of those days was that of the conflict between love and duty. It was a theme, too, which appealed to Allen, consciously or subconsciously, as interpretative of his own experience. And so he set to work on a story in which a monk should be torn between his vows and his passion for a woman. Three times he wrote and rewrote it before it satisfied Richard Watson Gilder, brother of the editor of *The Critic*, and came out in *The Century* for September, 1888, as a moving tale of fall and redemption. For Father Palemon's resistance was made to weaken before the insistent demands of the flesh, and love was made to triumph over keeping faith with God and the Trappist Order. But the story did not end with the monk's flight from Gethsemane. Significantly enough, he comes back; the world proves too much for him after the deaths of wife and child, and in his longing to get away from an emptiness too hideous to be supported by mortal ingenuity he returns to the place he had desecrated by infidelity but returns only to die, worn out by the anguish of remorse and grief. This is Allen's earliest use of the escape-from-reality *motif*, which is to recur over and over in his fiction, so often, indeed, as to hint strongly of being autobiographical in character. "The White Cowl" is Allen's first important story, self-conscious but, for all that, gripping. His writing arm was becoming more muscular. The chief defect in "The White Cowl" is immaturity of taste, revealed in its author's anxiety to make it literature; the descriptive phrases, particularly, are so forced as to remind a critical reader of the fine writing in a schoolboy composition. The conversation, too, is much too stilted; even in the 1890's people could hardly have talked so rhetorically as Allen's characters do. There are pages of propaganda against the monastic life, and whatever Allen's purpose in writing the story may have been—and he later contended that it was written for art's sake only—it cannot be denied that Catholics were right in believing that "The White Cowl" contained argument against secluded religious life. Other faults can be found with the story. For one thing, it makes use of the age-old device of having hero and heroine meet through the agency of a runaway horse. It contains too much symbolism, obviously learned from Hawthorne: Father Palemon, fleeing from temptation, soils the skirts of his cowl; the wounded head of Madeline leaves a bloodstain on his white bosom, just by his heart; in his uneasy dreaming that night the monk throws out his hand and twice strikes a crucifix hanging on his wall; dying, and placed upon his old cowl, his feet barely touch its earth-stains. In the use of Madeline as the name for the heroine, in an allusion to "The Eve of St. Agnes," and in the general richness of the pictorial passages Allen made it plain that he was fond of John Keats.

Since "A Home of the Silent Brotherhood" and "The White Cowl" centered about the same locality Allen now conceived the plan of pairing a descriptive or travel essay with a short story in order to capture the spirit of a place or time. He did not carry out this plan but he did write "Two Kentucky Gentlemen of the Old School," a tender and immediately popular story of the attachment between a master and his slave now known as "Two Gentlemen of Kentucky," to complement "Uncle Tom at Home in Kentucky." The design was interrupted by his finding other themes and by the second intrusion of death into the Allen household. In her seventy-fourth year Helen Foster Allen died, near midnight of the sixth of June, 1889, of a cancer which in those days never released its grasp upon a victim. The newspapers of that week were full of the horror of the Johnstown flood and of the measures being taken to relieve the destitute and suffering, but tucked away in the obituary column was a brief announcement of the death and of the burial service to be held in the home of Mrs. Ellen Martin on the eighth of June, at four in the afternoon. The notice was shorter than that for the father; it contained no word of eulogy and no statement beyond those of the dates of birth, death, and interment. But while Allen made no display of his grief his soul must have been heavy. What did he think as he closed the eyes of the woman who had borne him and folded the limp hands of the mother who had led him to a window to see his first redbird? Did the wedding ring on the left hand raise mocking questions in his mind? Did he reflect that the young bride of fifty-six years ago, dressed in her "white satin with ethereal silk overdress embroidered in an oak-leaf of green," had entered her married life with visions which had become less radiant year by year, that she who had been poised and calm had learned to be so through defeat? Did he ask himself why her courage should have brought her so little reward, why at the end she had not even a home—nothing but the love of two children? Did he see in her the tragic summary of human futility and ask himself angrily why such things must be? We do not know. But he did think of his sister. "Take good care of Annie," had been his mother's last injunction. And as he rode behind the hearse to the grave in the Lexington cemetery he must have said to himself that after all the world was for the living, that he must now dedicate himself to that sister as he once had to his mother. How little Annie had got from life, too! Beauty and family pride. But not the money which would have entitled her to the parties and other social affairs so dear to the hearts of Kentucky girls, and not the house and servants and carriage to uphold the family name; not even the happy romance which is each young woman's heritage; not the hope for a family circle including husband and children. He resolved that so long as he lived this sister should never want either comforts or kindness. He would try to make up for all that life had withheld.

And so back to his writing. In the month of his mother's death he saw in *The Century* his "King Solomon of Kentucky," a short historical story of a white vagabond who redeemed himself in the cholera outbreak in Lexington in 1833, the year of his parents' marriage; and in the following August and September he read his "County Court Day in Kentucky" and "Kentucky Fairs" in *Harper's*. In addition to these he had written minor papers for *The Critic*. These were busy, successful, and, apart from family bereavement, happy days for James Lane Allen. In three years he had pushed his way from complete obscurity to a position where his talents for the descriptive essay, for probing human passions, for defending the current idealism commanded respect for him as a writer of unusual freshness, learning, and grace; a writer who could hold his public alike with journalistic articles on this and that and with fiction meant to search the secret crypts of the heart. A glance at the bibliography at the

end of this book will show that he was producing material
with no ordinary energy, and this in spite of the fact that he
wrote slowly, corrected and revised painfully, and had difficulty in inventing action for his plots. He was making himself a writer almost by force, spending his nervous capital
with little thought of the morrow, and intent upon earning
money and reputation together. "Those days of toil were
so severe," he later informed a correspondent, "that when I
look back over them I cannot see why life could not have
been more kind to me, who would not have misused its kindness."

It is not surprising, therefore, that he should try to discover some means by which he might increase his income
from the pen, and the logical thing to hit upon then was the
lyceum platform. This was the conventional way by which
American authors might at once turn over extra dollars and
advertise themselves genteelly; at that very time, for instance,
Mark Twain and George W. Cable were proving a popular
team of lecturers and readers. But Allen had had no professional training or experience in the art of public speech and
was properly dubious as to his qualifications in that direction.
The sensible thing would be to put himself under the tutelage
of some good teacher of elocution, and so, while he continued
writing for the New York magazines, he negotiated with
James E. Murdock of Cincinnati for lessons in public speaking. Mr. Murdock, too old to undertake the instruction,
referred Allen to his granddaughter, a Miss Hollingshead,
who agreed to coach Allen for his new venture.

He was glad to spend part of the year in Cincinnati, for
the Ohio city offered advantages in books and music that
Lexington could not afford. In Cincinnati he lived at a fashionable boarding house kept by a Mrs. Bennett at the corner
of Park Avenue and MacMillan Street; here he found himself surrounded by a group of interesting talkers including

the Reverend Mr. Tinsley, rector of the Church of the Advent; the Reverend William McKibben, president of Lane Theological Seminary; Mr. and Mrs. James Foraker; and occasionally Judson Harmon, later governor of Ohio and prominent aspirant for the Democratic nomination for president of the United States. "The Professors of the Breakfast Table," they called themselves jocularly. Allen was scarcely one of the professors. As usual he withdrew within himself. He is remembered now as having been a courteous listener, a rare speaker but having something to contribute when he did speak, a reserved gentleman whose steady gray eyes enlarged by spectacles warned one not to overstep limits of privacy easily felt.

The lessons in speaking having progressed with satisfaction to teacher and pupil, Allen prepared for delivery a lecture on "The Literature of the New South," no copy of which is now extant. This he gave a few times in Chautauqua assemblies in Kentucky with varying success. The best contemporary account, written by Leigh Younge for *The Lexington Herald and Presbyter*, has this to say:

James Lane Allen, the rising Kentucky writer of whom we are justly so proud, and whose papers on Kentucky have done so much to call the attention of the North to our Bluegrass country, was one of the lecturers. And when he came with his carefully prepared paper on "The Literature of the New South," we felt that he knew whereof he spoke. He dealt with the Southern writers by classes, and while he gave to everyone full meed of justice and admiration, he yet began and ended with the famous statement of Emerson's at a Boston dinner, that the Southern literature was yet to come. The dialect story, the negro story, and the old French element which have been so charmingly treated, he told us, have had their day; they will take their places in the folk-lore of the country, and serve a part in the chronicle-making of the past, as nothing else can do; but the time for the interest in the reading of them is gone. And the coming subject of Southern literature is yet to be discovered. Who will be the fortunate Columbus?

Perhaps Allen dreamed that he might be the Columbus, for the phraseology of the latter part of this reporting suggests that it was based upon Allen's paper or on notes he furnished. He was not to be the discoverer. That honor was to await the advent of a woman of a sister state, Virginia; but although he did not himself chart the outline of the new southern literature he was shrewd enough and fair enough to give tribute to Ellen Glasgow when she made her findings known to the world.

The lectures did not yield Allen all that they had promised. He was not eloquent on the platform and he probably felt decidedly uncomfortable while trying to be. Once he confessed to Miss Hollingshead in a letter that he was so worn out by work and Cincinnati heat that "the truth is I could not be heard by those farthest away," but he added with pride that he had been offered an engagement "from Chicago for next winter." That winter he wrote again to his teacher: "The slight experience of this year has admonished me, that the financial returns are not compensation for loss of time from my especial work; and the pain of not satisfying part of an audience is greater than the pleasure of satisfying the other part—when the *honorarium* has to be taken from both." How deeply he was disappointed by his failure as a lecturer we do not know, but we do know that he never again made a similar trial.

Doubtless he was confirmed in his decision to devote himself exclusively to letters by the acceptance and publication of "Sister Dolorosa," serialized in *The Century Magazine* from December, 1890, to and including February, 1891. This story is easily bracketed with "The White Cowl" inasmuch as it tells of the tragic love of a nun for a young man of the

Bluegrass and thus reverses the central situation of the earlier narrative. It is in almost every way superior to "The White Cowl"; it is more compact and intense, its symbolism is less forced, its sentiment kept within discreet bounds, its general treatment more sympathetic. The author read Pauline Cambron's heart with clearer eyes than he had turned upon Father Palemon and he told her story with what is indeed remarkable intuition and with a pity that compels the reader to feel profoundly for the unhappy heroine. There are too many Pre-Raphaelite touches in style, there are too many tears, and the ending is singularly unfortunate—this last is to be one of Allen's chief defects throughout his career—although in justice it must be recorded that the tale originally ended where Gordon Helm saw Sister Dolorosa, unnoticed during his last visit to the Convent of the Stricken Heart. The printed ending was added at the advice of some unknown friend and proves that an author needs to be delivered not only from his enemies but also from such friends. The last chapter is a letter written by a Sister Agatha, who describes the leper colony at Molokai, makes enthusiastic references to Father Damien (these irrelevancies accounted for by the popular interest in Stevenson), and gives a short history of Sister Dolorosa's drowning before she had a chance to be disfigured by the plague, so that her beauty remained untainted in death. It is not, of course, the death which mars the ending, but the shift in point of view and in setting. Again it should be noted that Allen erected his story upon the escape-from-life *motif*. But the protagonist does not have a brief interval of happiness such as fell to the lot of Father Palemon; she has only resignation, exile, and death, and in this increasing somberness one divines something of the melancholy which bereavement had brought to the author.

The last month of 1890 saw his "Flute and Violin" in *Harper's Magazine*. This, one of the best known of his short stories and still admired by people who care most for his early work, is certainly sentimental enough to justify the criticism that Allen liked to wring tears from his readers. Men and women brought up on the kind of book which filled the shelves of Sunday school libraries two generations ago will doubtless feel an affinity between "Flute and Violin" and the popular moral tale of auld lang syne, even while they concede that Allen's writing has a dignity and a directing intelligence that the pious stories too often lacked. "Flute and Violin" has two heroes: the Reverend James Moore, whom Allen erroneously represented as a bachelor, and a little lame boy, David, suggested by a painting that Allen had stared at while waiting for his meals in one of the Lexington boarding-houses. The little lame boy was, like Laney Allen, empty of pocket, and, also like his creator, he had made a cornstalk fiddle on which he had learned to play "O Thou Fount of Every Blessing!" He likewise coveted a real violin and longed ardently for some kind of esthetic stimulus. When a traveling exhibition of wax figures came to Lexington, David, half-sick and goaded beyond honesty by his desire to see something artistic, stole a quarter in order that he might be admitted to the museum. The sight there of a rude painting of the Christ so troubled his conscience that he hurried out of town in a daze of remorse and fever and fell asleep in an abandoned rope-walk. Of course he died of his illness, whereupon the parson, accusing himself bitterly because in ecstasy over a woman's kiss he had neglected his protégé, performed an appropriate penance by hanging up his flute and playing upon it no more. It is not a great story. Many judges of fiction would deny that it is even a good one. But Allen liked it and gave its title to his first book, where it holds the place of honor. Faulty as it was, "Flute and Violin" had a quiet humor in certain passages, a distinction of style, a skill in the assembling of major and minor themes that presaged greater achievements and did much to encourage the Harpers to publish the author's initial volume. With the publication of that volume Allen's career as "magazinist" came to an end. Thereafter he was to publish much of his writing in magazines before it issued in books, but he was to do so to increase his income and not to keep body and soul together. For twenty-five years there was to be no more need to drive himself to hackwork or to pick up the crumbs that fell from editorial tables. For twenty-five years he was to live on his books. And then necessity sent him back to the magazine short story.

CHAPTER III

THE FEMININE PRINCIPLE

IT WAS A fortunate time for a writer with the gifts and limitations of James Lane Allen to launch his first work of fiction. The period described so amusingly by Thomas Beer as a Mauve Decade, noted for its pruderies, its gloved and scented manners, its sentiment and earnestness of purpose, was opening. Mid-Victorian ethics were dominant in the conventions which regulated social behavior and in the rules which made up the canon of good literature. In such a country and at such a time Allen was completely at home. Nursed, as we have seen, in an evangelical religion and in the chivalrous tradition that a woman was the noblest influence in a man's life, educated in the Greek and Roman classics (carefully selected) and in the graver productions of English literature, turning to the novel at first only to compliment such sound moralists as Hawthorne and George Eliot and Thackeray and Dickens, he had no hesitation in subscribing to the requirements for popular fiction in the nineties. So long as he could retain as a central point of view a belief in the virtues of self-control and in the innate goodness of a race which, contrary to Calvin's teaching, had the wish and the capacity to achieve its own salvation, so long as he could present man as an individual able to catch a glimpse of heaven, James Lane Allen was to make his name widely known as a representative American author.

The reading public then was largely feminine in sex and in taste. Even a hasty survey of the magazine articles written for its consumption will demonstrate the presence of an attitude which seems to later generations naïve and credulous, with a strong undercurrent of national self-consciousness soon

to bourgeon into imperialism. One result of this waxing national spirit was a demand for more books by our own writers,
so that Houghton, Mifflin & Company published in 1891
sixty-nine volumes by Americans as against seven by Brit-
ishers, and the Harpers put their imprint upon almost twice
as many books of native origin as upon those imported from
the mother country. Allen and his associates were perhaps
not unpleased to observe that writers not of Anglo-Saxon traditions were on the whole ignored by a public interested in
such matters as hypnotism, the rights and wrongs of convent
life, the propriety of riding a bicycle, the duty of Sunday
rest. Foreigners had such outlandish names. Moreover, too
many of them handled themes which called for bold and
straight thinking, and the public then preferred to do little
thinking of that kind.

It was not only the muscularity of the themes that
caused readers of the nineties to shy away from such men as
Ibsen, then being brought into the limelight by George Bernard Shaw. Foreign novelists and dramatists were also too
liberal in their mention of sex relations and in their views on
sex problems in the days when the word sex was itself taboo
in polite circles. Even at this short distance in time from the
Mauve Decade it is not easy to explain the fierceness with
which some of those writers were condemned, but it is easy to
see that decorum in dress, conduct, conversation, thinking,
and writing was expected of anyone who wished the approval
of the generality. Mark Twain was still looked upon with
suspicion by many a librarian and school teacher and Stephen
Crane's name was often whispered in scandal. Painting and
sculpture as well as literature were asked to conform to a
strict primness of taste. "It is only when she [art] attains a
more refined sense of delicacy that, as one that 'hath clean
hands and a pure heart,' she will ascend to the holy place
and her pure eyes will behold the ineffable," wrote Elizabeth

Stuart Phelps for *The Forum* in August, 1890; and a lady
viewing some paintings of the nude in an exhibition at the
Academy of Fine Arts in Philadelphia, March 7, 1891, wrote
in protest to a newspaper: "I hate these pictures with a bitter hatred." *The Critic,* potent in shaping our literary ideals
during that decade, was emphatically on the side of restraint
and decency, taking umbrage even at the outspokenness of
Grant Allen and comparing him with the Frenchman whose
name was then widely synonymous with evil: "Maupassant
at his worst could not do so much harm as Grant Allen."
And Charles Dudley Warner, alarmed by certain signs of
restiveness under the priggish authority of the time, warned
his large following that American fiction was falling into
"deep, unhealthy places," almost as Allen was to deplore the
same kind of change six years later. If a modern student
search in vain for the shocking fiction of the American nineties, he must remember that critical opinion was then so sensitive that William Dean Howells was thought iconoclastic for
proposing that "doesn't" and "can't" should, for the sake
of naturalness and smoothness, be used in reporting dialogue.
Standards were standards in the 1890's.

Nor was the public content to stop with a strong prejudice against fearless treatment of sex. As a natural corollary
of the axiom that sex was ugly it maintained that love and
courtship must be viewed romantically—that is, seen through
the eyes of the imagination rather than those of experience—
and that stories of love should end, after the principals
had run a rough course of obstacles, in marriage. The true
heroine must be invested with the beauty and innocence which
had become traditional in the English novel from the days
of Walter Scott; the hero, granted with some misgivings a
little more leeway in his actions, must nevertheless approach
the ideal of goodness, honor, and courage; to both young
people (and it is significant that they usually were young)

love must be a poetic dream remote from biological urge or social complexity. If the hero could begin as a poor young lad and end as a capitalist he gave an added fillip to the pleasure of the people who were then reading Horatio Alger's *Five Hundred Dollar Clerk* but who notwithstanding were soon to shout with glee over a president's denunciations of unscrupulous business men. American literature had outgrown the swaddling clothes of sensibility which it wore openly in the closing years of the eighteenth century, but a deathbed scene, shrouded in the right weave of pathos, could still make friends for its author. In 1886 *The Critic* had soberly conducted a symposium on whether a writer who aimed to make his readers weep should first weep himself and had received answers from T. B. Aldrich, Boyesen, Cable, Mark Twain (Mark replied in the affirmative), Eggleston, Robert Grant, Edward E. Hale, Brander Matthews, Amélie Rives, and Frank R. Stockton. Allen's eyes were open to the absurdity in much of the display of feeling in current fiction; he contributed to *The Critic* an essay called "On Novelties in Pathos," in which he demanded new methods in the technique of sobbing heroines; yet he did not, either because of personal melancholy or a wish to appeal to a feminine mood, successfully avoid all the pitfalls which he could point out to others.

Another circumstance that greatly favored Allen's venture in 1891 was the interest in geographical fiction. The best known novelists and short story writers were associated in the public mind with different sections of our country. Bret Harte had grown wealthy for a time by romanticizing the California gambler and miner. Cable's "'Sieur George" had appeared in *Scribner's Monthly* as early as 1873; Joel Chandler Harris's Uncle Remus got between book covers in 1880; Mark Twain had been celebrating the Mississippi in volumes ever since 1883. In 1871 Edward Eggleston had combined

pedagogy and narrative in his tale of an Indiana schoolmaster,
and in 1877 Sarah Orne Jewett published *Deephaven*. Ten
years later came Mrs. Freeman's *A Humble Romance and
Other Stories* and Thomas Nelson Page's idealization of ante-
bellum life "in ole Virginia." It could not have escaped Allen's notice that the nation was awake to the charm in reading of strange communities and strange customs, nor could he
have failed to perceive that attention was bestowed most
freely upon the South; it was easy, therefore, for him to
reason that his own state, always evocative of romance, needed
only a skillful and constant pen to be made as inviting in
print as any of its sisters. But he did not surrender uncondi-
tionally to the cohorts of local color whom he had once assailed. He would not rely too much upon dialect, peculiar
manners, and unfamiliar scene, as several of his contemporaries did, for those things he knew would have only a
transient value. He saw that all too often a writer tried to
conceal his dearth of story or of ability by advancing under
the camouflage of locality. He agreed with the *Edinburgh
Review* which, after surveying our novelists in 1891, declared
that "their works are deficient in creative power, and triviality
is their curse," and he resolved that no matter what might
be said against him he should never be termed trifling. To
Allen literature was an art to be regarded with the highest
seriousness. If a man wrote, let him proceed from his deepest feeling and profoundest knowledge, with no thought of
securing a passing reputation or of pandering to a dulled
taste. What he did should be greater than he was himself.
It was his purpose, even at the outset when he deliberately
made use of the prevalent interest in local color literature
and thus explored his "definite field," to eschew the shallower
treatment which would focus the gaze upon a locality's picturesque distinctions in speech and manners and which would

exalt setting above characterization in order to win readers. Hawthorne rather than Miss Murfree would be his model.

Flute and Violin and Other Kentucky Tales came out in January, 1891. The "other tales" were "King Solomon of Kentucky," "Two Gentlemen of Kentucky," "The White Cowl," "Sister Dolorosa," and "Posthumous Fame; or a Legend of the Beautiful," an allegory that does not fit comfortably into a collection of Kentucky stories and that strongly suggests Hawthorne. "King Solomon of Kentucky" and "Two Gentlemen of Kentucky" are founded upon real people and incidents and so make justifiable use of, although they do not rely on, dialect.

The reader who today picks up *Flute and Violin* will be impressed chiefly by three things: an excess of sentiment, a style too heavily adorned, and a puritanic point of view which is responsible for the weaving of allegories and symbols into the patterns of the narratives. To none of these stories is Kentucky any more indispensable than New England is to Hawthorne's romances; it is the souls of his people that Allen sets himself to scrutinize and to report; it is their moral problems that exercise his judgment and urge him to interpret the items of conduct involved. The ethical question is ever superior to the events which circle about it. Kentucky furnishes a *mis en scène* which conditions but slightly the actions and thoughts of his protagonists. The parson who neglected his duty under the spell of a woman's kiss, the nun and the monk who faced a conflict between loves and vows, the maker of tombstones who longed to immortalize the memory of his beloved—these are not sprung alone from Kentucky soil nor could the heroism of an outcast like King Solomon or the faithfulness of a slave to his master be found only in the Bluegrass state. Allen was clearly aiming, as he said a good writer would, to transcend the local color technique and to seize the universal in interest, to create the new type of writing of which he had made prophecy in his lecture on the literature of the New South.

Yet there were sufficient allusions to Kentucky's history and Kentucky's cycle of seasons to ensnare the average critic and the general reader and to persuade them that they were discovering virgin country that had so far been neglected by the local colorists. One or two reviewers detected a difference. The writer in *The Nation,* for example, said that "Mr. James Lane Allen's book of Kentucky stories shows that any jaded criticism is all wrong; that there was an imaginative height and a poetic depth to be touched which no previous hand had reached in this class of historic fiction."

As to the sentimentality, that was, on the whole, so much to the liking of the feminine taste that it aroused only an occasional protest, such as that of *The Chicago Times:* "Mr. Allen's chief lack as a story-teller seems to be in the element of humor. Not altogether that which makes people laugh, but rather showing in the prevailing tendency to stir the fountain of tears rather than appeal to any other human feeling." The style provoked no American cautionings, from which we may infer that it was regarded with equanimity, but a reviewer in the English *Athenaeum* wrote frankly that although it "is presumably intended to be elevated, it only succeeds in being crude and occasionally bombastic." To support his contention he quoted the following description of Sister Dolorosa:

She was still within the dim, half-awakened region of womanhood, whose changing mists are beautiful illusions, whose shadows about the horizon are the mysteries of poetic feeling, whose purpling east is the pallette of the imagination, and whose upspringing skylark is blithe aspiration that has not yet felt the weight of the clod it soars within.

No one will hesitate in agreeing with the Englishman to pronounce this a specimen of affected writing. But what the

English critic overlooked is that the nice balancing of clauses and something of the spirit of that sentence were borrowed directly from Thackeray's famous picture of Beatrix in Book II, Chapter VII of *Henry Esmond*. And in 1890 Thackeray was thought to be a pretty safe model to follow.

There was very little dissent to the praise that greeted Allen's first book, and as he read the hundreds of approving press notices which Annie cut out and pasted on sheets of stiff brown paper he had every reason to feel that his first step toward fame had been a sturdy one. With very little encouragement, with hurdles in the shape of poverty and sectional prejudice and indifference from his friends, he had won acclaim from reviewers and readers, had done something to make his name memorable, had even been compared to Hawthorne, an estimate that was to be more and more frequent during the next ten years of his writing. Yet he was not wholly content with his achievement; was, indeed, never going to be satisfied with what he had done, for he possessed the restlessness and irritability shared by all creators. He was always to long to put his name near the top of the roll of American men of letters and always to be conscious that his longing was unfulfilled, that it was, in fact, a futile presumption. "Mysterious complexity of our mortal nature and estate that we should so desire to be remembered after death, though born to be forgotten!" he cried out in "Posthumous Fame," that parable which might have been written by the lonely moralist of Salem.

Two minor annoyances ruffled somewhat the calm waters of self-satisfaction. Not all Catholics were able to read with complacence Allen's stories of priests and nuns who exhibited the passions if not the frailties of more worldly human beings, and some adherents of Holy Church attacked him as a betrayer of hospitality, one who had profited by the confiding charity of the abbot of Gethsemane in order to send broadcast an unfair account of monastic discipline and discontent. The charge of having repaid a kindness with an unkindness cut to the quick of Allen's sensitiveness and led him to fancy himself more disliked than he really was. Long after "The White Cowl" and "Sister Dolorosa" had been forgotten by the many he was to tell of an incident of the early nineties in which he believed himself the object of a mildly hostile demonstration in Cincinnati: with two young ladies he was watching an outdoor religious procession, the word passed about that he was James Lane Allen who had written stories that came near blaspheming their faith, people nudged elbows, scowled at him, muttered. Criticism of Allen did reach such a proportion that he thought best to meet it in a letter, printed in *The Century* for May, 1891. His stout defense was that he could have composed "The White Cowl" from such material as anyone could have secured from volumes like *The Rule of St. Benedict, The Centenary of Catholicity in Kentucky, The Life of the Rev. Charles Nevincky,* and Chateaubriand's *Vie de Rancé,* and that he did actually put together the plot of the other story, "Sister Dolorosa," before visiting the convent of Loretto. Finally, he submitted that like Balzac or Valera or Daudet or Dumas he was seeking not a good sermon but a good story.

Many members of the Roman communion, to be sure, found no offense in these two tales, but found rather that they dignified the tragedy of human affection at war with conscience and were able to submerge any thought of church differences in admiration of a skill which had uplifted faltering men and women to a plane of nobility. There is a story of a monk of the Trappist Foundation on the Campagna who was absolved from silence so that he might guide tourists through the buildings. Asked if he had read "The White Cowl" he replied, "Yes, many times." His brothers, he explained, did not read English and thought the story a religious work—"and it is," he added, "a religious work of the highest significance." Allen had, nevertheless, some reason for thinking that he had alienated Catholic readers; subsequently he would predict with irony that reviewers of that faith would be consistently adverse to his books. For his part, Allen cherished the antipathy, or suspected antipathy, unwisely; it bore fruit like Blake's poison tree. Isaac F. Marcosson, his closest friend then, says of him that he "had a profound dislike for Italy which was due largely to his obsession about the Catholic Church." The author of *Flute and Violin* was never to be attacked with impunity, especially if he knew himself innocent of intention to harm.

The second annoyance was something like a family quarrel. There was another James Lane Allen, a cousin who practiced law in Chicago, and since he also wrote for magazines readers had every chance to confuse the work of the two Kentuckians. As early as the eighth of September, 1888, the Lounger column of *The Critic* contained an announcement inspired by the Lexington Allen to the effect that he was not the attorney; three weeks later the Chicago Allen responded warmly. The two men, he retorted, were sons of brothers and had been named for an uncle living in Danville, and there had been a kind of gentleman's agreement that the uncle was to sign himself James L. Allen, the Chicago resident James Lane Allen, and the Lexington cousin was to be content with Lane Allen, which had, indeed, been the name under which he was commonly known until he began to write. The lawyer protested, therefore, that his Lexington kin had no right to complain if in usurping a name he had consented not to use he caused misapprehension among many readers. To this the author of the Harper stories replied tartly, whereupon the Lounger summarily dismissed the case, upheld the Lexington magazinist, and chided the lawyer for having perpetrated in his letter "a bit of prose so obnoxious to all the canons of literary criticism." And so when the first edition of *Flute and Violin* was put on the market it carried not only a fulsome dedication to his mother but also a biting foreword in which the author stated briefly the argument between himself and his cousin and ended by saying that "he now gladly asks that the responsibility of all his work be placed where it solely belongs." Thereafter the novelist was to be angered more than once by hearing and believing that the other James Lane Allen was not unwilling to borrow some luster from the identity of their names and that he was not above passing himself off as the writer of the subsequent popular novels.

Pleased as he was with this first book, Allen did not overrate it. He presented a copy to himself with the inscription: "To the Author, with his humble compliments and profound apologies." Already he was planning to devote himself to his career with a single-mindedness which was to make him the least known prominent man of letters of his period in America. Like Hawthorne he had gone through a rigorous apprenticeship in which, however, he had gained attention more easily than had the New Englander. To be nearer the truth, he was still in an apprentice's apron, for he thoroughly revised the magazine stories before issuing them in book form, blue-pencilling for compression—his outstanding fault being, in his eyes, a tendency to verbiage—for accuracy of fact and exactness of word, and for avoiding offense to the most scrupulous taste or prejudice.

Flute and Violin was published in January, and as soon as the proofs were out of his hands, the book on the stalls, and the reviews read, Allen began to make trips between Cincinnati and the Bluegrass while he assembled data for his last journalistic essay. This, "Homesteads of the Blue-Grass," appeared in *The Century* for May, 1892, and then joined the other travelogues to make up Allen's second volume,

The Blue-Grass Region of Kentucky, published later in the same year. This is not an impressive volume, although it had a second edition in 1898 and a third in 1900, each accounted for by the sales of *The Choir Invisible* and *The Reign of Law,* respectively. At its worst it is only fair reporting of landscapes and people and houses and manners; at its best it is a sympathetic interpretation of a population that Allen was anxious to have understood, even while he chid it for indifference to the arts. He was especially concerned to destroy the fiction that Kentuckians had an instinctive partiality for homicide. "Positively," he wrote in a kind of pet, "it is true that gentlemen in this State do not now get satisfaction out of each other in the market-place, and that on a modern county court day a three-cornered hat is hardly to be seen. . . . The fighting habit and the shooting habit were both more than satisfied during the Civil War." The book lingers fondly over a culture rapidly fading; it is plangent with a love of the outdoors, of simplicity and generosity of living, of refinement. As a chronicle of what Allen was to regard as a departed glory, as social history, it possesses a value which will preserve it from full obscurity. Its very nature, its requirements were a handicap to the author; yet its freshness and spirit make it fair reading today and assure it a place among the best books about a section of our country.

The greeting which this second venture received persuaded Allen that it was the writer of fiction who would receive the most popular and critical notice, for although *The Blue-Grass Region* was praised generally the praise seemed but perfunctory. *The Atlantic Monthly* alone found fault, expressing the unkind and surely erroneous opinion that "people will get little better idea of the region and its relation to Kentucky and will know little more of Kentucky"; and then added that it would have been better not to have printed part of the title-page in blue ink. That was in September, 1892. Over a year before Thomas Nelson Page had brought Allen to the notice of editors by including him with Mrs. Burton Harrison, Lafcadio Hearn, Amélie Rives, and Molly Elliott Seawell as one of the chief southern writers since the war, a compliment which pleased Allen but which is almost meaningless today when Mrs. Harrison's *The Count and the Congressman* is almost totally forgotten, Amélie Rives's *The Quick and the Dead* is no longer considered shocking, Molly Elliot Seawell's social comedies would be thought insipid were they ever read, and Hearn alone grows in stature. But in 1891 those were potent names to the public and to the editors who tried to give that public what it wanted, and so Allen was grateful for the praise and made a point of cultivating Page at the latter's home in Washington. The two had much in common and were drawn together until a thoughtless aside terminated the embryonic friendship. One day the conversation turned to bicycling as conversation then often did and Allen remarked that he rode and thought it good exercise. "Ah, yes," commented the Virginian, "it must indeed be good sport. I myself don't ride but I have a butler who does and he likes it very much." To anyone as morbidly sensitive as Allen that implied comparison was a direct insult. The acquaintance ended right there and no apology, if offered, could have renewed it. But that was years later, and in 1892 the effect of the publicity from Page was to encourage Allen to put the finishing paragraphs to a story on which he had been writing, a story which should have its setting in the scenery and history and legends of Kentucky and yet should serve notice to the world that he must not be classified as a mere local colorist.

Lippincott's Magazine, inspired by Page's laudatory item, had asked something of Allen for its Western Number, and to that periodical he sent his new story, "John Gray: A Kentucky Tale of the Olden Time." This was published in

June, 1892, accompanied by an autographed cut of its serious, professorial-looking author, able now to dress well, for his long coat was obviously lined with silk and his cuffs were as noticeably immaculate as they were thereafter to be to the end of his life. The plot of "John Gray" is slight. The hero, a schoolmaster in Lexington in 1795, is in love with Amy Falconer, a pretty but shallow girl who lives on the outskirts of the village with aunt and uncle. Through the machinations of one Stafford a misunderstanding between the two lovers arises and Amy marries Joseph Holden, another suitor. Humiliated and disillusioned, Gray thereupon goes east, marries, and eventually sends his son to Transylvania University as a student and with instructions to make the acquaintance of Mrs. Falconer, Amy's aunt. Amy drops out of the story entirely, John never describes his wife to his Kentucky friends, and there is the suggestion, elusive but arresting, that he and Mrs. Falconer loved each other, the man not realizing it until too late.

It is easy to uncover flaws in "John Gray." For one thing the reader is obliged to feel that it owes almost too much to other writers. The tenuous plot is indubitably a variation on that of *Henry Esmond*, in which the hero eventually marries not the girl he was first in love with but the mother of that girl; and when Allen calls John's son an "impudent young fellow" we are rightly reminded of Arthur Pendennis. Gray's name is the same as the hero's in Trollope's *Can You Forgive Her*, although that similarity is likely nothing more than coincidental. There is a schoolgirl who spends many hours in drawing tomahawks on a slate, and she makes us think of Traddles and his skeletons in *David Copperfield*. One chapter is entitled "One of the Weird Sisters," an allusion any schoolboy would identify, and another, "The Poetry of Earth," argues that Allen was acquainted with George Meredith.

More objectionable than the probable borrowings is the sentimentalism characteristic of Allen's earliest writings. It is evidenced in style, as when he describes clouds as "those dear Alps of the blue air"; it is plain in such episodes as that in which the villain is punished by a fall from a horse, is thereby made repentant, and before he dies is seen to weep and kiss John Gray's hand; it looms large in Gray's state of mind throughout, notwithstanding the author's declaration that his hero was not a sentimentalist. The last sentence, giving the reader a final look at Mrs. Falconer, illustrates neatly the tone of the whole story and lets the curtain fall in a way that was sufficiently agreeable to a *fin-de-siècle* audience: "She let the letter drop softly to her lap, and, folding her delicate withered hands on the window-sill, rested her forehead on them in prayer." Renunciation and resignation had brought their reward.

To support the frail plot, history was dragged in by a mighty tug; much enthusiasm was expended upon George Washington, even to the introduction of the hatchet story, and upon a eulogy of Bluegrass progress. Thus Allen exhibited at the outset a tendency to pad his tales with historical notes and didactic letters and lectures, a tendency that was to become more and more pronounced until certain of his short novels were almost to be swallowed up by preachments. As for conversation, his dramatis personae rarely get beyond a bookish speech, sententious and serious, delivered sometimes to the crack of a rhetorical whip.

When Lippincott issued *John Gray* in book form in 1893 Allen made but a few changes in the original text, and those as usual in the interest of condensation or of clearness. His revision was careful, however, down to exact selection of word and mark of punctuation. The new book aroused no enthusiastic comment, and from the fact that Allen kept no press clippings about it one can infer that he did not himself value it too highly, especially after it was forgotten when it re-appeared as the hugely successful *The Choir Invisible*. A second edition of *John Gray* was printed after *A Kentucky Cardinal* had taken its place among best sellers.

Allen's next production was his triumph of this first and romantic period and is, if present signs are prophetic, the story which of all his works is most likely to endure as a minor classic of our literature. "A Kentucky Cardinal" was a serial for *Harper's Magazine* for May and June of 1894. At once it put its spell upon readers, and Henry Mills Alden, who told Allen just before the younger writer was about to sail for Europe that it was "one of the finest things in American literature; it is something to which one will turn with joy when most contemporary literature is forgotten," was but voicing the verdict of the critic-at-large. Harper and Brothers at once made arrangements to put this idyl between the covers of a book, and after the author's habitually meticulous corrections had been made it came out, with two important alterations, in the same year. One variation was the insertion of two and a half pages in the fifteenth chapter to include the kissing of Sylvia, thus preparing the way for a complication in the sequel, not then fully in mind. The other was at the end, where in the book one finds a row of dots and the prescient sigh: "Ah, but the long, long silence of the trees," which, also demonstrating that Allen was looking ahead to *Aftermath*, must have fallen like a chill upon hitherto delighted readers.

Written in the first person—there are only two other such among Allen's novels—and partly in diary entries, *A Kentucky Cardinal* allowed the writer to express himself with unusual naturalness; he sloughed off much of the pedantry and many of the affectations which are so heavy in his more formal narratives. In *A Kentucky Cardinal* he let himself go and the result is an engaging story of young love quite unlike any-

thing else in our letters. Against a background of fruits and
flowers, on country places just outside Lexington, and with the
changing seasons giving color and atmosphere to the moods
of hero and heroine, Georgiana Cobb and Adam Moss meet
and love and suffer, their nerves exquisite and their ideals
finespun. Here for the first time in Allen's fiction we come
upon the test *motif*, for the girl gives Adam the choice of
capturing and imprisoning a redbird as a gift to her or of losing the chance to win her favor. Unlike the hero of the later
The Heroine in Bronze Adam weakens after a bitter struggle in which his love of all things wild is pitted against his
love for his beautiful neighbor. And then after he has captured and caged the cardinal Georgiana tells him what he
might have anticipated she would, that it was a mistake thus
to surrender his real self even to her. It is too late to redeem
the sacrifice of the bird, but the lovers marry, leaving us with
a lingering suspicion that all will not be well in this union
brought about by the man's allowing his fondness for a human being to outrun his devotion to nature.

It would not be fair to complain of such a story that its
protagonists are too brittle, too decorative, too languorous.
An author should not be judged for failing to do what he had
no intention of doing. Allen was not yet attempting realism.
He wished only to write an idyl of provincial life, a kind of
Kentucky *Paul and Virginia*, a romance in which the traditional hero and heroine should partake of something of the
nature of costumed figures in a tiny pageant, should move
with some of the stateliness and grace of a minuet through
a courtship whose tempo and details were considerably slower
and daintier than those of a generation or two later. And if
nothing else were to rise in defense of *A Kentucky Cardinal*,
its style, characterized by lightness, slyness of jest, and restraint of emotion, would be sufficient to win it an acquittal
on the accusation, as Lucy Lockwood Hazard accuses it, of

being neurasthenic. "Neurasthenic" is a word which might be reserved to describe much more recent fiction than Allen's and cannot with justice be applied to *A Kentucky Cardinal*. For once Allen touched his pen but lightly to the paper, and few readers will not be captivated by the resulting easy flow of narrative, the gentle insistence upon disciplined feelings. What happened was that Allen mixed in just the right proportions that reverence of nature which was one of the stock properties of romantic writers, and his more or less academic interest in people; that he injected enough measures of humor to dissolve the possible artificiality and so to create as if by magic chemistry a chivalric southern gentleman beloved by a southern girl who, for all her starched and crinoline ways, was playful, tender, and altogether human.

If it is easy to understand how *A Kentucky Cardinal* can be enjoyed now, why the *Golden Book Magazine* should have reprinted it in 1929, it is easier to understand why it sent the public to the bookstores in 1894. In that year the favorite novels in American homes were *David Copperfield*, *Ivanhoe*, *The Scarlet Letter*, *Uncle Tom's Cabin*, *Ben-Hur*, *Adam Bede*, and *Vanity Fair*, a self-evident tribute to the respectability of the readers of that decade. F. Marion Crawford, receiving as much as ten thousand dollars on the publication of a new novel, stood at the top of native novelists in point of sales. John Kendrick Bangs's *Coffee and Repartee* was in great demand. The timid were recoiling from Grant Allen's *The Woman Who Did* with an emphasis that obliged the English writer to return to safer subjects; Trilby's morals were being looked at askance; the next year the authorities were to suppress *The Police Gazette*. *A Kentucky Cardinal* struck a nice balance between such books as were frowned upon by the orthodox critics and such fictions as those of E. P. Roe. It was the first of Allen's writings to receive wide acclaim. Hamilton Wright Mabie, thereafter to be the Kentuckian's personal and professional friend, expressed the general reaction when he wrote that "*A Kentucky Cardinal* is the most finely conceived calendar of the year which the imagination has yet fashioned in this country: a calendar with sounds, sights, and fragrance for the senses, and with spiritual suggestion and hint of deeper correspondences for the soul." A note in *The Bookman* for June, 1895, recorded that it was "one of the most successful books of the year." Across the Atlantic, where Allen looked with pardonable anxiety for approval of his work, opinion was not unanimously cordial. After *A Kentucky Cardinal* had been published in London in 1896 by Osgood, McIlvaine and Company, a writer in *The Saturday Review* declared that although the book breathed "the charm of leisured sensibility" it was too elusive as to purpose, too philosophical and didactic, and that "after the lapse of a week a reader would probably have no very clear recollection of any part of it." *The Athenaeum*, with what must have seemed to Allen true British condescension, remarked that it was "not very far from being excellent in many respects," which is about as meaningless as criticism can become. Four years later *The Academy* gave what was to be a more lasting transatlantic judgment: " . . . in achievement it is exquisite; its wit, its humor, its wisdom must surely be among the best that ever came out of America. It is a radiant and marvellous little work, and from the playfulness of the opening to the austere sweet melancholy of the close it entrances and enchants. It may never be popular, but more than anything else it will help to sustain Mr. Allen's reputation with those few upon whose decision his reputation must ultimately depend."

In view of the eminence which this story holds among Allen's writings it is interesting to speculate as to whether he had read Victor Cherbuliez's *Le Secret du précepteur*, a third edition of which had come out in 1893. In the French novel we read of a doctor of philosophy, ambitious to succeed to a chair in the College of France, who tutors two young girls and falls in love with the giddier, Monique, just as Adam Moss at first thinks himself attracted to Sylvia. Both men are gardeners; the French professor surrounds himself with roses, tulips, dahlias, and geraniums with as much eagerness as Adam cares for his fruits; Monique, the younger sister, has difficulties with geography even as Sylvia, Georgiana's younger sister, finds the greatest common divisor baffling; the repartee in each book has a similar tone, sometimes with striking particularity as when Maximin Tristan is told he does not have a very cheerful name, while Adam Moss is teased for owning a green, cool, soft name. The matter, of course, cannot be pressed too far; resemblances may be wholly accidental, and nowhere is a critic likely to be more misled than in trying to demonstrate by parallelisms that one writer has imitated or been influenced by another.

A Kentucky Cardinal deserved a high place in Allen's regard. Within four years of its publication in the United States it sounded his name on both sides of the Atlantic; it earned for him the encomiums of critics; it sold well; above all, it projected much of his own personality, for his likeness to Adam Moss is unmistakable. Both loved flowers and birds, both had a lofty sense of honor, both delighted in a quiet but lively wit, both saw the conflict that invariably arose between a man's deepest passion for that thing which he knew he must do and must love and his obligations to a woman. Georgiana is probably an idealized composite of his mother and of Juliet Martin, who is said to have lost a toe in the manner described in the argument between Georgiana and her brother Joe. Finally, it was the only one of his love stories of this period, and one of two throughout his life, to be indited with freshness and with the power to create a complete illusion. Was it because, past the age when that kind of love was to be thought of as an actual happening to himself, he found a vicarious joy in Adam's winning of a spirited, sensitive, lovely girl? Did his maturity, his immovable melancholy dictate that this joy must be checked in a sequel that should display its untimely end?

The sequel was not written until Allen had made the first of his visits to Europe. A dozen years earlier he had celebrated the acceptance of his first ambitious essay by going to Cincinnati to hear *The Messiah;* now he would celebrate the publication of his first novelette by hearing the music and seeing the pictures and wandering through the cathedrals of the countries of the Old World. It would be a jaunt in which he would find some of the wonders he had read about all his life and in which he might take time to find himself, to breathe easily after furious rounds with editors and magazines, to forget briefly his sister, his renunciations for his mother's sake and for her sake. He would make no fuss about his going. There would be no public announcements, no letters to envious friends, no scurrying to meet foreign celebrities, not even a book about his travel. He was going to travel alone with James Lane Allen and what he discovered in himself and in foreign lands was to be no one's affair but his own. He was wise enough to know that nobody would understand, would fully appreciate him, that he could not even understand himself, and that the good life for him was one in which he would withdraw from the eyes of the world and be seen in what he wrote. He was now attired in the garment of the Genteel Tradition. "James Lane Allen," wrote his friend Nancy H. Banks in 1895, "is a writer whose innate modesty and pride have kept his personality in the background. We know very little about him and so we welcome a few biographical facts."

England drew him like a lodestar. It was the home of his ancestors. It had nurtured a race of literary geniuses from

the monk who told the story of Beowulf on parchment to
Rudyard Kipling, whose latest story was run off at top speed
by great presses. He could hear there the birds that Keats
and Shelley and Wordsworth and Arnold had matched in
song. He could walk along the river in which the boy
Shakespeare had fished, could sit in the chair from which Sam
Johnson had delivered pontifical rulings. May, June, and
July of 1894 he spent in England, most of the time in London, where he heard the cuckoo and the nightingale in Kew
Gardens; where he visited the Museum of Natural History,
and stood before Hogarth's "Marriage *à la mode*," Con-
stable's "Cornfield," and Romney's portrait of Mrs. Mark
Currie in the National Gallery; where he saw an exhibition
at the Royal Academy; where he attended a Sunday bird
market and was impressed by the English care for "those
lower creatures, which in binding man tenderly to the earth,
help to lift him tenderly to the skies." He also heard the
nightingale's song—one of the reasons, says Isaac F. Marcosson, for his going to England—near Box Hill in Surrey, and
one wonders whether he called on George Meredith, although it is very unlikely since he seemed to avoid literary
men rather than try to meet them. If Meredith invited him
to Box Hill that would be different, but Allen would certainly not make the first gesture toward acquaintance. On
the seventeenth of July he listened in the Hampstead Parish
Church while Edmund Gosse unveiled the American Memorial Bust of Keats, "who most of all the world's poets
felt the things that pass," he wrote over a decade later in
The Bride of the Mistletoe. Allen received a card for this
ceremony (he thought enough of the card to send it for
preservation to the Lexington Public Library) and he kept
in his trunk a copy of the *Hampstead and Highgate Express*
which gave an account of the proceedings, but strangely
enough he made no move to be introduced to Gosse, although

he could not have forgotten the Englishman's tribute to "Always Bussing His Friends." Gosse was not even aware that Allen was in England. On the Kentuckian's second visit to London Sir Edmund made direct friendly overtures, with what result we shall see. In August and September Allen was promenading down the Avenue d'Jena and strolling beneath the chestnut trees of Saint Cloud; then following a route planned by the British consul at Lausanne he walked, knapsack on shoulders, from the Lake of Geneva to Interlaken. And after that, home again.

When he returned to New York City he took up residence at 36 East Twenty-first Street but spent much time in the ensuing months in Cincinnati, Louisville, and Lexington, collecting data for two new works of fiction. One morning while he was lying in bed watching the sunlight stream through a window, the sequel of *A Kentucky Cardinal* resolved from nebular to planetary shape in his mind. Without being printed as a serial this sequel, *Aftermath*, was published in 1895 as a companion piece to its immediate predecessor and in time to compete with *Beside the Bonnie Brier Bush* and *The Honorable Peter Stirling* for Christmas trade. It is a custom quite honored in the observance to say of a sequel that it does not come up to the standards set by the preceding work, and much as one would like to dodge this cliché, it is too accurate in this instance to be avoided. *Aftermath* seems to have in its one hundred thirty-five pages no higher purpose than that of converting the comedy of the earlier book into a lavendered tragedy. One event could be relied upon to do this, but Allen realized that it must not be brought in too soon nor be foreseen too clearly. He was therefore hard put to it to keep his pages in motion: he introduced a touch of farce in the wooing of Sylvia; he inserted some verses which are obviously lifted from his juvenilia and which have nothing to do with the plot; he set aside ten pages out of the small total for propaganda against duelling—in short, he padded with a free hand. Hints of his changing character peep out here and there: his growing impatience with pompous ministers, his fear that a wife would interfere with a man's chosen work, his humanizing (was it the result of living in New York City and abroad?) to a degree where in picturing a baby's habits he could be almost Rabelaisian. The nobility of the Genteel Tradition is recovered near the end of the book when, after an account of the birth of the child, we are shocked by the abrupt opening of the seventh chapter: "A month has gone by since Georgiana passed away," an announcement which will stir the feelings of even the present-day reader who follows the love story from start to finish. After that, Adam Moss, released from the tie which had held him, unromantically enough, a chafing prisoner, goes back to his intimacy with nature, the eternal, Wordsworthian consoler. Always there is in Allen's work the escape from life.

Aftermath rounded out for the time the history of his hero and heroine, a history that was to be resumed thirty years later. After 1895 Allen, hopeful of performing bulkier and more lasting things in the art of fiction and instructed by much of what he had been seeing and reading, resolved to make himself over into a realistic writer, with Thomas Hardy for a partial model. But in those years immediately succeeding he wrote one more romance which, because it is an elaboration of *John Gray* and because of its fond idealism and lyrical style, is kin to the productions of this feminine period and must logically be grouped with them. The inspiration and purpose of *The Choir Invisible* (1897) are not far to seek. In 1893 Allen gave readers of *The Critic* to understand that he believed "with the new school of French symbolists that a new era lies before prose fiction in respect of exquisite form—form never yet attained by the English

novel." And a year before *The Choir Invisible* was published
he wrote an essay for *The Bookman* on "The Gentleman in
American Fiction" in which he lamented that the literature
which arraigned the "vices and weaknesses and failures of
men under the republic is not counterbalanced, or, as it should
be, overbalanced by a literature to set forth the virtues, the
strength, the success, the beauty of character, that men take
on under our civilization"—an opinion which he must have
viewed with some wonder as disillusion pressed upon him in
the next century. He thought it mortifying that Uncle Tom
and Uncle Remus should be the only characters in our fiction
universally known, that we had no gentlemen like Don
Quixote or Sir Roger de Coverley or Colonel Newcome. And
he added significantly: "A writer stands to his work as a
mason to his wall: they keep the same level; they rise together."

What he had in mind, therefore, was the presentation in
jewelled prose of a hero who should incarnate the highest
type of American, a Galahad in buckskins, because for
Allen the best example of native manhood was to be found
among our Anglo-Saxon pioneers, especially among those who
had widened Virginia's boundaries westward. Natty Bumppo,
it is true, had been brave and chivalrous and manly and a gentleman after backwoods standards but his standards were not
those of Virginia and Kentucky in the Mauve Decade. Allen's hero was awaiting him. John Gray, whose saga he had
sketched in 1892, could easily be remade into a knightly figure moving against the tapestry that was Kentucky in 1795—
a figure which should recall in valor and purity the best of
Malory's warriors; in moral firmness, in mingled pathos and
humor, the best of George Eliot's and Thackeray's. He
should be a man of whom Allen's mother would have approved. "Realism and commonplace, I believe, have seen
their day," he told a visitor, and added that his favorite nov-

els were *Vanity Fair*, *The Newcomes*, *Adam Bede*, and *The Mill on the Floss*. So he intended that this new book, whose title he took from a verse by George Eliot, should blend history and romance in perfect shadings.

To accomplish this he enlarged *John Gray* with a few scenes; he also changed the particulars of certain incidents. The new material is slight, and suggests that the two months spent in Maine during the revision must have been occupied chiefly with a characteristic recasting of sentences. The new episode which upon publication of *The Choir Invisible* drew the most comment was that in which Gray does battle with a famished cougar in a schoolhouse, an encounter based upon a Lexington tradition that had found its way into Collins's history of Kentucky. Stafford, the villain of *John Gray*, became in the new version O'Bannon, and although he was likewise killed by a fall from a horse he did not die in the near-maudlin fashion depicted in the earlier story. The frustrated love of Mrs. Falconer and John Gray was related in clearer but more poetic terms, and through their conversations and correspondence we learn more of Kentucky politics, of the national temper, and of international happenings, the purpose being to wash in as historic background considerably idealized the winning of the west.

Not all critics looked kindly upon these departures; Joseph Gilder, for instance, argued that almost all of them were injurious. He objected to the five pages descriptive of the appearance and habits of the dreaded cougar, to the careful recital of the early life of the heroine, to a two-page quotation from *Le Morte Darthur*. And he admonished the author sharply: "Even so conscientious a workman as he must find it difficult to disregard an advance sale of ten thousand copies and a paean of approval from the press." Allen never forgave the insinuation and from that time there was coolness between him and the editor who had introduced him to the literary public of New York. *The Nation,* which misspelled Gray's name, spoke flippantly of the whole book as "such a fairy tale" and called its historical matter a "not interesting revival of a really dead past." *The Saturday Review* thought it remarkably lacking in balance of objective and subjective parts; three years later *The Academy* offered the singular opinion that Mrs. Falconer "might be a composite of Gautier's de Maupin and one of Christina Rossetti's nuns." Even so recently as 1910 a writer in *The Sewanee Review* looked askance at Allen's revisions in general and his ethics in particular. The change of title, he held, was a bid for popularity that "strikes one as cheap and unworthy of an author who has respect for his reputation and love for his art." And with regard to the hero he continued: "The author must be held responsible for the moral influence of his books, and so Mr. Allen must be held responsible for the moral influence upon his readers of John Gray's immoral love for another man's wife. What good can such portrayals bring?"—which was applying Allen's own theory in a manner that must have been more than a little exasperating to the author. Such a criticism only amuses the reader of today, who is much more likely to find fault with the Tennysonian idealism of *The Choir Invisible.*

But these objectors were in a complete minority; Joseph Gilder used an honest phrase when he wrote of the "paean of approval" which the nineties raised for this romance. It met exactly a widespread demand for fiction which should have the renunciation of love as its theme; it also satisfied a request for bland humor that should decline easily into melancholy, for an inviting and strange locality, for strong hints of transcendentalism. Leading the chorus of approbation was Hamilton Wright Mabie, who proclaimed that "this latest story is as genuine a work of art as has come from an American hand." James MacArthur, editor of *The*

Bookman, made a comparison we have already noted and which will be made over and over: "Indeed we venture to say that it would be difficult to recall any other novel since *The Scarlet Letter* that has touched the same note of greatness, or given to one section of our national life, as Hawthorne's classic did to another, a voice that is far beyond singing." In February of 1897 the most popular books of fiction in the United States were *King Noanett, That First Affair, The Country of the Pointed Firs, The Honorable Peter Stirling, Marm Lisa* and *Child World,* but as the Macmillan Company was forced to print thousand after thousand of copies of *The Choir Invisible,* that novel jumped to first place in the year's sales; three years later *The Book Buyer* reported that two hundred fifty thousand copies had been sold. Mark Sullivan in *The Turn of the Century* rightly placed it among the ten best sellers of the entire decade.

The Choir Invisible was Allen's greatest popular and financial success; it made him famous, it swelled his income to one that equalled that of President McKinley, and today the title is, with the exception of *A Kentucky Cardinal,* most generally associated with his name. His publishers had every reason to congratulate themselves for having him on contract: for thirteen years thereafter each of his new volumes was to be designated as a literary event and could be counted on to contribute generously to the coffers of publisher and author. And although literary fashions have changed much since 1897, Mr. George Folsom Granberry, Allen's literary executor, still receives letters addressed to the writer of *The Choir Invisible* and asking for autographs. It was made accessible to the French public through a translation and to British readers by printings in London; American soldiers in France during the World War found it read by French officers, and it is still highly thought of in England. In 1927 no less a person than Radclyffe Hall wrote for *The Bookman* that the works of "the immortal James Lane Allen" were discovered after the fame of *The Choir Invisible,* that they were "read and reread in the homes of this island, indeed, in the homes of the whole British Empire. They are still being read here today."

Such a boulevard success as *The Choir Invisible* could not fail to inspire imitations and to attract an enterprising dramatist. Hard upon its tracks came many another rapidly moving tale of love and adventure in Europe or in America: Charles Major went to the time of Henry VIII for *When Knighthood Was in Flower* (1898); Mary Johnston made colonial Virginia exciting in *To Have and to Hold* (1899); Paul Leicester Ford, Maurice Thompson, and Winston Churchill vivified our early history in *Janice Meredith* (1899), *Alice of Old Vincennes* (1900), and *Richard Carvel* (1899), respectively. Booth Tarkington captivated the public with a French nobleman in disguise in *Monsieur Beaucaire* (1901) and Robert W. Chambers went to the past of New York State for *Cardigan* (1901) and *The Maid-at-Arms* (1902). Emerson Hough dealt with a period of national speculation in *The Mississippi Bubble* (1902). The list could be carried over several pages. If these mentioned and unmentioned historical novels did not owe their origin to the triumph of *The Choir Invisible* they certainly were not discouraged by it. We must not, of course, fall into the easy fallacy of assuming that they stemmed from Allen's book merely because they came after it, nor should we overlook the stimulating effect of the Spanish-American War, the widespread influence of Robert Louis Stevenson, the undying interest in Walter Scott, but we can feel pretty sure that more than one writer of this kind of fiction had noted the impressive record made by a book dealing with post-revolutionary Kentucky. *The Choir Invisible* did not, however, fare well on the stage. Allen feared that it would not, that it was too pictorial and too undramatic, that its value lay in words and their morality, and, to use his own phrase, he opposed the dramatization by Frances Hastings (Mrs. Henry Jewett) "most positively." Once the dramatization got under way he followed its fortune with natural interest. Miss Hastings cast herself in the rôle of Mrs. Falconer and her husband as John Gray. Both toiled enthusiastically to make the play as popular as the novel. Jewett haunted the studio of Orson Lowell, who was making the drawings for the illustrated edition of the book, and spouted scenes from the play while he asked the artist's advice on settings and took away a full set of the pen and ink sketches. The play opened in Washington, October 6, 1899, but held the boards for only two weeks. From there the company moved to Chicago and then to Indianapolis and Louisville. During the next season *The Choir Invisible* was produced in Boston, where it died after a month of performances, thus justifying Allen's forebodings. Jewett, formerly leading man for Viola Allen in Hall Caine's *The Christian*, was starring for the first time, and his lack of a following probably made failure all the more certain, although it is doubtful whether even a much better known actor could have carried on much longer in a part which was essentially unfitted for the theater. At any rate, Allen could console himself by reflecting that neither *To Have and To Hold* nor *Tess of the D'Urbervilles*, both of which kept booksellers busy, had done well on the stage. In 1929 Curtis Brown, Ltd., and Lionel Barton completed negotiations for a London dramatization and presentation of *The Choir Invisible*, and it is possible that John Gray's voice will some day be again heard from behind the proscenium arch.

Before long Allen came to regard the fiction of this feminine period with a kind of superior detachment. "In looking over these tales, written several years ago, the author feels like one who goes back to walk across a land he inhabits no

longer," he wrote in 1900. "They have for him the silence
of overgrown pathways, along which feet never pass again."
Yet they are among the most representative and, in the obvious sense, among the most personal of his writings. They
are the products of a scholar and gentleman, steeped in the
traditions of eighteenth- and nineteenth-century studies, who
turned dilettante and proceeded to draw upon his feelings
and upon books rather than upon objective life for his materials. They are the work, indeed, of one who, not afraid of
any man, was nevertheless afraid of men, timid before a vora-
cious American life which threatened to swallow him and his
kind and their sentiments. Compared with Ambrose Bierce's
contemporary mordant stories they seem to have wandered
far from actuality and to have retreated into the pleasant
fields of fancy. They are creations of a man whose manners
and bearing were as immaculate as the linen he wore (he
was once seen with soiled cuffs after watching a polo game)
a man who wrapped both physical and mental attitudes in
the dignified mantle of classicism. Allen's own phrase to
designate the motivating force of his literature of this period was "the Feminine Principle," whose characteristics were
refinement, delicacy, and grace—a phrase happily selected to
make clear his opinion of the most widely read fiction of the
nineties. None of these tales is more typical of his spirit than
is "Posthumous Fame," the apologue so admirably blending
Samuel Johnson and Nathaniel Hawthorne, so thoroughly an
index to the mind of this romantico-classicist who, disturbed
by the towering figures of Charles Darwin and Thomas
Hardy, was about to abandon a style dictated by his truer nature and, adopting a guiding Masculine Principle, was to try
even before the opening of the twentieth century, before
Dreiser's *Sister Carrie* had been read by anyone outside the
Doubleday office, to convert himself into a realist.

CHAPTER IV
THE MASCULINE PRINCIPLE

It needs no very acute critic to remark the turn taken by subject and matter in Allen's books dated immediately after 1895, excluding *The Choir Invisible*. Hitherto he had followed Alden's advice to survey a likely field and then plow it deeply; he had experimented with local color and attempted to do for Kentucky, only better, what other writers had been doing for Virginia and Maine and Louisiana and California; he had produced engaging love stories; he had outlined in *John Gray* the tale that later became his nearest approach to that great historical romance of his native state which he always aspired to write and for which his powers seemed ample, provided he could by exercise develop more masculinity in the management of plot. The fiction of his feminine period represents a well balanced combination of romance and sentiment, the most pleasing combination to be found in American literature up to that time. Cooper had offered romance suspended from adventure; Hawthorne had weighted romance with doubts of puritanism and transcendentalism; Melville had passionately mingled romance and despair; but no other important novelist had exhibited Allen's delicacy of feeling along with the same playful humor that shades off into seriousness, and no one had so consistently used so pure a tone.

To go, therefore, from the refinements of his first group of stories to the sensuous warmth of "Butterflies" as it appeared serially in *The Cosmopolitan* from the December issue, 1895, to and including the March issue of 1896, is as surprising today as it must have been to Allen's admirers at that time. And when "Butterflies" was followed by novels which attacked denominationalism and the revelations of the Christian religion, novels which showed a growing respect for Darwin and his work and an increasing tendency to speak of man's conduct in terms of animal behavior, which examined with more and more skepticism the sacredness of love and matrimony, and which showed an inclination to value the world less than it esteems itself—then the many who had wept over John Gray's renunciation and Georgiana's death must have asked themselves what had happened to the gentleman from Kentucky. His European trip had doubtless been a broadening experience and living in New York had expanded his points of view, yet the matters of travel and residence might not be a complete explanation of his change. Fortunately, Allen has himself answered the query, or at least furnished a clue to the answer.

The leading article in *The Atlantic Monthly* for October, 1897, was his "Two Principles in Recent American Fiction." It is highly valuable as throwing light upon what he must have been thinking for three or four years; it is, indeed, an *apologia* for his shifts in method and tone. He began by saying: "Not so very long ago—some twenty-five or thirty years—there reached our fiction a creative movement that must be identified as a wave of what is known in the art of the world as the Feminine Principle." Its three essential characteristics, he went on to say, were Refinement, Delicacy, Grace; three other characteristics were Smallness, Rarity, Tact. The Feminine Principle operated as a law of selection and as a law of treatment; that is, it suggested to an author that he take for his material things that would "secrete some essence of the rare" and then go on to invest minute things "with their due minuteness" and grace and tact. This type, he declared, had had its vogue but a reaction had lately set in against it:

Any complete expression of itself in art the human spirit can of course never and nowhere have. The very law of its own existence is the law of constant growth and change, so that what is most true of it today will be most false tomorrow. . . . Refinement is a good quality as far as it goes; but if you left out of American fiction everything that was not refined you left out most of the things that were truly American. Delicacy,—yes; but there was something better than Delicacy,—Strength. Grace,—true; yet of how little value are things graceful, in the United States, as compared with a thousand and one things that are clumsy or misshapen, but that are vital! The little things of our human nature and of our national society,—are they to be preferred to the larger things? As for the rare, give us rather the daily bread of the indispensable. And regarding the matter of tact,—that ceaseless state of being on guard, of holding one's self in and holding one's self back, and of seeing that not a drop overflows the artistic banks,—have done with it and away with it! Let us try for a while the literary virtues and the literary materials of less self-consciousness, of larger self-abandonment and thus impart to our fiction the free, the uncaring, the tremendous fling and swing that are the very genius of our time and spirit.

Brave words these! But he did concede one merit to the Feminine Principle: it enforced upon its devotees a necessity for writing good prose. And so Allen added a word of advice to the ambitious young author, pointing out that the "Age of the Carved Cherry-Stones" taught the value of deliberate and constant practice. Then, contrasting the Masculine Principle with the Feminine, he declared that the former possessed Virility, Strength, Massiveness; also the minor virtues of Largeness, Obviousness, and Primary or Instinctive Action:

. . . it is bent upon its subjects rather in the rough natural mass than in graceful detail, bent upon getting truth, or beauty, or whatever else may be wanted, from them as a whole, instead of stretching each atom on the graceful rack of psychological con-

fession, and bending the ear close to catch the last faint whispers
of its excruciating and moribund self-consciousness. . . . It may
well be, therefore, that we are about to be tested, as never in the
past, for our ability to wield with entire success this mighty principle in its solitary exercise. . . . In life there is no antagonism between virility and refinement, between strength and delicacy, as
any gentleman may know.   There is none between them in art,
as the greatest art of the world will bear witness.

To support this last statement Allen pointed out that the
Greeks and Shakespeare knew how to use both Principles,
and he suggested Kipling's "Recessional" as a contemporary
example of harmony and balance between the masculine and
feminine.   Another proof of the regard in which the author
of *The Light That Failed* was held during the nineties.

The length of these quotations is justified when we set
ourselves to the task of noting how far their writer applied
them to his subsequent composition and also because they are
worthy of more complimentary notice than they have yet
received at the hands of historians of American literature.
The whole essay is plainly enough a broadside against the
gentility and inanity of the bulk of American fiction; it is also
obviously directed in part against the school of Henry James
and William Dean Howells.   To be sure, some of our writers
had already broken with the Genteel Tradition.   Mark Twain
has been mentioned.   Then there was Joseph Kirkland's
Zury in 1887.   E. W. Howe told of dreary Twin Mounds in
The Story of a Country Town (1883); Hamlin Garland
described what midwestern farms were really like in *Main-
Travelled Roads* (1891); Henry B. Fuller satirized the Chicago scramble for social prestige in *With the Procession*
(1895); Stephen Crane paid to publish his tragic story of
New York slums, *Maggie* (1896); and Frank Norris applied
Zola's technique to explain the deterioration of a kindly den-
tist in *McTeague* (1899). But it is hardly necessary to say that

these books were unpopular, or exceptional if they won the public to their pages. For the temper of American readers was still prevailingly romantic and rebellion against that temper was not the commonplace that it is nowadays; four years were to elapse before Frank Norris would issue the first volume of his projected trilogy which was to paint the American panorama, and Theodore Dreiser did not publish *Sister Carrie* until 1900, and then it was suppressed. Allen's pronouncement, therefore, has considerable interest historically. He was clearly urging an abandonment of the gentle and the psychological novel and calling for what would seem to be a Zolaesque interpretation of American life, an interpretation, at any rate, which should be broad, sweeping, truthful, ruthless.

Now there was in those days, in those scenes, much to stir the blood of anyone as American as Allen. The genius of that "time and spirit" was indeed "fling and swing." To read any history of the period is to catch unmistakable echoes of the din which made the politics and social wars of the era noisy; the United States was swelling with national consciousness, girding itself for expansion, confused with a conflict between capital and labor. Discontent, especially in the West, had crystallized in the formation of the Populist party, which held a convention in Omaha in the summer of 1892. In the same month Pinkerton detectives clashed with strikers at the Homestead mills and blood flowed over heaps of slag; shortly afterward Henry Frick, a Titan of the steel industry, was shot and stabbed by a friend of Emma Goldman. During the spring, summer, and autumn of 1893 came a respite from domestic broils in the enthusiasm for the World's Columbian Exposition at Chicago, where the White City gave a decided impetus to our growth in the arts and sciences and also to national pride, for foreigners who came to scoff remained to admire. But the class struggle went on; in April of 1894 the remnant of Coxey's Army of the Commonweal of Christ straggled into the streets of Washington and brought to an empty end its crusade against tyranny. Two months later the Pullman strike, which was to make famous the name of Eugene V. Debs and to involve and ruin Governor Altgeld, began in Chicago. In California farmers came to grips with a railroad, an octopus which threatened to crush the life out of agriculture. Covetous eyes were turning again from the Capitol and from Wall Street to look upon Morro Castle. The whole country was in a ferment. Causes were being battled for with a fervor that called loudly for a novelist to transfer it to paper, and Allen knew it.

Nevertheless, the work which he saw needed to be done was work which he was clear-headed enough to realize lay beyond his powers. He was interested in humanity only in a perfunctory and academic fashion. He felt no throb of sympathy for the proletariat. Let every man and every class have justice but do not identify the cry for justice with the agitation of one class only. The masses that thronged American cities and clamored for their rights in mines and mills meant to him only the mob to be avoided. There was too little refinement about their ceaseless and vociferous activity. Stirring deeds of the past, especially if linked with Kentucky, appealed to him, but appealed as a spectacle, scarcely more real than the joustings of Arthur's knights. With the strainings and sweatings, the hardships and wrongs of his fellows he would have nought to do. Their problems, their groans, their triumph or defeat were, after all, things of transient importance only; beneath those appearances lay the tremendous significance of man the individual, man of any century of time and any rank of society, and that man he would study, that man he would write about. He had no urge to go upon the platform like Hamlin Garland or to advocate reforms like Henry George. At bottom aristocratic, he held himself mentally and physically aloof from the crowd, and the grand manner, which Ellen Glasgow was to observe harden into a pattern upon him, was settling upon his shoulders. He received few but the elect; denied himself to most reporters and interviewers; and one is persuaded that his fear of publicity was almost if not quite pathological. His name never appeared in a New York City directory. In 1895 *The Bookman* had declared that "Mr. James Lane Allen has been less written about than any other leading American writer, on account of his dislike of personal notoriety," and in 1900 Ellen Burns Sherman made in *The Book Buyer* the expected comparison: "Like Hawthorne, he holds himself *en cache*, living his own life as serenely and unheralded as the mutest and most inglorious of men." Charles Hemstreet's book about literary New York, published in 1903, had to be content with describing the window garden of Allen's "brownstone dwelling" on Madison Avenue; Henry van Dyke, acquainted with most of the authors of the day, was obliged to esteem Allen from a distance and to explain: "I always felt that he would be rather a difficult man to know well." More than ever, as the century turned, the man who had written *A Kentucky Cardinal* craved remoteness, space from the throng, the beggar, the heedless admirer, the designing flatterer, the curious. "I could no more have wished my home, when I should have one, to be wedded to any other man's home than I could have planned that my ribs should be nailed to his ribs," he has his hero say in *The Heroine in Bronze*, a sentiment which justly represents the author's spirit although not the fact, since he lived in apartments. He never had a home after leaving Kentucky. "Very few people knew him," explains Arthur Bartlett Maurice, former editor of *The Bookman;* "he was one of the shyest of men; and his actions always seemed shrouded in mystery."

The motives behind this passion for seclusion were mixed.

He was shy in a way, the outcome, doubtless, of early poverty. But shyness was far from being the strongest motive. It is not accusing him of priggishness to state that he felt, as we have already noted and accounted for, a difference between himself and the average American, for that difference was there and required no apology. His egocentric outlook, if one may use that contradiction in terms, also contributed heavily to his wish to be alone, for, after all, no one, not even his sister, was so important to him as himself. He seemed to have almost no interest in what anyone else was doing, rarely praised a book in print, and never allowed his name to be used in a campaign of publicity for another's work. To me, there is also in this withdrawal from life not only the fear that it might injure him and his art but also a subconscious longing for death, as though somewhere and sometime his heart had broken and left him with only the animal desire for life, while deep in the core of his being lodged a conviction of defeat and fatigue that only death could erase.

Certainly it is not to be supposed that his call for a masculine literature issued from the agony of his soul; that travail, futility, and dissipation shared with the horde of men and women prompted his demand for a realistic treatment of life in fiction; that, in short, his revolt sprang from a revulsion against personal gentility. He himself shed none of the armor of Sir Galahad. His demand came rather through the paler passion of literary imitation. The bulwark of what Allen thought of as Anglo-Saxon reticence in matters involving sex, for example, was slowly but surely crumbling under the ceaseless pounding of waves of naturalism that crossed the Atlantic, and he, ever alert to changes, was one of the first Americans to understand what was taking place and to help in the process of destruction. The flood of the new realism was not to be checked, especially the surge from France. Gautier and Flaubert, Maupassant and Zola were a last being read over here, probably *sub rosa* in many instances. Daudet's *Sapho,* which startled even Paris in 1884, was pirated by a New York publisher who was so anxious to out-strip his competitors that he divided the French volume into three parts for the sake of speedier translation and so at day-break following the afternoon when he had received the ro-mance was ready to publish, a feat that speaks loudly for American energy but also for the changing taste. The end of puritanism was in sight. *Trilby,* running from the Jan-uary number of *Harper's* for 1894 as a serial, should have been sufficiently shocking even in its censored form, but its chief effects, aside from tickling the desire for something mildly salacious, were to start a craze for the natural beauty of the foot and to enrage James McNeill Whistler, who saw himself caricatured in one of the characters. And the fact that the names of the Goncourt brothers and of Baudelaire are sprinkled through critical essays in the magazines shows an increasing audience for the French decadents. There were, to be sure, protests against this "unclean fiction." Joshua Caldwell spoke for the older prophets when he la-mented in *The New England Magazine* in 1890 that "the rapid multiplication and the undeniable popularity of the 'erotic novel' is a menace to American novels, and a disgrace to American letters," and for this degeneracy he blamed par-ticularly Sardou and "his high-priestess of indecency, Sarah Bernhardt."

If this kind of fiction had been confined to French authors only it would have been easy enough to attack as the product of a nation all English-speaking folk believed to be degen-erate, a nation whose ideals were as alien to the Saxons as were those of Tolstoi or D'Annunzio. But English and Americans were also breaking the constraint which had held them more or less tightly since the middle of the Victorian Period and some of them were handling sex in its less romantic aspects. Oscar Wilde, to be sure, might be dismissed as being too much under the spell of Huysmans, as George Moore assuredly was bewitched by Flaubert and Zola, but the idol of the decade, Rudyard Kipling, did not always use delicate words to tell stories of married men and women who sometimes forgot their vows. A still more powerful English-man had written pessimistic poetry, followed by novels of equal pessimism and irony. His "Wessex Folk" had been running serially in *Harper's Magazine* in 1891, and in De-cember of 1894 the same monthly began one of his novels entitled "The Simpletons"; today we know it as *Jude the Obscure.* Just before the decade opened, religion had been questioned by two women in *Robert Elsmere* and *John Ward, Preacher.*

A more liberal spirit in literature was imminent when so academic a writer as Brander Matthews would break away from classicism to write his "Vignettes of Manhattan" for *Harper's* to print in 1894, short sketches unimportant per se, but daring enough to be symptomatic of an approaching change. Allen, aware of what was going on and for the mo-ment stirred into departing from his earlier manner, resolved, as his *Atlantic* essay shows, to experiment with this new method, which was, after all, as old in English letters as Henry Fielding. But to do for America what Zola had done for France was, Allen knew, not for him. He was too dis-tant from humanity. Nor could he, like Kipling, describe the life of white men in a strange world which made almost nec-essary some alterations in the social code; Allen knew no Simlas, he knew only Lexington and the surrounding Blue-grass. He must therefore go on using his fondness for na-ture, which informs almost everything he wrote, and connect it in some way with the central situation of most of his novels the love, waxing or waning, of man for woman. Love was the *sine qua non* for the Victorian novelist, and Allen tardily outgrew his dependence upon it.

The great Englishman who emphasized so strongly the force of environment at work on personality, who used his settings with pronounced effect and who displayed the pitiless results of the duel between the sexes, was, of course, Thomas Hardy. The field which Hardy was exploring held acres which more than one writer might trample and in which Allen would not feel unfamiliar, and so in December of 1895, just one year after the tragic history of Jude Frawley had begun in *Harper's Magazine*, the *Cosmopolitan* printed the opening installment of Allen's "Butterflies," in which one may easily detect Hardy's influence.

This novelette, published later in the same year with the title of *Summer in Arcady*, represents the transition in Allen's work from one principle to another; it is not so feminine as *Aftermath* nor so masculine as *The Reign of Law* was to be. It discarded Refinement when at the outset the heroine was described as "lifting her rustling, snow-white petticoats high over the sheep and cattle traces in her path"; but it retained Delicacy and Grace in style and Smallness in scope. Rarity was abandoned in the study of two commonplace young people, and Tact was thrown high over the garden wall. Of the attributes of the Masculine Principle it may claim Virility, Strength, Obviousness, and Instinctive Action, but not Massiveness or Largeness—that is where Allen falls behind Hardy.

This story, the first of Allen's offering in the new realistic manner, called by Carl Van Doren (an unfavorable critic) his masterpiece and praised for having "at once rich passion and spare form," deserves some attention. It gets under way easily and moves quickly; it is the least erudite of Allen's fictions, there being allusions to only four classical figures: Epictetus, Solon, Dr. Johnson, and Pericles. A sententious

Prelude strikes the key for the whole performance and introduces butterflies as symbols of "the blindly wandering, blindly loving, blindly passing human race." Then in the warm June of a Bluegrass summer we meet Daphne, a buxom country girl of seventeen. When she is shrewdly described as having a "lithe, round figure, the unusual womanly development of which always attracted secret attention and caused her secret pain," we are reminded of how Hardy pictured Arabella Down as "a complete and substantial female form"; and when Allen goes on to say that the sight of this figure "could have made many a mother reflect upon the cruel haste with which Nature sometimes forces a child into maturity, and then adds to the peril of its life by covering it with alluring beauty," we are sure that Allen was acquainted with *Tess* and with Hardy's conception of nature as the agent of an inexorable destiny.

And that was the use that Allen made of nature in *Summer in Arcady*, and insisted upon our noting it, so that a present-day reader is often annoyed. Even in 1897 there was remonstrance: "Nature, with a big N, and in so many letters, is flung at us on every page, until we are sick of her," complained an English reviewer. Allen was too eager to prove that nature, having in mind only her own purposes, cares nothing for the peace of mind, health of body, or symmetry of soul of human beings so long as she can bring them together for the reproduction of the race. In his eagerness to make this thesis plain he employed his kinship with the outdoors and his decorative style to convey to his readers a series of lovely Bluegrass scenes. Yet even though Hamilton Wright Mabie exclaimed that "Mr. Allen's sharpest critic must confess that in no other book is atmosphere so pervasive, so potential, so charged with passion and beauty," it is likely that even some kind critics today must object to the laboring of the text.

Besides stressing the power of environment Allen made another concession to Hardy's example: he gave to hero and heroine unhappy parentage. Hilary, a farm boy of nineteen, like most of Allen's heroes, because somewhat like Allen himself, is "a heavy-limbed, heavy-built, handsome young fellow." In one of his rare bad sentences the author says of Hilary that "his father had died before he turned eighteen," and the lad, lacking the parent's restraining hand, has begun to justify the neighbors' expectations that he will come to a bad end. He has been expelled from the State College. He has thrilled at men's relation of sex experiences and made some explorations of his own in that direction; he rides wildly and drinks; he shocks church members by dancing. A thoroughly normal country youth he is: generous, curious, hotheaded, self-confident, strong in body and impulse, rebellious against the decorum of his family and his community. As for Daphne, she is in revolt against a home life dominated by a bigoted father and a drab routine, both of which combine to wash the color from her existence. Now when this young boy and girl, mutually attractive, warm-blooded, dissatisfied, live on adjoining farms and find in their meetings a happiness denied them elsewhere, and when above them and beside them and all around them nature sings in the dulcet voice which Allen could so well arouse from Bluegrass landscapes, and when this voice chants seductively the bliss of surrender and union in love, then there is reason for Allen to point out, as he does too frequently, that nature can be a betrayer and that the betrayal may be a calamity.

Daphne and Hilary do not bear the shields worn by most of Allen's heroes and heroines: a pride of family and a high refinement of mind. They follow Hardy's characters in being elemental. Hilary's education was interrupted after a school fight and consequent expulsion; Daphne's schooling is left in discreet silence. Their conversation is carried on in dialect; their ideas are simple, their manners homely. They are inclined to horseplay. When in trying to prevent a sportive kiss Daphne presses a tilted plate against her bosom and sauce begins to trickle down the front of her dress, she pays Hilary back by pitching a dumpling at his head.

He dodged, but some of the flying sauce struck his cheek; it glistened as though coated with gum arabic.

"Look at you!" he shouted again, "a-spoiling my clean shift and a-gorming me up like a baby."

While reading this incident one cannot forget that Arabella first won Jude's notice by striking him in the neck with a piece of thrown offal.

Symbolism appears not only in the title but also at the outset of the story, and accompanies the march of the plot. When Daphne enters the scene she walks gingerly because "she remembered that she was unfortunate about stumbling." After Hilary has been put out of church membership because he danced at a picnic he is accosted by Daphne's father, who complains that the lad's bull has been breaking through fences. Whereupon Hilary retorts hotly that "a bull that didn't have spirit enough in him to jump *some* fences wouldn't be of any use to me"—a bit of symbolism that recurs at the story's climax.

In this climactic episode the girl's self-control is swept away by the fact that Hilary returns to their rendezvous when she least expects it; she runs to him, kisses his hand, presses it to her bosom, and lays her cheek upon it.

And this in her was so sudden and so maddening to him that, taken off his guard also—his long self-restraint swept away—with a low answering cry he threw his arms around her and drew her form in against his. Then bending her slowly backward, his face close over her face, with a helpless sense of surrender he pressed his lips to hers. Daphne lay in his embrace, her eyes closed, no longer resisting him now.

*   *   *   *

The young trust themselves alone with Nature, who cares only for life and nothing for the higher things that make life worth living. To them who understand her deadly approaches she can come least near with her power to harm. When her low storm threatens, they can rise to higher strongholds, perhaps to the great calm crags of spiritual retreat, and look down with pity upon her havoc in the plain. But the young, who have not learned and do not suspect, these from the creation of the world she has been engulfing as those who once walked between walls of water.

*   *   *   *

How still the woods were all around! How still the woods were overhead. For centuries their roots, their boughs and buds and heart fibres, had witnessed the love histories of the irresponsible little creatures of earth and air that had come and gone, countless and forgotten, like their own leaves. Never had Nature driven to them such an earthly pair, two ephemera of immortal destinies.

How still the woods were, except that not far away, in Hilary's pasture, a wild, dangerous bull, whose blood was raging, paused once as he roved nearer and listened, his head in the air; then with a deep answering roar came hurrying on. . . . Straight on toward the still trees he moved, with the lash of his feet through the grass, and the snapping of vines across his resistless brows—straight on toward a panel of the fence where the briers were short and the top rail broken. The pause of an instant there; then his awful weight was lifted, and came crushing down.

Readers who have been misled into thinking of Allen as a writer only of sentimental and innocuous tales may well be startled at finding in these paragraphs a frankness and daring very rare in American fiction prior to the twentieth century. He was going to leave no doubts about his turning to realism. Yet because he had not abandoned the tradition of gentility he felt some hesitation over the length to which he had gone, and when "Butterflies" was published in book form as *Summer in Arcady* he modified somewhat the wording of the first version. The phrases "with a helpless sense of surrender" are deleted in *Summer in Arcady;* so is the sentence reading "Daphne lay in his embrace, her eyes closed, no longer resisting him now"; and there are no asterisks, so that it is possible to read the book with a misunderstanding which leaves behind a slight bewilderment. Moreover, to the book the author wrote a preface, one of the strangest things from his pen. In it he lamented that our "separate, wholesome, altogether peaceful and rather unambitious world of books" had been invaded by an army of "black, chaotic books of the new fiction"; he protested against this "downward-moving fiction" and asserted that in writing his story he had tried "to wrest a moral victory for each of the characters." He went further: he expressed a hope that fathers and mothers might derive instruction from his tale, and in that connection made the curious statement that "the fallen women of the race are in a measure set apart to that awful doom by the inherited immorality of their fathers."

The moral victory spoken of seems to lie in the fact that Daphne escaped "that awful doom" because of the timely appearance of a bull and because she and Hilary elope to Aberdeen, Ohio, where they are married. Of the morality of the situation a critic is not called upon to speak. But there is no doubt of Allen's position. To him human nature was a battleground for two opposing forces: that of the physical, which recruited its troops from selfish desires, and that of the spiritual, which acquired its strength from a nobility partly innate and partly absorbed from surroundings. The boy and girl were caught up in this immemorial struggle between the impulses and, says the author, only something instinctively sound in each saved them from catastrophe.

But though the critic may not be asked to have views on the morality of Allen's dénouement, he may fairly be asked whether that morality obtrudes to the place where it interferes with the art of the story. The answer must be in the affirmative, and it is a pity that this should be so, for *Summer in Arcady* has many merits. As already averred, it is as spontaneous as anything Allen wrote; it moves rapidly and carries us along with its motion; it displays the most natural dialogue to be found in any of the author's books; it has verbal richness and vitality. But throughout it all is the ominous preaching of a text, the cautioning of the writer's puritanism. In a sense, *Summer in Arcady* deserves the trite comparison to a palimpsest with religious reflections constantly blotting out an original pagan document.

Not every reader could agree with Allen's point of view or approve of his departure from idyllic romance. A reviewer in *The Athenaeum* said that *Summer in Arcady* was "not at all equal to his *A Kentucky Cardinal*. The preface condemns the book." The opinion of *The Saturday Review* was that "never was anything more free from useful moral teaching." *Vogue* thought it "the first distinctively American novel of the 'problem' school," but suggested that it best be described as "unclean." And the *Chicago Times-Herald*, agreeing that the novel was "gross," went on to say: "Nothing in fiction or out can warrant a writer in dwelling upon the minutiae of a daughter's ministrations to her father with a fine-tooth comb," —this being an allusion to Daphne's removing the dandruff from her parent's hair.

Although now definitely committed to the cause of realism, Allen published in the next year *The Choir Invisible*, after which came reputation and moderate wealth. Indeed, he found himself thereafter a national, even an international figure, mentioned with the greatest of American men of letters. He was at last free from the anxieties attendant upon making a living with his pen; he was able, if he wished, to seek social relaxation, to expand in the sunshine of appreciation. Advancing years, however, admonished him to set himself to the accomplishment of greater things; he was about to enter the fifties. Eight months after the publication of *The Choir Invisible*, *The Bookman* printed his pair of sonnets with the not very fortunate title of "Forget Me, Death! —O Death, Forget Me Not," in which he expressed the fear, common to creators, that he might be halted midway up, that he might be "cut down" in the full heat of his "soul's mounting purpose."

Perhaps he was not very clear about that mounting purpose. The wavering back and forth from romance to realism and realism to romance would intimate that he was not sure that he had found the central position from which he could look about with the greatest confidence. His natural sentimentality and refinement, his conscious partiality for short fiction, were at odds with a desire to do big novels in a big way, to be American *à la mode*. So he urged himself on, and set to work upon two novels, one of which he meant to surpass anything else he had done and which gave him so much trouble that he finally laid it aside and finished first the other, *The Reign of Law*. Two years passed before this book, which was to plunge him into his first serious controversy and to make him many enemies, was ready for the bookseller. In the meantime David Harum and Mr. Dooley captured the public, the dramatization of *The Choir Invisible* failed, Allen received an honorary degree of Doctor of Laws from Kentucky University, and the Spanish-American War aroused the country in a flare of patriotism. The invasion of Cuba and the victory at Manila Harbor failed, however, to elate Allen, and this despite the fact that he always looked upon war generally as a stimulus to literature and to the national health, that he cherished the memory of he roic deeds done during our Civil War, and that twenty years later he was to be violently anti-German. He could find little justification for our seizure of Spanish colonies, for our fighting a country obviously no match for our strength, and so he declared in an interview given to a representative of the *Louisville Courier-Journal*. "The Spanish War," he was incoherently reported to have said, "so far has touched the whole American people in but one way as being rightful, and this was the destruction of its battleship." Allen's sympathies being completely bound up with the agrarian culture from which he had sprung, he was naturally cool toward an enterprise which looked to him like imperialistic aggression on the part of the industrialized portion of his homeland.

In 1900 Allen had passed into his fifties; physically and mentally he was at the peak, equipped to perform work that should stand for his maturity. He was eager to climb on, to achieve an eminent place in the history of his country's literature, to give to the world something which should live after his death. But in seeking a subject he again ignored contemporary events and, still intent upon the drama of a soul rather than the epic of national expansion, still with his eyes turned fondly upon Kentucky's past, selected his material from a part of the life to be found in the Bluegrass immediately subsequent to the Civil War. He passed over our war in Cuba, our Rough Riders, our heated debates for and against manifest destiny, the pacification of the Philippines, the waxing discontent created by the growth of trusts; of these and of the developments in South Africa which were leading up to the Boer War he makes no mention in any of his stories. The new novel, instead, was to turn back some twenty years to show a young man's conversion to skepticism in things religious; it was to link Allen's name with "the heretical trinity" of Mrs. Humphry Ward, Margaret Deland, and Olive Schreiner; it was to cost him the friendly admiration of his own state. Now that attacks through fiction upon a Church, and narratives of young candidates for the ministry who become assailed by doubts are no longer novelties, the reader of *The Reign of Law* will be first impressed not by its theme, not by its critique of what Allen denominated "wrangling, sarcastic, envious creeds," but by its workmanship. Technically it is a considerable improvement upon *The Choir Invisible*, for its unity of purpose is admirably maintained. From the first sentence of the introductory chapter, "Hemp," to the last sentence of the final page of the book in which the likeness of growing hemp to the enlarging soul of man is again set forth, there is scarcely a line we could wish to erase if we overlook the sentimental touches more highly regarded in 1900 than now. Allen marshalled his details with authority and set them marching in close order toward his objective, which was to persuade his readers that our lives can be explained by a parable teaching that we are but as seeds of hemp, sown upon selected ground and springing up and growing in mystic ways that are beyond our control. It is only when we keep this purpose in mind that we can forgive the long introductory chapter on hemp. In writing this lyric prelude of twenty-three pages Allen meant to begin his book in the most significant manner. Hardy's opening of *The Return of the Native* had set the key for that work by its interpretation of Egdon Heath as the controlling element in the lives of those who dwelt upon it, and it is easy to see that Allen was attempting the same thing, only with more spiritual implications and with the symbolism more frankly tagged. Through a brief account of the history of hemp-raising in Kentucky and of the methods of cultivating this plant we come to the last paragraph of the chapter:

Ah! type, too, of our life, which is also seed-sown, earth-rooted; which must struggle upward, be cut down, rotted and broken, ere the separation take place between our dross and our worth—poor perishable shard and immortal fibre. Oh, the mystery, the mystery of that growth from the casting of a soul as a seed into the dark earth until the time when, led through all natural changes and cleansed of weakness, it is borne from the fields of its nativity for the long service.

And after we have watched the career of the young man who is the great-grandson of the builder of the first church for toleration in Kentucky, and who is the son of an ignorant and colorless mother who cannot appreciate him (the dark earth in which the seed was sown), we read with a sense of satisfied completion the last sentence in the book:

O Mystery Immortal! which is in the hemp and in our souls, in its bloom and in our passions; by which our poor lives are led upward out of the earth for a season, then cut down, rotted and broken—for Thy long service!

Looking backward, we can see how unified the whole has been.

That introductory chapter served another purpose, a stylistic one. *Current Literature* for August of that year lifted it from the book and printed it as a specimen of good contemporary prose; Dr. Finley put it into type for the blind. The following paragraph is typical of Allen's manufactured cadences:

Some morning when the roar of March winds is no more heard in the tossing woods, but along still brown boughs a faint, veil-like greenness runs; when every spring, welling out of the soaked earth, trickles through banks of sod unbarred by ice; before a bee is abroad under the calling sky; before the red of apple-buds becomes a sign in the low orchards, or the high song of the thrush is pouring forth far away at wet pale-green sunsets, the sower, the earliest sower of the hemp, goes forth into the fields.

If we read these lines aloud we note that, soothing as the rhythms are and pleasing as are the images evoked, they leave the impression of a self-conscious and slightly stilted writing. We note, too, as we proceed, a gravity, a dignity in tone not to be found in Allen's earlier nature passages; his increasing seriousness is weighing down the earlier spontaneity and cooling the earlier warmth. Nature, at first represented as the living background for noble heroes and heroines, as a colorful prop to pageantry, had in *Summer in Arcady* become a Mephistophelian prompter to sin and had lost some of its divinity. In a way Allen had betrayed and caged his cardinal, and it never sang again quite so sweetly.

For there are two motives running throughout *The Reign of Law:* the desire to show man as merely one of the natural creations of the universal life-force, akin to animals and trees and birds, and the wish, firmly rooted in Allen's puritanism but slowly withering from the top, to find in this same created being some meaning, some reason for existence, some worth surpassing that of beast or bush. Science and religion combat openly in the narrative and furtively between the printed words, and despite the poetry of the final paragraph, science has much the better of the conflict. It was this victory, together with what was thought to be an unfavorable treatment of clergymen, that promoted the controversy over *The Reign of Law* and made it historically important as being the first notable anti-fundamentalist novel to come from the pen of a southerner.

Allen had long been pondering the evolutionary concept, even, as we have seen, from college days. In the introduction to the revised edition of *A Kentucky Cardinal* and *Aftermath* published in 1900 he sketched some of the youthful impressions which he felt lent strength to his writing: the sight of his father sowing hemp; his own planting of corn and cutting of weeds; his knowledge, common to all farm boys, of the breeding of animals and fowls; his watching of the hemp through all its changes. He went on to say: " . . . these same experiences taught me, and have always compelled me, to see human life as set in Nature: finding its explanation in soil and sky and season: merely one of the wild growths that spring up on the surface of the earth amid ten thousand others. I hold this to be the only true way to write of Man in fiction, as it is in science." Back in 1886 in his essay, "Local Color," he had stated that "in truth, human life becomes to him [the local colorist] a part of nature and must be depicted as such."

This respect for Darwinism as he understood it grew until in 1908 he was to make the sweeping assertion that English literature could be divided into two periods, one before Darwin and one after. He was asked in that year to write an address to be read at the dedication in the Lexington cemetery of a monument to King Solomon, the vagabond he had immortalized in "King Solomon of Kentucky." The paper concerned itself less with this old hero than it did with what was a defense of his new point of view; one can even suspect that he had some intention of mildly shocking, perhaps of "educating" his auditors. After making this separation of our literature into two parts he argued that it was no longer possible to produce a satirist like Thackeray, since we no longer have faith in man's sudden redemption, that our knowledge of man's slow growth through the centuries prevented our renewing that faith, and that novelists must henceforth be cast in the mold of George Eliot, who illustrated positivism and evolution in her novels. "You can satirize a fallen angel who wilfully refuses to regain his paradise," he declared, "but you cannot satirize an animal who is developing through millions of years his own will to be used against his own instincts."

What has been said will raise the question of whether *The Reign of Law* is autobiographical. Undoubtedly much of it is. Allen like David, was a poor boy who went to Kentucky University in 1868; he must also have had his thinking revolutionized by the Darwinian volumes. His religious doubts were nursed, as David's were, by the hatreds among various denominations. David's search for an explanation of the universe was Allen's; both he and his hero shared the belief that man was but an animal and that the world was not created for his enjoyment only. When David announces to Gabriella that "the time is coming when the churches will be deserted by all thinking men, unless they cease trying to uphold, as the teachings of God, mere creeds of their ecclesiastical founders" and that "men do reject and have a right to reject what some man writes out as the eternal truth of the matter" we are surely hearing Allen's voice—and at a great distance that of Henry David Thoreau. But the correspondences cannot be pushed very far. Allen did not study for the ministry, did not have a disagreeable home life, was not expelled from college, did not marry a Gabriella. As we shall presently note, being drawn into an argument over the book he explicitly denied that David's adventures were to be taken as his own, and he assured his old college friend William B. Smith that David was largely drawn from him.

The Reign of Law was James Lane Allen's first thoroughly masculine novel; it possessed, according to his prescription, Virility, Strength, and Massiveness, nor did it lack some of those feminine elements which the author thought should be compounded with the masculine. Characters and settings have the vigor of reality. The sturdy hero rebelling against dogmatism; the sullen sick father; the shiftless but sympathetic mother; the heroine, a victim of the new social order after the Civil War, facing poverty and accompanying exile from her class—these are the strongest characters Allen had yet drawn. Admirable, too, is the presentation of the milieu in which the latter part of the comedy is played: the drab farmhouse, the tasteless cooking, the decay in buildings and stock, the tense, inarticulate hostility between father and son (the most dramatic thing in any of Allen's novels), the heart-breaking toil. Obviously Allen was familiar with Hardy's description of furze-cutting in *The Return of the Native* and with the story of Tess laboring in the fields; possibly with the pictures of Zola's drudging peasants; obviously, too, he was influenced by the whole direction of the local color school. Nor should we overlook the fact that Barrie was founding the "Kailyard School" in the nineties and that Eden Phillpotts was writing of the people in Devonshire and Cornwall; Allen was acquainted with the work of both men. But however strong these influences may have been, they cannot subtract from *The Reign of Law* the credit of being one of the first substantial novels in the American saga of the soil, which was to be given fresh impetus thirteen years later by Willa Cather's *O Pioneers!*

Seventy thousand copies of *The Reign of Law* were at once sold on faith, and abuse and denunciation broke forth simultaneously. It was not to be supposed that orthodox clergymen and laymen could read such heresy and remain passive:

The universe—it is the expression of Law. Our solar system—it has been formed by Law. The sun—the driving force of Law has made it. Our earth—Law has shaped that; brought Life out of it; evolved Life on it from the lowest to the highest; lifted primeval Man to modern Man; out of barbarism developed civilization; out of prehistoric religions, historic religions. And this one order—method—purpose—ever running and unfolding through the universe, is all we know of Him whom we call Creator, God, our Father. So that His reign is the Reign of Law. He, himself, is the author of the Law that we should seek Him. We obey, and our seekings are our religions.

For such an utterance Allen was attacked from the pulpit and through the press, by friends and foes almost impartially, with the churches naturally leading the van of the onslaught.

"Mr. James Lane Allen has done a very silly thing," declared *The Church Standard* (Protestant Episcopal), while *The Catholic News* (Roman Catholic) disapproved by saying that "Mr. Allen presents the spectacle of a man trying to carry water in a sieve."

Most interesting of all was the outcry in Lexington, seat of the university upon which Allen had trained his guns. President McGarvey, Allen's old teacher, immediately sprang to the defense of his institution and of the Christian faith. In a sermon preached in the first week of October, 1900, he reproached Allen for writing a book made up largely of personal experiences, and in an unfortunate moment for himself impeached the truthfulness of the novel by denying that a student had ever been expelled, as David was, from the College of the Bible. He also denied that professors of that college so taught God's Word as to make infidels of the students and that the university had fallen into ruin, as Allen maintained, through insistence upon dogmatic beliefs. He called attention to Mr. Allen's "conceit" in arrogating unto himself knowledge on a subject in which wiser men confessed themselves ignorant; he struck a cunning blow by suggesting that the chief purpose of the book was to degrade Christianity; and he wound up by proclaiming that there was no such thing as a "reign of law" and by defending belief in miracles.

That Allen was stung by this and other assaults is shown by the sharpness of his reply, printed in the same newspaper which had displayed Dr. McGarvey's criticism and given about a month after the President's arraignment. First he refuted the charge that he wrote autobiographically: "I can only tell the President that I do not publish my personal grievances as fiction." He seized quickly upon the assertion that no real David had been expelled from Kentucky University:

Conceive of an archbishop of those days as hurrying to his cathedral and hurling against a great satirist the accusation of being a liar for writing *The Tale of a Tub*, because there was no tub! Imagine the Duke of Wellington calling Thackeray a liar for saying that a certain young chap was killed at the Battle of Waterloo, when there was no such chap in the British Army! I hasten to assure the President—who is troubled with the idea that I may have too good an opinion of myself—that I am not comparing myself to Dean Swift or Thackeray any more than I should dare liken him to a great church scholar or a born leader of men.

No love lost there! And he continued by saying that he had made no attack upon the professors; had, rather, represented them sympathetically if not attractively; and he advised his former teacher to read the book he was presumably finding fault with. He wisely refused to argue the theory of evolution but, becoming more irritated as he proceeded, vented a sarcasm which he rarely employed in writing. In President McGarvey's classes, he felt sure, must be "many quick-witted boys of common sense and the rudiments of a public school education" who could answer their executive's contentions, and he advised his antagonist to "call confidentially upon his professor of natural science and talk with him half an hour for the common credit of the faculty and the good name of the institution." As to miracles, he believed what David believed.

. . . such theology as the President has shown in his address, coupled with such ignorance of the intellectual condition of his age, helps to drive young men out of the church. In all probability it would have helped to make David an infidel. It would certainly make me one.

Nor would he withdraw his charge that the university was a ruin, for he pointed out the proud purpose for which the college had been founded and how far it had fallen short because of denominational and factional disputes.

The Macmillan Company, probably wishing to pour oil upon troubled waters and at the same time take advantage of an excellent opening for publicity, printed in the same year a thirty-two-page pamphlet entitled *Mr. James Lane Allen's The Reign of Law: A Controversy and Some Opinions Concerning It,* in which most prominence was given to clerical opinions supporting the author. *The Literary Digest* took notice of the sensation under the caption: "Is Mr. Allen's Reign of Law an Infidel Work?" After announcing that *The Reign of Law* had "created a somewhat extraordinary amount of controversy in the religious world" it gave the opinion of Dr. Chadwick (Unitarian) to the effect that the book had done more for the liberal cause than all the sermons preached in liberal pulpits throughout the past year. Magazine and newspaper critics lined up pretty solidly behind the novelist, although several pointed out his error in having David read *The Descent of Man* three years before it was published. Richard Le Gallienne, however, must have caused Allen to forget this mistake when he averred in the *Boston Evening Transcript* for the eleventh of August that "No writer using the English language is at the moment writing so beautifully about nature."

Naturally the furor over Allen's views caused the sales of his book to proceed briskly. It had to compete with *Red Pottage* and with the historical novels, *Alice of Old Vincennes, To Have and To Hold,* and *Janice Meredith,* but it sprang at once into the list of best sellers, far outstripping, for example, Edith Wharton's *The Greater Inclination,* published the year before. *The Bookman* for August, 1900, recorded that *The Reign of Law* was at the head of the list of novels in popular demand; *The World Almanac* for 1900 said that 112,-000 copies of the novel had been run off in that year; *World's Work* in March of the next year put it among the most popular books, although it gradually gave way before Marie Corelli's *The Master Christian*.

The vogue of *The Reign of Law* was not confined to the United States. The Macmillan Company issued it in England as *Increasing Purpose* (borrowed from the familiar line in Tennyson's "Locksley Hall" in order not to conflict with a scientific volume with the same title by the Duke of Argyll). Despite some unfavorable criticism the novel leaped into the front rank among the favorites in the tight little island. The *Illustrated London News* remarked that it had "little value as science and the faintest possible interest as fiction," but *The Athenaeum* found descriptive passages in it as good as anything in *Lorna Doone*. By November *The Literary Digest* was able to report that *The Reign of Law* was the fastest-selling novel in England and that *The Academy* put it first in its roster of popular fiction. To prepare the British for Allen's newest book the Macmillan Company had issued *A Kentucky Cardinal*, *Aftermath*, *Flute and Violin*, and *The Blue-Grass Region of Kentucky* in England a few weeks before *Increasing Purpose* appeared, and Allen found himself literally introduced *en masse* to literary Englishmen.

The Reign of Law is one of the most enduring of Allen's works. It demonstrated what had before been a matter of doubt—that he could at will handle realism convincingly, even when he chose to variegate it with tints of idealism and romanticism. It showed a steadily developing maturity of style and thought; it stimulated thinking among the author's enlarging audience and drove an entering wedge for liberalism in American religious thought. Incidentally, it contains the best lyric that Allen ever wrote, "The Song of the Hemp."

Three years elapsed before he completed his next novel, first announced as *The Crypts of the Heart*. In the meantime he had been moved to oppose our efforts to "pacify" the Filipinos, a struggle in which he felt ashamed of the great disparity of the powers involved and which he argued would call forth no American literature. Wars in the past, he pointed out, had stimulated our national letters; fiction and poetry had followed the flag. The first good American novelist was Cooper, following the Revolution; the second great movement in our literature had begun some time after the Revolution; the third movement was a direct result of the Civil War; but the wars with Spain and with the little brown islanders could stimulate no first-rate writing. "I challenge," he wrote in a syndicated article, "any one to make any sort of collection of American literature that celebrates our long war of two years to subjugate an innocent people who never wronged us but by desiring the same liberty which we ourselves would die to defend." But such temperate words were, of course, drowned out by Senator Beveridge's ringing call to the United States to embrace its destiny and by the less publicised but none the less potent counsels of certain captains of industry. That was in 1901, and in the next year Allen contributed, with William Dean Howells, Hamilton Wright Mabie, and John Kendrick Bangs, to a symposium on a question provoked by Jules Verne's prediction that newspaper narratives would supplant fiction as reading matter. Allen held that novels would not be suffered to disappear; that they would always be needed to satisfy the longing for escape; that even though they were declining in merit the very falling off was a presumption that the quality would eventually be raised—a bit of reasoning which the editor of *The North American Review* apparently printed without an uplifted eyebrow.

Then in 1903 came *The Mettle of the Pasture*. There is every reason to believe that Allen meant this novel celebrating the sterling character of Kentucky manhood and womanhood to be his most ambitious contribution to his country's

iterature. He toiled at it long and patiently, keeping notes
n a red, paper-backed book such as a schoolboy might have
used for composition exercises. His writing is almost unde-
cipherable, intentionally so; the sentences and phrases are
scrawled at all angles and few of them throw any light upon
the growing story. Of Mrs. Conyers, he made the comment
that she stood for "individual variability produced by excess
of food"; "evolution" and "devolution" occur frequently;
there is clear indication that the delightful book on courtship read by Marguerite is Allen's invention; on the last
page, in bold firm hand, is the cryptic line: "Yes, I thank
you, Harriet." These fragments, of no value in reconstruct-
ing Allen's processes in putting his plot together, are such
as any writer might jot down in random reverie. Nor did he
confide much more of his plan to inquisitive friends or interviewers. He told Arthur Bartlett Maurice in 1900 that the
works prior to this were the fruits of apprenticeship; two
years before he informed a representative of *The Bookman*
that he was not going to desert Kentucky as a field of action
but was, on the contrary, placing there "the first novel of my
life," a novel that was to unite "the humor of *A Kentucky
Cardinal*, the philosophic frankness of *Summer in Arcady*,
and the spiritual seriousness of *The Choir Invisible*," a novel
to be twice as long as anything he had previously attempted.

The Mettle of the Pasture is the longest but it is also the
dullest of Allen's writings. The title, derived from King
Henry the Fifth's address to his soldiers before Harfleur, is
meant to apply particularly to Isabel Conyers's distorted puritanism which prevents her from accepting the man she loves;
the theme, a variation on *Tess of the D'Urbervilles*, is that a
pure woman is justified in rejecting her affianced if he has
been guilty of "sin" before knowing her. Isabel recedes from
this hard position, but not until Rowan Meredith is desperately ill; and to make the moral unescapable Allen lets

the hero die, so that grief and frustration fall heavily upon both man and woman as the consequence of a single unpremeditated misstep. The mercy thus extended at the close of the book is but disguised cruelty; Allen had no wish to condone and did not condone sexual irregularity, however slight. The text of the sermon is to be found in Isabel's cry to Professor Hardage: "Cannot you see them standing all through history, the sad figures of girls who have only asked for what they gave, love in its purity and its singleness—have only asked that there should have been no other before them? And cannot you see what a girl feels when she consents to accept anything less—that she is lowered to herself from that time on,—has lost her own ideal of herself, as well as her ideal of the man she loves? And cannot you see that she lowers herself in *his* eyes also and ceases to be his ideal through her willingness to live with him on a lower plane?"

Since the book was dedicated to his sister it is likely that this plea for the single standard took its origin from her unhappy experience. It is a plea that is typical of the sentimentality which informs *The Mettle of the Pasture*, a sentimentality that expands through stiff dialogue, fine writing, and overdrawn episodes into sheer melodrama. If any of Allen's writings warranted *The Nation's* accusation in 1925 that he was melodramatic, it was this one. From the garden setting of the first chapter (love trysts in Allen's stories are preferably out-of-doors) to the death scene of the silly last chapter, the hypersensitive protagonists move through page after page of unreality. To give the impression of quickened actuality Allen put into this novel more people than are to be found in any other one of his: six love affairs go on simultaneously and one unhappily married pair chant a kind of Greek chorus. If any part of the book is autobiographical it is the recital of the early ambitions of Professor Hardage who bears a certain resemblance to his creator, and in the picture of the breaking down of class barriers in the post-bellum South. On the other hand and even though Allen used in this novel names taken directly from his family connections, as late as 1923 he wrote to a student in Lexington: "I never put myself into my stories, any of them," thus reiterating a denial he wished to have believed.

Devoted as the book was to exhibiting American idealism of the brand of the nineties, it contains a character who by virtue of her malevolence is one of the most memorable in Allen's sheaf of fictions, his vicious women being exceedingly rare. Isabel's grandmother, crafty, vengeful, worldly-wise, is not to be forgotten, even though her chief purpose is to serve as a foil for her pure granddaughter. She stands out so sharply that an English critic, looking for evidences of reality, seized upon her with some satisfaction: "The old lady enjoys iced cream and strawberries or a cooling sherbet in her 'parlours,' where she sharpens her nails on the furniture. Nothing much results from the sharpening or the diet." Most of Allen's heroines linger in the mind like music when soft voices have died, but this grandmother, destined to defeat, dominates the action by force of ill-will and makes the fourteen other principal characters feeble by contrast, although Pansy Vaughan and Harriet Crane have their moments and the interviews between women whose interests are clashing are specimens of Allen's humor at its best.

In its totality *The Mettle of the Pasture* is, despite its heavy priggishness, anti-romantic in effect, for the hero, Rowan Meredith, is forced to pay with premature death for a mistake which Allen attributes to the fact that man is an earth animal, played upon by resistless forces of breed and place. Through Professor Hardage the author speaks: "But this particular phrase—the mettle of the pasture—belongs to our country rather than to his [Shakespeare's], more to Darwin than to the theater of that time. What most men are

thinking now, if they think at all, is of our earth, a smal
grass-grown planet hung in space. And unaccountably mak
ing his appearance on it, is man, a pasturing animal, derivin,
his mettle from the pasture." Symbolic of this attitude whic
robs his protagonist of true tragic quality is the scene i
which Rowan looks at the portraits of two of his ancestor
one a puritan and one a good liver, and then blows out hi
candle, thus signifying that on the question of the freedom o
the will versus the potency of environment there is no ligh

The Mettle of the Pasture was another best seller fo
Allen and another object of critical acclamation. Said the r
viewer in *The Outlook:* "Mr. Allen's work, as it is graduall
presented to us, seems to indicate that he will probably tak
in our generation the place which Hawthorne occupied in h
own—the place of the patient, gifted devotee of his art, whicl
though not versatile, has in addition to restrained power th
note of inimitable charm, and charm abides when flashy orig
inality becomes trite through imitations." Certainly ther
can be no questioning Allen's patience, the high order of h
talents, or his devotion to literature. But in view of the shif
in his technique and themes and manners it is surprising t
have him rated as lacking in versatility. Unlike most Amer
can writers, especially if they become financial and popula
successes, Allen was not content to go on repeating the pe
formance by which he prospered; he was intent upon growtl
even though that growth, like most development, was base
upon imitation, conscious or non-conscious. From the paste
of *Flute and Violin* to the comparative robustness of *The Me
tle of the Pasture* was no slight advancement, and no stude
of the volumes lying between these two will fail to note tl
maturing expression and thought, the increasing substitutic
of vigor for dreaminess of language, of skepticism and mil
cynicism for youthful acceptance of idealistic conception
Whereas death had been gently used in *Aftermath* to evok

no more than emotional response, it was employed in *The Mettle of the Pasture* to illustrate the pitiless course of physical devolution. That Allen should have been the first notable southern writer of fiction to champion Darwinism is testimony to his courage in putting aside his laurels to quest for truth. He was trying to grow as America grew, in bigness, in energy, in understanding.

He made a gallant attempt to assume Virility, Strength, and Massiveness in this period. But to become a masculine writer in his sense required more than imitation; required greater powers, it must be conceded, than he could muster. Intellectually and emotionally he was feminine—and that is not meant as a reproach—and by no amount of determination or industry could he change his nature. He could not drive himself into showing a ruggedness, a daring, a control of material which he did not possess. Of the three novels in this group *Summer in Arcady* is the best technically; even *The Reign of Law*, held together by a factitious unity, breaks into two parts which fail to cohere completely, and *The Mettle of the Pasture* became so unwieldy as to pass beyond management. *The Reign of Law*, tardy though its attack upon orthodoxy was, might have been a potent indictment of the religious and moral biases of the post-war South had Allen been capable of combining expertly its two elements; it failed because, like all regular Victorians, he looked upon love as the supreme thing and therefore abstracted from the novel the ultimate sincerity which would have given Strength to the stories of David and Gabriella. David's progress in disillusionment should have been carried over from religion to love between the sexes, but that far Allen was unwilling to go—as yet. In a few years he was to make the logical and complete step and the consequences were to be disastrous to him.

The Mettle of the Pasture fails for the same reason. And it has other weaknesses. In it Allen surveys with a more dubious eye the human affections, he is not sure marriages are made in heaven, he allows his hero pre-marital sex experience, yet love is still the thing for which the world is well lost and it is through love that Rowan Meredith and Isabel Conyers are wounded. It is not the vulnerability of a loving girl that is objectionable to us; it is the mingling of a now outworn theory of heredity with the story of passion that divides the novel into halves that are never quite brought together. To increase the confusion the halves are dissected into parts, so that the five other love affairs may present Kentucky society after the Civil War. Unfortunately, all the scenes and all the people except the grandmother suffer from a coolness and artificiality of treatment resulting from the author's aloof-ness. He was too far away from his characters and his scene. His heart was given to the evolutionary hypothesis, not to his weak, suffering people. Every line he wrote, whether for publication or for the eyes of his friends only, whether de-scribing John Gray or Hilary or Rowan, proclaims him the idealist who could convincingly create an Adam Moss but who had little understanding of the erring and distorted.

If he wished to write massively and vitally he could have found no better area for observation than New York City, now fixed upon as his home since Kentuckians had failed to approve his *Reign of Law;* yet it was to be nine years be-fore he abandoned Kentucky as the scene of his fiction. He was living in the past. He planned to record the clash and din aroused by champions in stirring times, yet he turned to the tranquil Bluegrass and through a haze of memory at-tempted to put peaks of experience into a region where he had noted only the gently rolling hills. He was keen enough to realize the ambiguous nature of his position, and to a man of his earnestness the knowledge must have been a cause of some self-questioning; the incongruity between his training and temperament and his desire to be a realist was too pronounced to be overlooked. "My impression was that Allen's life, at least in New York, where he was cut off from his natural environment and hereditary associations, did not have a good effect upon his mental processes or his quality as an artist in letters," declares Henry van Dyke. "It did not make him morose, for he was always courteous and affable, though naturally of a reserved disposition. But it inclined him perhaps to think too much about himself and too little about other people. The sane and gentle humor which irradiated *A Kentucky Cardinal* and *Aftermath* seemed to be drying up at the roots. Consequently he gave the impression of being a misunderstood man, with something of the quality of Hamlet in his temper." In the same letter Dr. van Dyke recalled a dinner for some thirty or forty literary people at the Aldine Club, with Allen making a speech in the course of which he gave his hearers to understand that gentlemen no longer engaged in literature, and since Thomas Nelson Page, F. Hopkinson Smith, and George W. Cable were at the table that part of the address fell upon embarrassed ears.

At about that time Sue Porter Heatwole, wife of a distinguished Virginian educator, met Mr. Allen while he was summering in Asheville. Her comments on the author, whom she admired greatly, make very clear the angle from which he was looking at himself. "Mr. Allen," writes Mrs. Heatwole, "must have been about fifty years old when I first met him. There were no marks of age, and he looked not older than thirty-five [a fact which some psychologists would deem an evidence of neurosis].

"He seemed to cast that golden glow over everything that he touched and brought to the surface the best in the heart of people and things. He related simple everyday things with that fairy-like touch, a kind penetrating psychology or a sort of sorcery that baffles analysis. His personality was a fusion of life and dream, the very charm of poetry animated his being. . . .

"He promised to visit me, told me how he had to conserve his health because he *must* finish the work he had in his head and heart to do. . . .

· "He was in a way shy. I think that was rather due to the feeling that he had a real gift; he felt he was a person apart from the thousand and ten thousand commonplace mortals; he did not scorn them, but felt he must not let this precious gift of the gods—whatever that may be—become less precious by too much exposure. He was full of humor and wit and loved to be happy. He loved beauty in every form. He disliked pretense and insincerity in people and things. He always impressed me with being able to see through the flesh into the very heart of one's soul. He was always perfectly dressed, perfectly poised, and by far the most distinguished looking man it has ever been my pleasure to see. No one could think evil in his presence, and I think he felt the need of high atmosphere in which to let his spirit live. He did not like many people. I regarded this carefully and introduced him to but one person."

Through this letter one catches again the note of the paradox that was Allen, a paradox he expressed most neatly in *The Alabaster Box* when he had one of the clubmen say ". . . the first and greatest wish of every man worth his salt in this world is to be let alone; his second and next greatest wish is—*not* to be let alone!" The letter reveals another matter: Allen was obviously still feeling himself exceptional, an upholder of the tenets of humanism even while he was flirting with the new naturalism. His pecuniary success could not help contributing something to his self-satisfaction, but beyond that was the conviction that had been with him for years—that he was spiritually separate from most of his contemporaries. He was contemplating himself as a force surviving from the earlier American virtues, as almost if not quite the last apostle of the Genteel Tradition in American literature. The Genteel Tradition was to be very lonely in New York in the twentieth century.

CHAPTER V

"THE LITERATURE OF SCIENCE AND ART"

For six years following the publication of *The Mettle of the Pasture* James Lane Allen was strangely silent. Although at the height of his popularity, with every chance to capitalize his name, with editors and publishers and public eager to read anything from his pen, he seemed to scorn every opportunity to exploit his reputation, and to leave the lists of fiction open to such active writers as Robert Chambers, who published eight volumes during this six-year interval, David Graham Phillips, who was responsible for nine, and Jack London, whose name appeared on twelve. Not even Reginald Wright Kauffman's squib in *Life* could make him break his silence:

> Mix metaphors, and while the sun still shines
>> Make hay with highly sentimental dames;
> The public favor suffers quick declines;
>> 'Tis a long Lane that has no turning, James.

The unfairness of the second verse angered Allen but moved him to no reply. If he had plans for future work he kept his counsel about them; for a time it looked, since during this interval he wrote only one thing of any importance and that for a magazine, as if he were about to retire gracefully and hang up his laurels. One can only speculate upon the reasons for this non-productivity, for he never discussed it. Possibly, as the preceding chapter intimated, he was unsettled and dissatisfied concerning his artistic principles. Perhaps he was written out, physically and spiritually, and despite the impression he gave of being unusually fit, was in real need of a period of recuperation. He was described in those years as being "a little over six feet in height . . . and broad-shoul-dered, with something of a military bearing. His hair is thin and gray, and he wears a gray mustache. . . . His eyes are gray, large and bright, and his features are regular and good." But the tone of his letters from this time on belies the suggestion of stamina; he complains of illness, of fears for his sister's health; he betrays weariness and nervousness —the nervousness of one who found it difficult to unbend, who would not even cross his knees in conversation, who took everything, most of all himself, too seriously. Like George Eliot the mercury of change was in his veins and he felt urged to go from place to place. He found New York irk-some and made short trips to the South in winter and to the Northeast in summer. The new South with its willingness to ape Yankee industrialism, caused his spirits to droop a lit-tle; he lamented the loss of the polish and leisure he had seen about him in his youth and young manhood. He found the early largeness and simplicity of living superseded by a growing desire to succeed in business, and over the resultant strife and hurry and hypocrisy he shook his head irritably.

"For twenty-five years I have been an invalid trying to take care of another—and to do a little work," he fretted in a letter to M. A. Cassidy in 1923, revealing that in the early years of the twentieth century he had felt his forces al-ready on the wane. It was as if the energy expended in climb-ing from poverty and obscurity to a state of moderate af-fluence and of considerable fame had left him querulous, over-fatigued, and worst of all, skeptical of that which he had achieved. The bright truth which he had once set his heart upon imprisoning within the circle of his writing was as far away as ever, and instead of guiding humanity from the broad highway of error he had done no more than produce a few stories which served as temporary amusements and gen-tle sermons. Loneliness of course accentuated the bitter

mood induced by self-examination. Although a man
strong feeling, he was too self-conscious to be able to find
satisfactory outlet for his needs by contracting numero
friendships. He was constitutionally averse to the expressi
of whatever warmth he possessed, was prevented by son
powerful conditioning from exposing that generosity of spi
which makes a man widely beloved. He was devoted to
sister but found her sometimes a drain upon his patience.
the bottom of his heart he possibly craved wife and chi
yet knew the craving would never be strong enough to bre
down his reluctance to divert attention from his work. "
the mariner steers for the lighthouse, as the hound runs dov
the stag, as the soldier wakes to the bugle, as the miner di
for the future, as the drunkard drains the cup, as the sai
watches the cross, I follow my work, I follow my work,"
has the professor cry in *The Bride of the Mistletoe,* and t
accents are indubitably Allen's own.

Yet he made diffident gestures for friendship, sometim
in unusual ways, and he was always on the lookout for tho
countless little actions which pass daily before the eyes of t
world but which are noted only by the sympathetic observe
of human life. On New Year's Night of 1905, while he w
taking dinner in the Grunewald Hotel, New Orleans, he w
charmed by the face and bearing of a little boy at a near-
table. Shrinking from actual acquaintance, he wrote the fo
lowing note to "A child on New Year's Night":

When I, Stranger, am gone the waiter is asked to give to y
this candy—Should your Mama and Papa have ever heard of t
"Choir Invisible" they may know one of the voices was a ch
such as you—and fame sometimes comes from a divine voice-
JAMES LANE ALLEN. I am incognito—ask them to consider it

The parents respected Allen's curiously mixed desire for se
effacement, for it was not until fifteen years later that t

mother wrote to inform him that the boy's name was Earle Cotter Crumb, and that their family admired the author's works; she enclosed, for identification, Allen's old note, which she had preserved. Since he kept the correspondence with a packet of clippings relating to *A Cathedral Singer*, and since he hinted at the child's possessing a good singing voice, it may well be that Earle Crumb was the inspiration for the young hero of the story which centered about the building of the Cathedral of St. John the Divine.

Other things treasured by Allen in those years were a clipping which praised hidden lives deliberately withdrawn from the tumult because they did not deem worthy of strife those things for which others were fighting, and a clipping of Richard Burton's poem "Those Who Walk Alone," two items which characterize much of his contemporary mood. One stanza of the poem again raises the question of whether it interested Allen because it reflected his own experience:

> Women there are on earth, most sweet and high,
>   Who lose their own, and walk bereft and lonely,
> Loving that one lost heart until they die,
>   Loving it only.

The Macmillan Company even found it expedient to give publicity to his disposition, and when in June, 1900, it issued its Book List it emphasized the retiring nature of the "aristocrat of American letters," a shyness all the more admirable since he was "perhaps the greatest of living novelists in America." Loneliness, however, drove him to keep a journal; he ridiculed the idea of setting "Emersonian dripping pans under my eaves," and had no need to be reminded of his literary projects, but did feel the desirability of having a confidant, all the better inasmuch as it should be mute. On the first page he put down: "Notes unintelligible to anyone but myself—so written on purpose—to be used later on—

James Lane Allen," and then did his best to make good his caution. The jottings that can be read are unimportant but revelatory of a temper that was indeed very like Hawthorne's.

For the twenty-fifth of January he related how a crippled boy who "hardly came up to my waist" helped him on with his overcoat—"*me*, six feet one, weighing 200. The thought stayed with me late and lasted that night." The next day he amused himself by asking the laundry boy if he were a good judge of noses; on the twenty-seventh he entered the fact that he had walked at twilight in Central Park. The notes show that he was steadily dictating in the mornings and going out for walks in the afternoons, little journeys in which he would be discreetly curious and observant and willing to open conversation with a child or a workman; he seemed most at ease—again like Hawthorne—with the young and inferior. On the tenth of February he recorded, doubtless with a smile of amusement, that a chance acquaintance at table confided the information that Kipling had died in the very hotel in which they were eating; two days later he varied his walk by going up Riverside Drive from the Park; on the fourteenth he described a group of men and women, gesticulating excitedly at a distance, who turned out to be deaf mutes.

The men closest to him at this time were Isaac F. Marcosson, to whom he was to dedicate *The Heroine in Bronze* and toward whom he was eventually to cool, and T. S. Jones, Jr., for whose *The Voice in the Silence* he was to write a preface. Frequently he walked and dined and went to the opera with these companions. "James Lane Allen was a splendid gentleman," is Mr. Jones's tribute to his friend, "handsome, generous, chivalric, fine; of great pride and reticence on personal matters (he never discussed his friends nor deeper attachments and I naturally did not probe into his affairs); he had the sense of understanding that the average mind is jealous and prefers the negative position, wherefore he protected himself; he was isolated, which was natural; he had a loving heart and was easily hurt . . . but he covered this . . . I only wish he had been a bit tougher toward things, had a bit more laughter . . . though he had a delightful sense of fun —had been a bit happier. . . . He was of the best spiritual breed, of that I am certain."

Whatever feeling of mental and physical pain, of inadequacy or superiority, may have contributed to his reasons for remaining aloof from the swifter currents, certain it is that he proceeded, now that his income would allow him to live like a Kentucky gentleman, to make himself comfortable. A few days before his birthday in 1908 he took an apartment at 130 West Seventy-fifth Street, the residence which was to be associated with his prosperous years. Here through the windows of a large living-room he could look out upon the crowds bustling along the sidewalk in front of Dr. John Roach Straton's Church, a building, however, which he did not enter; if he attended religious services it was usually to hear Dr. Charles Parkhurst preach. Here he could retreat, if he chose, to quiet and security behind a mahogany desk over which hung a picture of Balzac, his favorite novelist, whom he so little resembled; here, attired in a scarlet dinner jacket and white flannels, he could entertain his friends at ease, except that his sister must always be kept out of sight in another near-by apartment; the cancer which was disfiguring her face sent her into complete seclusion. On the floor he laid a Kirman rug and carpet; at the windows were silk curtains made especially for him in France; he set off the Circassian walnut furniture with silver plate and sparkling glassware; he occupied a large teakwood chair while writing. On the walls were a tapestry and five carbon prints—Turner's "The Fighting Téméraire" and "Dido Building Carthage," Michelangelo's "The Creation of Adam," Titian's "Nymph and

Shepherd," and Botticelli's "Spring." Signed works of a
also hung on the walls: a large print entitled "The Fath
of the Forest," inscribed "To James Lane Allen, Esq., wit
appreciation for his interest in my work, Ernest Haskell";
signed silver point landscape by D. W. Tryon; and an etchir
by Gravesand. Prominent also was the bronze figure of
young girl, two feet six inches high, whose outstretched han
held two sockets for candles—an item of furnishing whic
was to play its part in a novel not yet contemplated. "Th
big things of life cost suffering and after they are won com
relaxation," he told John Wilson Townsend in 1912, thin
ing, doubtless, of his own struggles for recognition and of th
desire for rest he felt after more than a decade of steady e
deavor. In the midst of this comfort one regret gnawed lil
the envious worm; when a visitor from Lexington con
mented upon the fine style in which Allen was now living tl
latter sighed with some bitterness: "Ah, yes, but it mea
nothing now. If only my mother could have lived to sha
it!"

At about the same time he moved into these quarters tl
Saturday Evening Post printed (December 5, 1908) a ta
generally overlooked even by Allen's admirers today but or
of considerable value as a vane to indicate the direction
which his thoughts were blowing. This was "The La
Christmas Tree," another of the grave moralities which Ha
thorne's spirit might have communicated to the Kentucki;
had the earlier writer known the scientific theory upon whic
the story rests, that of a gradual extension of cold northwa
and southward from the polar caps and downward from tl
sky, ending in the extinction of every living thing upon tl
earth. The idea was not, of course, original with Allen n
very new; Camille Flammarion had, for example, stated
clearly in *The Contemporary Review* for April, 1891.
But to Allen the question of what might happen to ol

sphere when surrounded and invaded by utter frigidity became also the deeper inquiry of why it should happen, why something fair should be created, set in motion, populated, and then wholly obliterated. Unable to find a satisfactory answer he could only say in cheerless refrain that all is mystery; that the conduct of Destiny is as far past mortal comprehension as any problem that agitates the human mind. Even our behaviour, he reflected, is past understanding. Why are not men, condemned to brief existence on a grass-grown ball in space, charitable the one to the other? Why do they not turn to each other for happiness instead of recoiling from each other in quarrels? Why does a race which demands first of all justice, in practice measure it out last? He found such seekings unanswerable; he went on, logically, to doubt man's immortality, to ponder sadly over the impermanence of science, art, youth, and love. Written in prose as pure, cold, and beautiful as the snow and ice it pictured, prose that compels the reader to feel the gradual descent of deadly cold in each flicker of the falling snowdrops, "The Last Christmas Tree" is stylistically one of the best things Allen ever did. It must have caused at least a few of the critically-minded to wish that he would confine himself to the essay and venture rarely, if ever, from the short tale or sketch or prose pastel into the complexities of invention made necessary by the requirements of a full-length novel. Nor could the close reader have missed the swelling note of disenchantment arising from a conviction of the inevitable futility of all human effort and aspiration, a note struck long ago in "Posthumous Fame" but sounded now with scientific precision and in deeper tone. "Here was his conflict, which no Freud can understand," is the comment of T. S. Jones; "his heart knew there were worlds on worlds, as Christ and Socrates and Gautama knew; but he was confused by temporal philosophy. . . . His eyes were ever lifted to the mountain-tops, to

the stars; he doubted as Arnold doubted . . . but he
longed to the great company." When *The Last Christm*
Tree was published by Mosher in 1914 Allen dedicated
"To those who know they have no solution of the unive
yet hope for the best and live for it." His attempt to synt
size science and art ended in spiritual disorder.

Of equal interest with the display of his growing disil
sionment is the indication in the tale that Allen was study
the symbolism of evergreen trees, an examination soon
have far-reaching consequences inasmuch as it brought
his public a shock so strong as to alienate many of his devot
readers and thus lose for him the popularity upon wh
much of his content and income depended. For the res
of the research was *The Bride of the Mistletoe*, published
the Macmillan Company in 1909, six years after *The M*
tle of the Pasture. The research had obviously led him
The Golden Bough and from the anthropological data the
assembled he had spun a symbolic tale of modern marriag

The Bride of the Mistletoe sold well at the outset; it h
to compete with such best-sellers as Elinor M. Lane's *Katri*
Richard Harding Davis's *White Mice*, and F. Marion Cra
ford's *The White Sister*, but Allen's name carried it along
successful rivalry. Only for a time. Then the storm bro
in the form of loud clamor from both press and public.
is hard to believe that all the critics who heaped obloquy up
Allen's Christmas story were as thin-skinned as their o
cries suggest; perhaps they were but manifesting the alm
unavoidable reaction of opinion against any author who stan
prominently among literary favorites for more than a d
ade, especially since this author had neglected to capitali
his reputation by building up friendships that diploma
might have recommended and since he had first come to t
fore in the preceding century. Be that as it may, influent
spokesmen among reviewers minced no words in condemni

both author and book, while other critics, benevolent but bewildered by Allen's change of front, stood helplessly by, not certain whether to praise or blame. Few even of the friendly were bold enough to give more praise than might cautiously be bestowed upon the style.

The disapproval was emphatic, ranging from pedantic fault-finding to severe arraignment upon moral grounds. *The Athenaeum,* as an example of the first, pointed out that Allen had on page seventy-four of *The Bride of the Mistletoe* used "him" for "he"; the *Chicago Record-Herald* complained that "raisonner" had been misspelled in the quotation from De Maupassant that stands on the page just before the Preface. But the moralists were more vindictive. "As a piece of writing," said the *Chicago Evening Post,* "it is bastard, with its queer mixture of anthropology, portraiture, and rhapsody." The *New York Times* deplored "its poisonous purpose." The *Boston Transcript* protested that "it is not poetry nor is it sensible prose. It is merely an unending series of words, words, words." The *Philadelphia Press* avowed: "It is a miserable, sordid, repulsive subject—Faugh!" *The Independent* declared: "A crueler book for women has not been written before this time," and *The Bookman* warned that "it is not—and this is a point that cannot be too strongly emphasized—a book for the 'jeune fille.'" *The Saturday Review,* ready to concede something to a novelist it had always admired within reason, remarked that "the effort is sublime, the result ridiculous." *The Congregationalist,* perhaps not unwilling to return some blows dealt orthodox religion in *The Reign of Law,* asserted that "the book reminds one of the performance of a man half drunk." *The Nation,* henceforth to set its face sternly against Mr. Allen, assailed him viciously:

We have had occasion before now to call attention to the "sentimental voluptuousness," the gauze-veiled eroticism, which has given its peculiar note, and line, to Mr. Allen's work. There is a touch of unwholesomeness in the particularity with which he is wont to appeal to the lust of the fancy. He will not let us think of an attractive woman without bearing constantly in mind the existence of a body under her clothes. He deals not in the nude, but in the provocatively draped; his imagination finds something too ravishingly improper in the idea of nakedness. Sterne had the same kind of fancy, but redeemed or half redeemed it by humor, of which Mr. Allen has not a gleam. And in this day of the world, humor or no, the Peeping Tom method must be considered as pretty definitely relegated to the "Amusement Parlors" and their literary equivalents. Mr. Allen's code is of the age when ladies walked with limbs, and men wore inexpressibles. No seriousness of intent can greatly avail Mr. Allen as long as this taint remains. When are we to have done with this harping upon the physiology of marriage?

We do not know what Mr. Allen's reaction to this illogical outburst was, but it can safely be assumed that he was silently furious. That he who had early guided himself by the chivalry of Arthur's knights, who had grown up in the South's aristocratic traditions, who had in his personal life been as free from reproach as Bayard himself should be thus abused with innuendo and direct charge—how could he who had once hurled his croquet mallet through a porch lattice treat these slurs with the contemptuous humor they merited? Even justly hostile criticism made him, like many another artist, ill, and the scurrility which now descended upon him must have made him wish that the day of duels was not over.

That he had anticipated an explosion, although certainly not so violent a one as he came to hear, seems evident from the fact that shortly after *The Bride of the Mistletoe* was published a single sentence, obscurely placed in the *New York Times*, announced his departure "for an extended trip through Europe," where he again effaced himself with characteristic shrinking. "I was anxious," wrote Sir Edmund

Gosse in response to an inquiry, "when James Lane Allen was over here some twenty years ago, to see him. I wrote to what I was told was his address, but I received no answer. I was answered afterwards that he had not wished to form any acquaintances in London, and that, in fact, he repelled all advances. I am very sorry that I can give you no further information. I fancy that Allen's brief visit to this country left no mark of any kind on anybody, not even on himself." Moreover, Allen wrote to John Wilson Townsend immediately after returning from abroad: "You may know that the story [*The Bride of the Mistletoe*] has veered into the center of a discussion widespread and by me expected. Not until the work is completed can this first part be finally judged: I have no fears of what the judgment then will be."

Today the reader of this maligned volume will look vainly for either startling scenes or ideas in that writing, although after finishing his perusal he may well be in the dark as to the author's intent. He will find in it a short preface which admits that there is no purposing to write a novel but rather a short story of unquestionable unity. "There are two characters—a middle-aged married couple living in a plain farmhouse; one point on the field of human nature is located; at that point one movement is directed toward one climax; no external event whatsoever is introduced; and the time is about forty hours." The expectant reader meets first a man "with a quietude in him that was oftener in Southern gentlemen in quieter, more gentlemanly times," a man "with instant courtesy—rather obsolete now," writing in his study; to the study comes a queenly woman soon identified as the wife of the writing man, Professor Ousley. Through their uneasy, constrained dialogue it transpires that all is not well in this household; that husband and wife are haunted by some fear. Presently we learn, however, that the wife is unhappy because she is almost convinced that she has been but an Incident to her mate, that he no longer really sees her. Years before he had brought her to this house on Christmas Eve, their wedding night, had playfully named her his Bride of the Mistletoe, and had loved her fondly until in the past year his ardor had cooled and he had seemed to seek satisfaction in his work instead of in her. Too proud to question him, she had been deeply hurt by his turning from her; now, unable to endure her suspense longer, she insinuates her fears into her speeches. He evades her thrusts but agrees that they should celebrate one more old-fashioned Christmas with their children, to whom the mysteries are dear. After a tree has been cut, set up, and trimmed, he explains why he has neglected her for his studies: he has been penning a book for her which is to answer one of her random queries as to the meaning of the Christmas tree.

Here follow twenty-three pages of a kind of lecture in which the professor accounts for the use of an evergreen tree at the celebration of the Nativity; he also explains the significance of the ornaments upon the tree: the cornucopia, the star, the candle, the cross, the dove, the bell, the fruits and flowers, the tinsel, masks, and dolls. Then Mrs. Ousley, fascinated but aloof in manner, asks about the mistletoe—what is its meaning, its connection with the Christmas festival? The husband demurs, then refuses to reply. Alarmed by some vague suggestion in his demeanor, she insists upon his going on with the treatise. Finally he acquiesces, sternly disregarding her sudden volte-face when she sees that he will do what she wishes, and continuing his "wandering tale," divulges that the use of mistletoe is a survival of Druidic rites of sacrifice involving the free play of sex. In a flash of intuition the wife realizes then what she has meant to her husband: she has been only a bride of the mistletoe, a bit of ceremony in his general career, and her value to him has now declined sharply with the passing of youth. Going to her room she gives way to despair and fury. In her first rage she resolves to quit the man and his house forever; she even entertains thoughts of murder; but as she sits through the vigil of an entire night she gradually becomes resigned to the defeat of her womanhood and resolves to stand by her trust. "Only the heroic, among both men and women," is Allen's reflection, "losing the best as their first choice, fight their way through defeat to the standard of the second best and fight on there." But she does allow her mind to linger momentarily upon a neighbor, the family doctor, who, she realizes, loves her. And so the story ends, with Mrs. Ousley broken-hearted over the collapse of her marriage but waiting gallantly for what the future may bring.

There is nothing in all this to give the slightest qualm to the most sensitive reader today. It is true that Allen alluded without any necessity to the wife's "warm, foam-white thigh"; true that a psychoanalyst would find openings for cogitation upon Allen's repressed sexual life; and it cannot be denied that Allen looked candidly at the longevity of sex attraction between a wedded couple. But the reader who picks up the story twenty years after its printing finds nothing new or exciting in these particulars; he is more likely to examine them in a kind of wonder that they should once have been held sensual and disgusting. And he will probably realize that in reading *The Bride of the Mistletoe* he has met a genuine esthetic experience.

For this tale leaves an almost weird impression upon the imaginative mind. Its style does much to create this feeling. A writer in *The Bellman* expressed the opinion that Allen was "probably the greatest living master of cold and classic English," a view pretty generally shared in that day, even to the point of inspiring some waggery. John Kendrick Bangs, for instance, wrote for the *Chapbook* as early as March 1, 1898: "Can you fancy what superb work could be expected

from the joint efforts of Mr. James Lane Allen and Dr
[Harry Thurston] Peck? How the classical beauty of Mr
Allen's English would soften the rugged rhetorical crag
upon which the antelope of Dr. Peck's fancy disports itself
and how, on the other hand, the seething vitality of Dr. Pec
would melt a little of the ice which hedges about the greate
part of Mr. Allen's writing. . . . Surely Mr. Allen does no
wish to stand so far aloof from his fellows that none but
literary Nansen would dare brave the perils of his acquaint
ance." *The Bride of the Mistletoe* justifies this critical pos
tion. It is one of the coldest books in American literature
as though its pages had been frosted by the bleak winds tha
blew about the professor's house that Christmas Eve. Th
frigidity is reinforced by the author's remoteness from hi
two characters; he reveals no moiety of humor, no hint o
sympathy, no hope for a kindly solution to a desperate sit
uation. In addition, the apparent but far from transparen
symbolism leaves the reader uncertain whether he has had
peep at life or whether he has seen only papier-mâché figure
through a glass darkly.

Reviewers who made a conscientious endeavor to under
stand *The Bride of the Mistletoe* agreed that it derived some
thing from what William Winter had branded five year
before as "the slimy muck of Mr. Ibsen and the lunacy o
Mr. Maeterlinck." This is not an unfair inference. Al
though there is no external evidence that Allen had rea
Ibsen carefully, the relation between the Norwegian's Nor
and the American's Mrs. Ousley, both of whom meditate
flight because their husbands slighted their individualities
seems obvious enough, nor can the likeness of the preternat
urally wise children in *The Doctor's Christmas Eve* (seque
to *The Bride of the Mistletoe*) to Little Eyolf be overlooked
Maeterlinck's influence can be more confidently traced. Th
Belgian was receiving much attention in the magazines of th

opening years of the twentieth century; *The Reader's Guide to Periodical Literature* lists eighty-nine references to discussions of the dramatist between 1900 and 1909, and Allen, who was a consistent if not wide reader, could not have overlooked the prominence given to the author of *Monna Vanna*. Moreover, Allen, an inveterate opera-goer, interested in Oscar Hammerstein's challenge to the prestige of the Metropolitan Company, must have heard Mary Garden and Jean Perier in *Pelléas et Mélisande* at the Manhattan Opera House in April, 1908 and been entranced by the mystery and atmosphere of the action as well as the calm forebodings set forth by the musical score. Finally, there is direct evidence that he had purchased Richard Hovey's translation of Maeterlinck's plays, so that we have good reason for searching Allen's Christmas trilogy for what may be the foreigner's finger-prints. They are there, in the clipped sentences, the pregnant phrases, the eloquent silences of the dialogue in *The Bride of the Mistletoe*; Allen's conversations prior to this book had been, whether playful or serious, full-rounded and nearly oratorical. In this new work, however, he compressed the speeches into tense and dramatic arrangement which is strikingly reminiscent of Maeterlinck's mannerism. There are other parallelisms: the oak tree beside the professor's house is invested with a fateful meaning which suggests strongly the symbolism of the vaults in Arkël's castle; the precocious children already alluded to, especially the doctor's son, may owe something to Yniold.

Any novelist would have been somewhat daunted by the reception given to *The Bride of the Mistletoe*. But Allen went on with the announced sequel, first called *A Brood of the Eagle* but published as *The Doctor's Christmas Eve*; indeed, he picked up the glove thrown by some of his critics for on the title page of this new novel he put a quotation from Francis of Assisi which read: *Secretum est mihi*. This second volume of the Christmas trilogy came out early in December, 1910, so as to appeal to holiday shoppers whose eyes would naturally be caught by the title. But by this time many of Allen's former admirers, persuaded that he had bargained his early ideals for pieces of silver, were of a mind to give the new venture a greeting less than cordial, and the critics, having once bearded the lion with impunity, prepared to review his latest book with a curtness that could have impressed him as only brutal, especially since the new novel held no revolutionary thesis.

The Doctor's Christmas Eve continues the story begun by *The Bride of the Mistletoe*, but from the point of view of Dr. Birney and his family. We meet first the doctor's children, a boy and a girl, trudging through the snow on the morning of the twenty-fourth of December; they are walking across the fields to the Ousley house, where are another boy and girl who are to be host and hostess for the holiday. From that scene the novel offers retrospective views which reveal the doctor's character—including an excellent chapter which takes pains to present his heredity and environment as nearly equal factors in his development. In the same long chapter we learn that his domestic life, too, has been unhappy: that he had fallen in love with the bride of his best friend, Fred Ousley; that he had married in the hope of being able to stifle the illicit affection; that his heart proved stronger than his will; that his little son had discovered his father's preference and was beginning to be troubled by it. Then we return to the quartet of precocious children and a tedious, stilted description of their Christmas play; after that we pass rapidly to springtime and an embarrassing episode in which the Birney boy blurts out at the family table that Mrs. Ousley should have been his mother. From that instant the pretended peace of the doctor's household can no longer be maintained, and so Allen, in what looks at first like an evasion of the problem his plot had contrived, has the little son die in a scene not unrelated to similar scenes created by Dickens. Later the parents draw diffidently together, but there is no clear prediction that their future will hold anything but mutual coolness and regrets.

The sequel to *The Bride of the Mistletoe* is, therefore, written much after the formula of his earlier books: it provides a love story (although the man and woman are married), it introduces nature as a fateful force interfering with the movements of man, and it ends on the note of pathos. But the spontaneity and zest of the earlier productions are missing here; the tragedy that culminates in the death of the child is not to be taken as the personal tragedy of Dr. Birney and his wife but is to be seen rather as an accidental effect of and a possible remedy for a complication that is universally distributed—the instability of marriage based upon physical attraction chiefly; the sombreness of this theme gives an inevitable heaviness to the pages in which it is handled.

Nevertheless, not all reviewers were to be mollified by the more conventional story. The *New York Post* dubbed Allen's imagination "decadently Gallic"; the *New York Times* regretted the "abysmal lack of sense of humor." *The Nation* reasoned that there was "something mawkish and morbid in the processes of a mind perpetually preoccupied with the 'mystery' of the sex relation. We seem to be eavesdropping at a private confessional, or sharing the dreams of an anchorite," this last taunt probably with reference to Allen's impenetrable reserve. W. E. Bradley in *The Bookman* decided that *The Doctor's Christmas Eve* was "very much inferior to *The Bride of the Mistletoe*, absurd and ridiculous as that book was in many respects." Unkindest cut of all, a paper of Allen's home town, the *Lexington Herald*, rejected the story as stupid, denied the truth of its picture of Kentucky life, and believed that "dirt and dust" were "ruining" the author's mind. Discouraged by such attacks, conscious that much of what had called forth abuse was the result of his awkwardness in treating of matters of sex, brought face to face with defeat for the first time, Allen suspended the trilogy and gave no later hint in writing of how he would have rounded it out, although it was his purpose to complete it after a lapse of years had helped the public to understand or forget.

Since 1910, therefore, the question that has remained uppermost in the minds of Allen's followers has been, What did he try to say in *The Bride of the Mistletoe*, that strange, chilling, rhapsodic "story" and what did he try to say in the lighter, warmer, but equally strange sequel, with its hero who had married the wrong woman and who longed to express his sex-frustration by giving one roar like that of a beast in the jungle? The first volume of the trilogy had been dedicated "To One Who Knows"—"too much," added one squeamish reviewer—but what was there to know? What had been the theme of the truncated trilogy and how might it have ended? The questions have constituted one of the most interesting of the minor mysteries of American letters of the present century and might have remained without any credible answer had not Allen left, perhaps intentionally, some clues to the solution. In an envelope containing papers relating to the trilogy he placed a few clippings, one of which, entitled "Old Stories of Christmas," is so important that it must be reproduced verbatim:

There is a legend in Germany that when Eve plucked the fatal apple the leaves of the tree immediately shrivelled into needle points and its bright green turned dark. The nature of the tree changed and it became an evergreen, in all seasons preaching the story of man's fall through the first act of disobedience. Only on Christmas does it bloom brightly with lights and become beautiful with love gifts. The curse is turned into a blessing by the coming of the Christ child, and thus we have our Christmas tree.

This sheds some light upon Allen's plot but an examination of two other items in the envelope makes the illumination brighter. Both are unmistakably in Allen's handwriting. One, pencilled on the back of a bill presented to him at the Hotel Frascati, Havre, is an outline. The bill, undated but originating on his trip to Europe in 1909, shows that Allen was charged 10 francs for *location*, 11 francs fifty for *diner*, 1 franc fifty for *vins*, and 2 francs fifty for *omnibus*. Why he stopped over night at Havre instead of going on to Paris, his favorite foreign capital, is a matter for conjecture. Anyway, on the back of this bill, perhaps after having received it and while he dawdled over the *vins*, he drew up the outline for the Christmas trilogy as he then conceived it:

> THE DAY WE EARN
> A Three-Part Story
> II   The Bride of the Mistletoe
> —the Woman
> note of the mortal
> II II   A Brood of the Eagle
> —The Children
> note of the immortal
> II II II   The Pledge of the Evergreen
> —The Man
> Mortal and immortal
> Notes—The day we all earn—we have
> earned ours together

The other outline holds a similar synopsis, with no important variation but with this addition: "This his last note—all peace, all goodness something we earn."

The two synopses are neatly arranged, but at the bottom and to the left of the first one (the divisions being caused by two foldings of the paper) are notes which have meaning only for the person who has read the two volumes of the trilogy and which are sometimes too incoherent or carelessly scrawled to have meaning even for him. "In Ch. the Festival of man's Youth—the mortal youth that passes; the immortal that comes—on this night—I pledge you—? As I pass with you into—This was the festival of woman. All races meet here. See 'Individual.' 'When all her illusions are over'— she *knows*—" These jottings below the first synopsis refer definitely to the content of the trilogy. To the left is an outline, almost illegible, of a story dealing with suspected illegitimacy; the details cannot be gathered, and the only phrase which may connect the fragment with the books Allen was writing is the last one: "mystery of the influences affecting the origin of life and personality."

Combining these bits of evidence we are ready to hazard a hypothesis which may explain Allen's objectives. *The Bride of the Mistletoe* was to show, through a wife's realization that she was not all in all to her husband, the sense of change inherent in our spiritual environment, the evanescent delight in sex and youth, the turning of the green into dark when youth and sex have been plucked. The rejection of Mrs. Ousley's person was to be associated poetically with the Christmas holiday and those ancient ceremonies which symbolized the urge and potency of sex, and the several strands were to be woven deftly into a pattern of mortality. Into *The Doctor's Christmas Eve* he wished to inject the idea of a child's turning a curse into a blessing, the concept of a Christ-child, and it was this intention, not Allen's sentimentality, that required the death of the doctor's son. Not a word of the third volume has been found; probably none was written. But it seems quite likely that this part of the trilogy, which was not to be fiction and which may be hinted at in *The Last Christmas Tree*, would have been an essay or memoir composed by Dr. Birney and given to his wife to read, possibly on the Christmas Eve following the little boy's death. This paper might have combined mystically the Ger-

man legend and their own experiences; certainly we are justified in assuming that it would have ended with a text to the
effect that if they had at last through misunderstandings and
grief arrived at a day of trustful content it was because they
had earned together that day of goodness and peace. All
that we know certainly of this third volume is that Allen
announced in 1909 that it would be called *The Christmas
Tree: An Interpretation.*

It is therefore a fine irony that an attempted trilogy with
a theme thus platitudinous should have evoked for its author
so much condemnation and abuse. One additional bit of
vilification must be mentioned. Since in that twilight of the
Age of Innocence anyone who did or wrote incomprehensible
things was liable to the accusation of being a drug fiend it was
not long until underground gossip, persisting to this day in
Kentucky, had Mr. Allen addicted to the use of drugs; that
was supposed to account for what the ignorant considered his
vagaries of style and thought. The accusation is best refuted
by Dr. Rolfe Floyd of New York City, who as personal
physician, was in regular attendance upon Mr. Allen from
the thirteenth of February, 1911, until 1925. With respect
to this gossip Dr. Floyd wrote curtly and emphatically: "The
rumor that Mr. Allen took dope is entirely unfounded, so
far as any knowledge that I ever had."

The truth is that far from being the half-drunken sensualist or drug addict that some imagined, Mr. Allen was a
Victorian pursuing apart his vision splendid, the vision he
had kept before his eyes ever since his period of apprenticeship in the eighties, the desire to set before Americans the
ideals of courage, the conventions of morality, the fashions of
poise and gentility which he thought belonged to Anglo-
Saxons of the hardy pioneer and early republican days—the
direct message of the agrarian South to its cruder (thought
Allen) and harsher neighbors north of the Ohio river. But

the North turned a deaf ear to his praise of an eighteenth-century civilization and the South drew back from his union of science and truth and fiction. The Christmas books cost him dear in both sections, and the huge popularity which had been attached to the author of *The Choir Invisible* shrank alarmingly. It was never again to reach its former dimensions.

"I got *The Bride of the Mistletoe* for you, but after reading it burned it instead," wrote a friend to Sue Porter Heatwole, both women having been admirers of Allen's works and Mrs. Heatwole remaining so. "What has happened to our precious James Lane Allen?" This shocked query is symptomatic of the change which was to bring Allen close to want and unhappiness, a change which was not, as we shall see, due entirely to the effect of the Christmas books upon his readers. It was a change entirely unjustifiable as far as the morality of *The Bride of the Mistletoe* and *The Doctor's Christmas Eve* is concerned. If readers of 1909 and 1910 had possessed some of his patience, if they had been as devoted as he to the hope of expressing a noble Christmas idea in symphonic prose, if they had been given an inkling of his purpose and so had the opportunity to discover and examine the rich implications of these Christmas stories, then they must in all justice have given them a truer rating. Allen himself had a partiality for *The Bride of the Mistletoe* to the end, and it is pleasant to record that the greatest Kentucky novelist since his day, Elizabeth Madox Roberts, believes that book to be Allen's best. Even in torso the trilogy is a unique achievement in American literature, and its sincerity, its beauty, and the sharpness of its vision make it possible to think of it as our best symbolic fiction.

CHAPTER VI

DECLINE AND RECOVERY

STRANGE THAT idealists still believe and write that solitude
will add sweetness to the flavor of life, that one can satisfy
the insatiable longing to find one's identity by losing oneself
to the world. Almost all experience is against them. The
solitary, as any amateur psychologist can tell us, runs the risk
of becoming morbid and paranoiac, of suffering from manias
more or less disastrous, of becoming at the very least crochety
and misanthropic. Comparative solitude was no kinder to
James Lane Allen than it had been to William Wordsworth
and Henry Thoreau; it was, indeed, less kind, and the years
he entered after 1910 were the most unhappy of his life, unhappy because of the ever growing sense of isolation from
his fellows, even from his fellow-craftsmen; because of his
loss of affluence, literary reputation, and health; and because
of the conviction of futility that coiled like a reptile about his
heart. Against this misery he battled with fortitude, arming
himself with his code of honor, his stoicism, and his humor,
a quality which became somewhat worn as he stepped over
the threshold of his sixth decade. One sign of his unhappiness is found in his fitful moving from place to place, not
only to bring about an adjustment to seasonable changes but
also to find, as it seems, some room or rooms where he might
at last feel at rest.

Authors, said George Henry Lewes, are an irritable race,
but much of Allen's irascibility was due to his solitude and
his dissatisfaction with the temper of the times. What had
formerly been in him austerity became too frequently suspicion, wrath, something closely related to obsession. The
slightest infringement of his own rules of politeness grew to

mountainous proportions in his eyes. John Wilson Tow
send has told of how on a visit to New York City he anger
Mr. Allen by calling "Come in" to him instead of openi
the door of the hotel room to the visiting author, and C
Young Rice relates a similar experience. Since Allen h
been encouraging to both Mr. and Mrs. Rice when they
gan writing they hoped, when they were in the metropo
to make known to him their appreciation of his kindne
After Allen and the Rices met, the former suggested that
call upon the poet and his novelist wife, but Rice, eager
show all respect to the older man, replied that he wou
instead, pay the first call, which he did. At the end of
agreeable chat and as he prepared to leave, Rice w
astounded, therefore, when Allen said: "I'm sorry Mrs. R
doesn't approve of me"—so astounded that he could or
ask the speaker to repeat his words. "Why, what can y
mean?" cried the husband. "What do you mean when y
say Mrs. Rice doesn't approve of you?" "Evidently," w
the host's frosty answer, "she thinks I should be an unsat
factory acquaintance since she has refused to let me call up
her!"

Further testimony to this truculence, this sensitiveness
unintended slight or insult, is given by Ellen Glasgow. M
Glasgow first met Allen "about 1910—or perhaps 1909"
a dinner given by Ruth McEnery Stuart in New York, a
the two began a sudden friendship cemented by an int
mittent correspondence and occasional meetings. To ma
tain that friendship, however, must have been a trying bu
ness, for Miss Glasgow soon discovered that Allen, after s
ing her frequently and writing charming letters every wee
would refuse for months to speak to her because she had
some way and without meaning to be rude done somethi
that displeased him and that he considered an affront to
dignity. As the years passed it became more difficult to avo

a rupture with the aging novelist who seized upon the most trifling lapses as evidences of intentional neglect. In February of 1918 he wrote to her: "I allow myself to believe that I know you better, know *more* of you, than any other human being in this stupid, harsh, blindfolded, and largely contemptible world"; yet in the following May he sent her this note:

I am wondering whether a letter written some weeks ago found you in Richmond or has found you at all. If it has not reached you, this is a letter. If it has reached you, this is not a letter.

Sincerely yours,
JAMES LANE ALLEN.

And since she had received the letter but had been unable to answer it a long and haughty silence on his part ensued.

Miss Glasgow excused much of this capriciousness. After all, Allen was a man of one generation being tried and found wanting by another generation, and just as his novels failed to meet public taste in the post-war period so did the stateliness of his manners appear to the younger set as so much superfluous pomp and circumstance. He was an ill man, too, and by this time had a pathetic craving for appreciation; and not only was he ill and disappointed but he also saw his resources dwindling at a rapid rate. "Yet he bore all this," comments Miss Glasgow, "with superb gallantry. Taken all in all, he was, I think, the most gallant figure I have ever known." Finally, she explains that the real trouble between her and Allen was that, try as hard as she could, it was impossible for her to admire his style of writing as ardently as all the impressionable young men of the nineties had admired it. "Since," Miss Glasgow added rather maliciously, "we were both bred in the southern tradition, I tried, in the classic feminine manner, to do what was required of me in the way of adulation—but I invariably failed!"

Less normal than the desire for esteem was Allen's co 
tinuous suspicion of Catholics, the conviction that they we 
banded together to do him despite, if not harm. Dr. Rol 
Floyd, his physician, described the mental quirk thus:

> It is true that he had an unalterable belief that he had offend 
> the Catholic Church and that wherever he settled down in o 
> place for a period of a few weeks or more, he could see evidenc 
> of Catholic enmity. How well grounded this idea was, I nev 
> had an opportunity to find out. At any rate it never produc 
> any marked influence on his outward conduct because, though 
> lived in furnished apartments and used to move from one 
> another every year or so, I never knew of his changing his pla 
> or taking trips or in fact making any other important modificati 
> of his life because of this supposed persecution.

And then there is the dubious anecdote to the effect th 
Allen complained to a friend that Irish policemen showe 
him discourtesy, even to the point of jostling him, steppi 
on his toes, rudely abandoning him in traffic. When t 
friend escorted Allen to the chief of police that offic 
listened to the novelist's censure and then angered him st 
further by exclaiming with some pertinent profanity that  
men had never even heard of James Lane Allen.

The picture has, of course, its reverse side, for the m 
who was trigger quick to take umbrage at a profanation of t 
code was meticulously careful to live up to the high standar 
of politeness in bearing and speech which were already pa 
ing into the limbo of forgotten fashions. He never ask 
others to do for him what he would not do for them, and  
attitudes, his words were as punctilious and circumspect 
1918 as they had been when he shone among the *fin de siè *
group. After a two hours' visit with Allen one evening, t 
young writer Richard Burton came away with the impressi 
of a ripely-cultured southern gentleman, whimsically s 
over the drab realism of the day and above all things rese 

ing what he regarded as the vulgarity that dominated themes, motives, methods, and leading individuals of the new century. "There was [Mr. Burton remarked] in Allen—as a personality emanating atmosphere—something of the old-time gentility that I recall in Aldrich, Higginson, and Charles Warren Stoddard: it is passing, or has passed, that genial Attic elegance—like an aroma too evanescent and too delicate to survive in this harsh, raw, democratic air! . . . I don't recall one human being still living who clearly illustrates that benign golden expression of the humanities caught in a character setting."

One new friend Allen made during this last stage, one who was to stay with him, except for an occasional interruption owing to his own sensitiveness, to the end. This was George Folsom Granberry, an energetic director of a Piano School in Carnegie Hall, a young man half Allen's age. Mr. Granberry, like Allen, was a southerner, but unlike Allen too young to have had his enthusiasms and ideals weakened by buffets of experience. For years he had admired Allen's writings and had longed to meet the author; once the distinguished looking Kentuckian had been pointed out to him on the avenue. Then, sometime in February or March of 1910 Allen walked into Granberry's office looking for someone to set to music the words of a song he had written, a song about "mother." Mr. Granberry saw but did not say that the song was weak in the elements which make for popular appeal, but he did confess that he was not a composer. The young man's sparkle and freshness, combined with admiration and the manners that Allen favored, brought the two together at once in friendship, although the elder was, as would be expected, slow about admitting Granberry to anything like intimate comradeship and never did reveal himself or attempt to reveal himself clearly so that his personality might completely emerge from the trappings he had laid upon it. Two entries from Granberry's diary show why he was drawn to the man whose books he had been partial to:

Wednesday, March 23rd, 1910

I spent a part of the day with Mr. James Lane Allen. He had many interesting things to say:

"I am an unmarried man, but not a bachelor.[1] It is a splendid thing to have an ideal that remains unmarred. I could not get the one I wanted so I would marry no one. I am absolutely free and I am happy. Everything that I really wish for, I have. The only sorrow I know is for the lack of strength which prevents my doing as much work as I should like to do."

I could not help wondering if he meant a special person, or just an ideal when he said he could not get the person he wished.[2]

I tried his new Steinway piano. Played Schubert's *Rosamunde*, which is one of Mr. A's favorite musical compositions. When I took my leave Mr. A. urged me to come in soon for an entire evening and he said: "I never allow business to come here nor will I ever see persons whom I do not like. I am too open and candid to prevent a person's knowing it when I do not enjoy his company, so I make no pretense. This is the place where I live, simply, quietly, and I will not be disturbed by curious or meddlesome persons."

Wednesday, May 4th, 1910

I spent the evening with James Lane Allen and played some songs he had written. He had great pleasure in this side-issue of writing vocal music. He had a great deal to say in regard to the work of many composers and writers, who mistake a high *appreciation* for the *creative* faculty and so produce much work that cannot live. . . . In the course of the evening an occurrence took place which was truly characteristic of Mr. A. He was going to present me with a copy of his latest book *(Mistletoe)* when he found a slight imperfection on the fly leaf, caused by a special

[1] This doubtless was Allen's playful way of announcing that he lived with his sister. It is incredible that he should have made a confidence implying any other kind of relationship.

[2] Mr. Granberry inserted here a notation: "I found later that it was an *ideal* person and not a certain individual, which Mr. A. meant."

pressure in binding. He examined several copies and found the same slight defect, so he said: "I will get you a new, *perfect* copy. I could never inscribe an imperfect book to a friend."

This is, perhaps, the place to contradict published statements that Allen was a performer on a musical instrument. Mr. Granberry explains that his friend could do no more than pick out an air—as in the instance of the songs mentioned in the diary—on the piano, but that he did have the intuition and sympathy which made him in a sense a musician. Once while they were listening to *Tannhäuser* Allen leaned over to Granberry and, shielding his mouth with his white-gloved hand, whispered apropos the song contest in Wartburg Castle: "Tableau!" Another time, contrasting Bach and Wagner he argued the former's superiority because Bach "did not wear through." Neither of these opinions demonstrates a nicer power of musical discrimination than the person of general culture is likely to have, but they do direct us to a fact, that music constituted throughout his life one of James Lane Allen's chiefest joys.

By 1910 Allen was definitely on the decline in popularity, in literary skill, and in nervous power with which to sustain prolonged creative effort. Stung and saddened by the failure of his Christmas tragedy, he was now to watch helplessly a change in public manners and literary taste which left him stranded almost alone on the rock of the Genteel Tradition and which greatly reduced the sale of his books. Most of his last seven works were brief, three of them being scarcely more than short stories and the last being a collection of tales. Fondly he planned long novels, romances which were to be laid down with the greatest art of which he was capable, romances in which he was to reconstruct the kingdom and the glory of the Old South. Some he began and left incomplete, some he left unwritten save for a title and a few tentative notes. His writing arm weakened because his heart failed in discouragement. It was hard to belong to one generation and to be judged by another. How could he write for Americans of the pre-war era? For readers who were preferring in ever greater numbers the raw meat from Jack London's stockyard, the naturalism which Dreiser had illustrated in *Sister Carrie?*

Henry James once grieved that it seemed to be America's mission to vulgarize the world, and in the days of Theodore Roosevelt there was much to justify the Mandarin's grief. Perhaps no historian has yet properly estimated the influence the President himself exerted in the alteration of what might loosely be called the American spirit. No person old enough to have been aware of what was going on before 1914 can forget the impact of Roosevelt's personality upon our collective life. Since the administration of Abraham Lincoln our presidents, whether Republican or Democratic, gifted or mediocre, teetotalers or drinkers, had been men of a degree of public dignity which in the opening decades of the twentieth century could certainly be called old-fashioned. There is no intention here to intimate that "Teddy" lacked dignity or that he was vulgar in any connotation of that word; what is meant is that he, more than anyone else, dramatized the new American who was loud to the point of violence, aggressive to the point of dishonesty, democratic to the point of what might formerly have been called uncouthness. We had in the first Roosevelt a "practical" man who could swing the "big stick" over a "trust" or a South American republic; a Rough Rider who could say that any man "worth his salt" would be proud to fight Spaniards; a statesman of somewhat demagogic tendencies whose gritting teeth punctuated his denunciations of "malefactors of great wealth"; a writer who championed "the strenuous life"; an outdoor man who punched cows, shot lions, discovered rivers, and indicted "nature fakers"; a student who added picturesque words and phrases to the vocabulary of "Mr. Common People." Dynamic, crusading, magnetic, apotheosis of American energy and might, the President gave the appearance of setting the tempo for the dance of American twentieth-century life. He was what we all wished to be. Trusted or distrusted by adults, beloved or hated as the case might be, he was nevertheless as inspiring to the American boy of that day as Samuel Smiles's *Self-help* had been to his father. And Roosevelt did add to the din of the nation. Once Allen told Granberry that he contemplated writing an essay on "The Great Silences." "Roosevelt has no silences," he reflected grimly. With all his respect for the chief executive's integrity and militant Americanism, Allen perceived that Roosevelt and he represented two antithetical social types and that his own kind was rapidly vanishing. The two men were utterly unlike, and one of them had become the idol of the American people. The fate of the other was inescapable.

It was, to be sure, not Mr. Roosevelt who had brought about the tremendous acceleration of speed in all our goings and comings; he simply embodied to the imagination of the men of the street our nation-wide spirit of doing things speedily, vigorously, colorfully; he loomed heroically, indeed epically, because he was the incarnation of our genius for what Allen had called "fling and swing." It was rather the scientist, the inventor who gave us the means with which to attempt to satisfy our inexplicable, irrational, and eventually destructive passion for speed. We longed to move faster, eat faster, read faster, write faster, live faster. Everyone was bent upon serving Mammon with breathless zeal; the man who had read *The Gilded Age* had a son who chuckled over *Get-Rich-Quick Wallingford*. To annihilate space we turned from the bicycle to the automobile and the motorcycle, to the telephone and the airplane. We explored the bottom of the sea in submarines. We struck off curt letters on typewriters and read papers and magazines, printed in bulk, devoted to a new kind of journalism called "muckraking." We used Mr. Edison's electric lights to brighten streets of theaters and night clubs. We clutched our partners in dances called "turkey trot" and "bunny hug"; we tapped our feet to strange rhythms in "Alexander's Ragtime Band." We exercised our jaws with chewing gum. We began to cultivate the cult of bigness, being assured that two are always better than one.

To Allen America must have begun to resemble a Mad Hatter's tea party. The generation he knew, the only one he could write about with confidence, had been, whatever its sins, a profoundly and instinctively decent one. At least, that is what he thought, allowing many of his own fine qualities to be transferred into the past so that they might be fitted upon his memories of that generation. Now, he saw, times had changed so decisively that he was left far to the rear. He could not raise his voice in self-praise nor bid for publicity. He could not possibly call for the bright calcium light. The worst of it all was, so far as the change affected him, that from this welter of what he regarded as sensationalism, vulgarity, crass pushing and shoving, from this mad scramble for wealth and notoriety, this explosive destruction of the leisure in which a gentleman should be able to invite both his soul and his body, from all this emerged a new species of woman, one who viewed his heroines with amusement or contempt, one who found herself unable to care for the high-minded and scrupulous ladies who bore their problems with fortitude and shy grace throughout his pages. The Gibson girl was waning, along with the Genteel Tradition. In her place came a young lady who marched in parades, acted in photodramas, campaigned for the vote, addressed prohibition meetings, rode a bicycle or drove a car, played tennis instead of croquet, did not hang her head at thought of either babies or divorce. She had vim, dash, pep, go—favorite words on her tongue. She sat beside man in business offices and in the ball park. She climbed mountains and swam rivers. Occasionally she shot her husband. And she was to James Lane Allen a creature he had never known, so utterly emancipated from formal manners and etiquette, that he refused to have anything to do with her; from the end of 1912 until his death in 1925 he wrote no story in which the love of man for woman was the prime theme. He did not understand the new ways of courtship and the new conception of love, and the old ways and the old dreams were now laughed at. He had never heard in the nineties of hormones and gonads. Could they possibly be as precious as the sweep of hair from a forehead, the line of a soft arm, the eye which betokened a noble and trusting heart? The women readers—upon whom any novelist must depend largely for his support—disapproved of him and his heroines as much as he disapproved of the new women. The sun had almost set upon the languishing female who died of a broken heart, even upon her who believed the world well lost for love. The new woman was bent upon a career and service. Strange words, these, to Allen.

The novel, ever the mirror to popular fashions, had begun to reflect this fling and swing, this new woman, this demand for fast action and heightened realism. Writers like Eggleston, Kirkland, E. W. Howe, and Hamlin Garland had already rubbed off some of the nap of romantic fiction. Henry James and William Dean Howells, still living but publishing with difficulty, were retreating sadly to their Valhalla, and in their stead arose new gods: Frank Norris with his Amazonian Moran, captain of the "Lady Letty," his good-natured McTeague, who had to kill his wife; Jack London with a dozen heroic miners, woodsmen, hunters, and their vigorous, strong-limbed, and full-breasted sweethearts—Jack London, who in 1905 was preaching the world revolution; Upton Sinclair, whose *Jungle* shocked the public and Congress in 1906; O. Henry, whose fantastic slang in *The Four Million* delighted the same public in the same year; David Graham Phillips, who adapted muckraking methods to the novel; Ellen Glasgow, who had developed into a realist after her half-romantic *Battle-Ground;* Booth Tarkington, whose political and historical romances set no one's teeth on edge but whose partiality for horseplay, as in *Cherry,* placed him outside the Genteel Tradition. Robert Herrick, Henry B. Fuller, Harold Frederic filched from the American woman her sweetness, her tenderness, her patience, and with a few waves of their pens transformed her into a monster grasping and devouring; and Theodore Dreiser saw his *Sister Carrie* suppressed because it admitted what everyone knew, that women were not sexless and that sin was not always punished in this naughty world. Only one novelist beside himself seemed to have escaped the contagion of bad taste in the United States, and Allen found little comfort in Mrs. Wharton's deftly ironic studies of social parasites in New York, Newport, and Paris. Nor was the novel alone in reflecting the new spirit (there is always a new spirit!) for by 1910 James Gibbons Huneker was writing such criticism of the arts as would never have occurred to Charles Dudley Warner, and in three or four years Vachel Lindsay and Carl Sandburg were to scandalize poetry-lovers whose criteria had been taken from Keats and Shelley and Tennyson, and *Reedy's Mirror* was to print Edgar Lee Masters's parody on the Greek *Anthology.* Only the drama, shackled by the cleverness of Clyde Fitch and the near-melodrama of David Belasco, lagged behind the procession of American literature.

But writing drama was something with which Allen had nothing to do and which he was to try but once and then quite unsuccessfully. It was the novel which had brought him fame and wealth; it was poetry which he wrote to relieve a short sharp pang of emotion; and he was fully aware of the mutations both forms were undergoing. Indeed, by one of the most curious contradictions in his life, he had himself done much, as we have seen, to destroy the comparative innocence of the American novel of the nineties and to introduce American readers to French and English naturalistic technique and theme. He had attacked revealed religion in *The Reign of Law* and had toyed with the possibility of letting his heroine in *The Bride of the Mistletoe* commit adultery. He had stopped her in good time. Now, like Grant Allen in England, he drew back, convinced that he had gone too far at the very moment when almost everybody else was getting ready to believe that he had not gone far enough. Wounded and puzzled by the failure of his Christmas trilogy, doubtful what road to take next, he showed his faltering step in the nature of his next novel, *The Heroine in Bronze.*

Back in July of 1897 a reviewer in *The Saturday Review* had written of Allen: "As the painter of love scenes he would not easily find his master." Two years later an article in *The Nation* deplored the decay of literary allusion. Whether Allen saw these statements, or having seen them, remembered them, we do not know, but he did begin work in 1911 on what became his longest love story devoted to one young couple only and he did make it the most ornamental of all his writings by gilding it with many allusions to literature and other arts. We should be on firmer ground in our surmises, however, if we assumed that the postponement of the Christmas trilogy put a period to Allen's progress in realism; that he sought now to return to the mood of *A Kentucky Cardinal* and *Aftermath* and thus to reconquer his readers; and that the great number of allusions is evidence of the need for covering up gaps in narrative content. That a bronze female

figure should have been the immediate inspiration for this
story is further proof that his plots were becoming thin and
brittle and that he refused to look to life—life, that is, as
London and Dreiser were picturing it—when he cast about
for material out of which to build a tale.

In April of 1911 he wrote from Denver that he expected
the Macmillan Company to issue a uniform edition of his
works (an expectation which was disappointed); thereafter
he labored over the new manuscript, interrupting his concentration to prepare a Foreword to T. S. Jones's *The Voice in
the Silence*, to contribute to the November issue of *Munsey's*
a mediocre essay on "The National Spirit of Thanksgiving,"
and to attend on the second of March, 1912, a dinner to Howells at which the dean of American letters celebrated his
seventy-fifth birthday. Meanwhile several bits of flattery encouraged him at his task. For one thing *The Choir Invisible*
was translated into French and published in 1911 by Fischbacher of Paris as *L'Invisible Chœur*. This was the second
of his novels to put on foreign dress, the first having been
The Reign of Law, which was rendered into Danish by J.
Christian Bay in 1902; there had been a rumor that *A Kentucky Cardinal* was to appear in Japanese, but nothing came
of it. For another thing, he was requested by Orlando Rouland to sit for a portrait. Most flattering of all was a sentence
in Arnold Bennett's "The Future of the American Novel,"
printed in the January *North American Review* for 1912:
". . . the future is big with possible developments of the various schools of fiction represented by writers like Mr. James
Lane Allen, Mr. Frank Norris, Mrs. Gertrude Atherton,
Mrs. Edith Wharton, Mr. Hamlin Garland, and Mr. Theodore Dreiser." Such notice, even from one so opinionated as
the author of *The Old Wives' Tale*, fell like manna upon the
desert. Having delivered the manuscript of the new novel
to the Macmillans Allen went to Montreal in July in order

to escape the heat of the metropolis. That fall, almost simultaneously with the publication of *The Heroine in Bronze*, he was attacked by his familiar enemy, eye-strain, the aftermath of the typhoid and overwork of long ago, and, overcome by a revulsion against all claims of property, sometimes against all claims made by life itself, he gave up the apartment he had decorated so cheerfully, stored the furniture, and moved into The Burlington at 10 West Thirtieth Street, New York. Then with the three thousand dollars he received as advance royalty he went to Philadelphia and Atlantic City for the Christmas holidays.

He was reading Nietzsche for the first time.

The Heroine in Bronze marks another turning-point in Allen's life, for with it he began his decline and with it he left the state of his birth and laid the scene in New York City—additional proof that he was nettled by Kentucky's rejection of *The Reign of Law* and the Christmas trilogy. But the hero, Donald Clough, is a Kentuckian, a novelist who, like Allen, kept over his desk a copy of the Boulanger portrait of Balzac and on the desk a bronze statuette of a girl two feet, six inches high whose outstretched hands held sockets for candles. Clough is twenty-two, idealistic, religious, poor, and homesick for "a rich, wide-rolling, pastoral region several hundred miles away," a "a beautiful country, the like of which was not to be seen elsewhere in the world." He is in love with Muriel Dunstan, daughter of a wealthy and influential "Commodore" who lives in "the most beautiful, the most celebrated, and the most fashionable quarter of the city. A house that can stand where it stood must be a strong house." To Muriel comes Donald Clough with an idea for a new book which he discusses with her as they walk in a lovely garden—the garden of the Rockefeller house was the setting for this dialogue—and, aglow with enthusiasm as he is, he immediately divines her hurt withdrawal from him and his plan when she learns that he is about to use an incident taken from her girlhood. All her maidenly instincts, her aristocratic wish for privacy, are outraged by this threat to make public property of her history, and she lets him understand that if he goes on with the story she will be lost to him, especially as she is about to leave for Europe, where her beauty and wealth will attract the siege of many suitors. It is again the test *motif* of which Allen was so enamoured: shall Clough write his book in his own way and thereby lose his beloved, or shall he yield to her wish and thereby win her and happiness? Beyond that is the suggestion of a problem which was more lively then than now: has a novelist the right to introduce in his fiction his knowledge of the experiences of his friends? Allen's answer to the latter question, often expressed privately, was an emphatic negative, and he once destroyed a partially completed manuscript because an acquaintance objected that he was being put into the narrative. However, Donald Clough is made of sterner stuff; he holds to his purpose to write the story as he had conceived it, and the two lovers part in a quarrel without words but not without emotion, a quarrel which seems to puff mole-hills into mountains but one which the author handles with fine restraint: "She spoke trifles about this flower and that flower; I replied with trifles. She laughed at nothing, I laughed at nothing. She sought calmness, I sought calmness. I had offered her my best and she had made the worst of it; and as we faced our tragedy, we laughed and spoke of blossoms broken from the bushes."

All that hot summer Donald Clough perseveres desperately with his story, looking for help to the bronze statuette which takes the place of a flesh and blood ideal. One insupportably torrid day drives him to the seashore, and here Allen writes well, with deep but controlled feeling, of the ocean and of Donald's going to sleep on the sands and dream-

ing of Hero and Leander. Then Muriel, enfeebled by illness, returns from abroad and renews the interrupted friendship. At last Donald is ready to read to her his finished tale,
with an ending which he knows will pain her and produce another and doubtless final estrangement. Resolutely he reads
through to the last word. And you and I are as much surprised as he when Muriel, hurt as she is, confesses her love
and promises to marry him. Later she explains that although he had twice wounded her she could forgive and admire, and that if he had not wounded her, if he had surrendered his will to his desire for her, she might at first have
been elated but would have ultimately rejected him, for "a
man's work—not work that is forced upon him, but the work
that he deliberately chooses to do—must be first with him
because his work is his character." In playful revenge for
these tests Donald tells her that he has been inspired all
summer by "another" who shared his loneliness uncomplain-
ingly. Muriel receives this confession with a horror that al-
mosts plunges us into the morass of an anti-climax, but on
Donald's explanation of the identity of the heroine in bronze
all is well and the novel ends on a rather absurd note.

To many readers in 1912 *The Heroine in Bronze* must
have been as nearly perfect a love story as American literature
had yet offered. Its plot is quiet, if not entirely serene, and
nothing raucous or cynical or shabby, nothing to indicate that
men and women and love cannot be mixed while libido is
forgotten, was allowed to intrude. Its tone is symphonic;
its hero chivalrous, determined, even pious; its stage set with
the color of two summers so that light tragedy and light comedy may be played with equal facility; its sentiments the
highest and most delicate; its style poetic to the verge of
oratory. Yet it did not, as so many of Allen's books had
done, lead the best-seller lists for it was surpassed by Margaret Deland's *The Iron Woman*, Harold Bell Wright's *The*

Winning of Barbara Worth, and Gene Stratton-Porter's *The Harvester.* The first of these ministered to a respect for a dominating personality and a moral epilogue; the second appealed to a bourgeois sentimentality; and the third capitalized the love of the outdoors which was called into being by Theodore Roosevelt, John Burroughs, John Muir, Dan Beard, Ernest Seton-Thompson, Madison Cawein, and lesser figures; and since Allen had offended many of his followers by his heterodoxy and his willingness to admit the presence of evil in nature *The Heroine in Bronze,* in spite of the trumpetings of his friendly critics, lagged behind in sales. Frederic Taber Cooper in *The Bookman* contrasted Allen's novel with Dreiser's *The Financier* and declared that the author of the first knew "just as every really big artist knows, what the small type of craftsman will never learn, that great art is independent of size"—thus administering at once a compliment to Allen and a rebuke to the unwieldy Hoosier. H. W. Mabie, who could always be depended upon for comely praise, avowed in *The Outlook* that "there are phrases of such verbal music in this story that one rereads it for sheer delight in the beauty of its English," and a reviewer in the *St. Louis Mirror* said rather ambiguously, "It is the most stylistic piece of literary workmanship since *The Chevalier of Pensieri-Vani.*" The *New York Daily Tribune* felt, on the other hand, that "Mr. Allen is becoming the victim of his style, that elaborately polished style of which he is so proud, and which has brought him so many admirers" and went on to protest against the "speeches" made by the dramatis personae. No one found fault with the many allusions to books and the arts, although in no other of his writings did Allen pour out such allusions in such profusion—to Theocritus, the *Odyssey,* Gray's *Elegy,* Cicero, the labors of Hercules, *Othello,* the fable of Diana and Acteon, the Bible, Goethe, Rousseau, *Don Quixote,* Shakespeare, Burns, Horace, Balzac,

Paul and Virginia, The Arabian Nights, Gibbon's *Decline and Fall,* Leander and Hero, *Paradise Lost,* the Apocrypha, Renan, the fable of the fox and the grapes, Socrates, Aldus, Elzevir, Longfellow, Helen of Troy, *Carmen, Tristan and Isolde,* the Ring operas, Beethoven's *Pastoral Symphony, Lohengrin, Tannhäuser,* Botticelli, a Watteau fan, an Aubusson tapestry. This garnishing of a story had lost much of its former appeal to the American taste, but in England Allen's public still held true to him and *The Heroine in Bronze* shared in popularity with Amundsen's record of south polar exploration.

For once Allen had a joke on the critics, although it was a joke so equivocal that he must have been undecided whether to chuckle or to grow angry at their lack of discernment. One of them was shrewd enough to see that the narrative centered about the idealization of the bronze girl—an idealization possibly Allen's own—but no one understood, as Allen confided to Mr. Granberry, that the point of the whole book is that the boy had not written his story about Muriel Dunstan, that she had simply assumed that she was the hub of his life and thought—"but that," Allen remarked, sagely enough for a bachelor, "is one of the chief characteristics of women." He meditated writing a sequel which should make the point clear by producing the story Donald Clough had published, but this plan he abandoned.

Let us not linger too long over *The Heroine in Bronze.* So much space has been given to it because, as already stated, it marks the beginning of Allen's decline. The novel is, let us say flatly, deservedly a failure. Its story is without the value of depth, it does not clarify our interpretations of life, it climbs to the bottom of no well in the search for truth; its hero and heroine are exotic young people conjured up by the imagination of a lonesome man who, like them, had little commerce with actualities; its dialogue is as strained and un-

natural as is the style of the whole. Let the description
the heroine serve at once to measure the qualities of the sty
and the characterization:

She sat there under the blue sky of the summer morning with t
freshness of the blue and silver sea in the air about her; an Ame.
can vestal of the college in her land and race and time. Yet li
a Greek vestal on the Greek-like seat; Greek-like in the softne
of snowy vestments which we in our day touch only as the har
ness of marble; Greek-like in symmetry, grace, health. Not :
ornament; not the simplest band of linked gold around her ne
bared low; not a gem in the ear, nor bracelet on the arms bar
to the elbows—arms the chisellings of which were as of alabast
and the flesh tones of which were as alabaster shadowed by r(
leaves. A comb of palest amber out of an old Greek sea caught
the soft gleaming gold of her hair: across the top of the comb l
a little garland of shaken windflowers. In her eyes the one bl
of the sky and of the sea for the gladness of that day.

Surely this was a heroine who should also have been c;
in bronze.

Busy as he was with his latest novel, Allen had kept l
eye upon political developments, which usually interested hi
only as a bystander. In 1912, however, the situation w
unusual: the powerful Republican party had been divid(
by the acrimonious personal quarrel between Taft and Roo:
velt and the Democrats had the best chance in a generation f
winning the presidency. Three men were mentioned m(
loudly for the Democratic nomination, and of these thr
Allen preferred Governor Woodrow Wilson of New Jerse
Bryan he despised as symbolical of all that was erratic a!
non-intellectual among commoners, and Champ Clark,
we have already noted, had long been in his bad graces. W
son was a southerner, and Allen was still sectional enough
throw up his hat when the band played Dixie; Wilson, •
professor and ex-university president, was a gentleman of c\

ture; Wilson was a Democrat who might be expected to fight special privilege and redeem the government of such scandals as those connected with Ballinger and the dismissal of Pinchot from the forestry service; and so Allen rejoiced when the Virginian was elected in November of 1912 and inaugurated on the fourth of March, 1913. But his joy and his allegiance did not live long. When Wilson, hard-pressed by foreign encroachments upon our rights, made his famous protestation that a nation might be too proud to fight, Allen was through with him, and no later bravery in word or action could atone, so far as he was concerned, for that utterance of retreat. Thenceforth Allen assured his friends that Wilson was "an inferior who got the honors at school." The use of the scholastic comparison suggests a deep-rooted and unconscious envy on Allen's part, an envy which also explains, at least to a certain extent, his attitude toward many of his literary contemporaries. At this time, for instance, he was fearing that his fellow-Kentuckian, Irvin Cobb, would be seduced from the straight way of honest authorship by large royalties, and he was declaring warmly that he would not read Bernard Shaw, whose genius for self-advertisement must also have antagonized the retiring American.

The last word of *The Heroine in Bronze* left Allen depleted nervously, and in the summer of 1913 he went with his sister, as he had been going for the past five summers, to Boston, "a cool, green, fresh city." Here in satisfying isolation at 141 Newberry Street, with a good library near, he planned to write other stories which should have their setting in New York City instead of the Bluegrass. His own no longer received him. Kentucky did not appreciate him, he thought and said with the emphasis of profanity; Kentucky "never did appreciate its best people." "A great calm" subsisted down there, he believed, a calm in which people lived in a kind of vacuum, grew without understanding how

or why, and even if, like John Wilson Townsend, they read
his books they failed to comprehend them and so wrote
hostile reviews for the newspapers. He would forever shake
off the dust of Kentucky, never set foot upon its soil, write no
more of its inhabitants. That, it seems, was the cumulative
effect of his resentment at various slights and attacks, but
while his anger gave fuel to the flame of disappointment in
his soul it came near breaking his heart.

For with the meadows and streams of the Bluegrass region no longer nestling in his affections, what remained for
him to love? The dearest person in his world, his mother,
had been dead almost a quarter of a century; his recollection of her was cushioned against sorrow too severe and the
nature of his love for her had become almost impersonal;
he dedicated no more books to her. His sister, ill and unhappy, was not even a good companion; he almost never
introduced her even to his intimates. The Old Guard who
wore the same uniform as his, who had confronted with him
the ranks of vulgarity and indecency, were trooping from the
field and could no longer give him spiritual comradeship:
Charles Dudley Warner had died in 1900, Stoddard in 1903,
Aldrich in 1907, Stedman in 1908, Richard Watson Gilder
and Edward E. Hale in 1909, Thomas Wentworth Higginson in 1911, S. Wier Mitchell in 1914. Henry James lived
on in England but publishers were no longer anxious to receive his manuscripts; Howells was reclining wearily on essay and biography; Cable was scurrying about with projects
of reform in Northampton; Thomas Nelson Page had not
been his friend these many years; Henry van Dyke no longer
steered critical opinion. The heroes had dropped with their
faces toward the wall, but the forts of folly had not fallen;
those citadels were, indeed, stronger than ever, and from
their portals issued a horde of Goths and Vandals who gathered the plunder of appreciation and spread the terror of

their ruthlessness. Allen saw himself left almost alone, with his ideals waving forlornly from the tip of his ashen lance. These heroes, had they after all fought in the right cause? Had they fought truly, with armor unsullied? Even that memory was denied him, for not all the guardians of the Genteel Tradition had pleased him—had not Stedman been dismissed from Yale for good reason and had not Gilder written one mortifying line of verse about his wife's clothes? Were not Allen's remaining companions failing to live up to the demands of his code? There was Marcosson, for example—had not Marcosson, to whom he had dedicated *The Heroine in Bronze,* written some things about Allen which though harmless were not quite true? He would break with Marcosson. And he did.

"Free from the happiness of slaves, redeemed from Deities and adorations, fearless and fear-inspiring, grand and lonesome: so is the will of the conscientious." This he had read in *Also Sprach Zarathustra.* Certainly he found himself lonesome enough. The inhabitants of "this largely contemptible world" had lost the virtues of their parents, and not content with lessening their nobility, they even refused to believe nobility could exist; they believed that he, the conscientious, the puritan in behavior, was a sensualist, a drug addict, one who leered through a peephole at human passions, one who wore the mask of gentility in order to disport with the fauns. They believed it and they declared it openly. Wrathful, disillusioned, ill, too old to see fresh visions, knowing that his earning power had deteriorated because a *Choir Invisible* could no longer stampede the American public, Allen let himself fall into fits of misanthropy. And in this mood of discarding the rags of his confidence in mankind he decided to write no longer about Nietzsche's "animal with red cheeks" but to write about children, a trilogy about children—the buds, the promises of a better day, the beings in whom one could find joy and innocence and honor trailing in their clouds of glory, the beings from whom one could not rationally expect too much gratitude and loyalty. And so while he recovered in Bronxville from an illness and wrote an introduction to Townsend's *Kentucky in American Letters* and informed the *New York Times* that Dickens's *A Christmas Carol* was, "for all its faults," the best short story in English—a choice revealing his present temper, his turning to the child—he laid down the groundwork for a mother-and-son trilogy. Not, it should be noted, stories dealing with the relations of fathers to sons but with the mutual feelings of mothers and sons. In his loneliness his attitude toward children became purely emotional, and the emotional directed him properly into the maternal point of view, but since Allen knew little either of mothering or of children the attempted trilogy was to fail miserably. Nothing else he wrote is today so complete a failure.

The first part of the trilogy was "A Cathedral Singer," a long short story printed in the *Century Magazine* for May, 1914, and published by the Century Company in 1916. Its immediate inspiration was the Cathedral of St. John the Divine, whose noble apse Allen had watched a-building as he sat with a book in Morningside Park. This edifice expressive of man's longing to bend the knee to divinity cried out for someone to catch its spirit and to give it back to the world in words that would point out the way to the good life here and to immortality hereafter. So reasoned Allen as he searched his mind for the mood in which to enwrap his theme. In that year of illness and defeat he felt most of all the bitterness of losing those things for which we strive with all our might, losing them by a narrow margin and despite our righteous deserts. Immortality! That was what he had striven for, immortality through fame, and he had come so near to seizing it. Now, with an overwhelming sense of helplessness, he felt it slipping through his fingers and his mood began to blend again with that of Thomas Hardy, the stern teller of Wessex tales who never allowed us to forget the tricks that a malignant chance plays upon us. The influence of Hardy had not been discernible in Allen's work since 1903, but now the Kentuckian returned in spirit to the householder of Max Gate, capturing there the conviction of human tragedy but refusing to take on the same protective indifference toward that tragedy. Hardy could by no stretching of fancy be thought of as the author of *The Heroine in Bronze;* neither could he be thought of as the author of "A Cathedral Singer," because although its action and theme are such as the Englishman might have conceived and selected, its style is sugared in a way that would have turned the older man's stomach. "A Cathedral Singer" has some kinship with Hardy's *Life's Little Ironies* (1894), and we shall presently find Allen experimenting with a dramatic conversation called "Heaven's Little Ironies," pretty clear evidence that he was dipping again in the acid bath of pessimism; it also makes a paraphrase, as we shall see, of Hardy's sonnet "Hap" (1866); but its freely sentimental wording so jars upon its story as to make the latter quite incredible. We recall some of the incidents in *Life's Little Ironies:* a girl who, because of a plighted word to a suitor, does not keep a rendezvous with her foreign lover and so indirectly causes him to be arrested as a deserter and shot before her own eyes; a son who, having risen from the shop-keeping class, ruins his mother's chance for happiness by forbidding her marriage to a man of that same class; a man who goes bravely to death with his two sons so that his wife may have money; two sons who let their drunken father drown in order that his disgraceful condition may not interfere with their sister's opportunity to catch a husband; a lady who writes love letters for her illiterate maid, wins the man's love for the maid, and then realizes that she has been caught in the toils and loves of the same man—all underscore the means by which man is compelled to live his days in darkness and terror and to end them in ignominy and failure.

Man is defenseless against whatever weapons unreasoning chance may hurl at him. That was the philosophy Hardy had pounded out upon the anvil of his great novels of character and environment and that is the philosophy at the heart of "A Cathedral Singer." Yet Allen does not leave man defeated utterly, for he allows him to lose all but honor; with honor intact man's head need not bow. Character will outlive time, will defy chance. Thus does Allen go beyond Hardy in mysticism in the brief story of Rachel Truesdale and her little son. She is a southern widow living in New York City; she ekes out a tiny income by posing before a life class in the National Academy of Design. Her manly and outspoken son, Ashby, sells newspapers to help lighten the burden of poverty. Singing at his task, he is overheard by the choir director of the cathedral, who is so much struck by the boy's voice that he visits the mother to arrange for Ashby's taking free lessons from him. Everything is settled satisfactorily, but a few days later the mother, watching through the window for her child's coming, sees him run down and crushed by a speeding car below. Ashby dies, Mrs. Truesdale returns stoically to the art class, and the volume closes in prophetic strain as Allen links the sacrifice of young life with the glory in marble and glass rising on the rocks that overlook the East Side.

The whole thing is so devoid of motivation as to be almost pointless. It looks, therefore, like a blind wandering behind *Life's Little Ironies,* and the connection with Hardy is made plain by a sentence which paraphrases the octave of the sonnet "Hap." Allen's sentence reads:

Often during the trouble and discouragement of years it had seemed to her that her own life and every other life would have more meaning if only there had been, away off somewhere in the universe, a higher evil intelligence to look on and laugh, to laugh pitilessly at every human thing. She had held on to her faith because she must hold on to something, and she had nothing else.

Compare this quotation with Hardy's lines:

> If but some vengeful god would call to me
> From up the sky, and laugh: "Thou suffering thing
> Know thou thy sorrow is my ecstasy,
> That thy love's loss is my hate's profiting!"

> Then would I bear it, clench myself, and die,
> Steeled by the sense of ire unmerited;
> Half-eased in that a Powerfuller than I
> Had willed and meted me the tears I shed.

But Allen, unlike Hardy, iced his grimness with saccharine words that cause "A Cathedral Singer" to remain indigestible. One example will be sufficient. As Mrs. Truesdale stands at the bedside of her sleeping child she murmurs: "My heavenly guest! My guest from the singing stars of God!"— which, it must be obvious, sounds more like Marie Corelli than Thomas Hardy. Surely Mr. Allen never heard a mother, no matter how fond of her offspring, deliver so rapturous a soliloquy; it wasn't done even on the stage in 1916. And if he had against all likelihood heard such a murmur he had no business putting it into the mouth of a woman in a story, for while it might have been a fact it could never have been the truth. Mother love is not so maudlin. A real mother would have kissed the sleeper lightly so as not to waken him and would have said to herself that he was looking pretty fine tonight.

But Allen did not know that, and his intuitions were loaded with chains of poesy. His loyal friends did not cor-

rect him—he was a hard man to correct—but instead exclaimed over the melodramatic scene in which the swooning
mother hangs with bleeding hands thrust through the broken
window pane, and since "A Cathedral Singer" did not come
out in book form and thus give the critics a chance to condemn it, Allen, pretty well content with the beginning of the
trilogy, proceeded to go on with his plan.   Other projects and ideas crowded in upon him, bringing the discomforts
of strain and tension.   He knew he had still to write a really
great novel, one as substantial, say, as those John Galsworthy
was turning out across the Atlantic.   He knew, too, that his
writing was becoming stiff and his plots anemic.   The arteries
were hardening.   But memories kept thronging his consciousness, calling for release in a lengthy work of fiction
which should preserve the days of long ago and also place
upon his brow the ultimate wreath of fame.   Yet Fate had
another trick up her sleeve, a deadly one, it turned out, which
was to sweep off all his winnings.

    Not two months after the *Century Magazine* printed "A
Cathedral Singer" an Austrian archduke was murdered in
Sarajevo and an inferno soon flamed high as jealous, snarl-
ing nations sought to establish through war a new balance
of power.   As government after government was drawn into
the struggle President Wilson called upon American citizens
to remain neutral in thought as well as in deed, and so genuinely pacific was the intent of the American people that he
was reëlected on the platform of having kept us out of war.
To maintain that neutrality, however, became ever more
difficult in the face of interference with our commerce and
rights on the sea, of spy plots and a deluge of propaganda,
of intrigue to stir up Mexico upon our border, and Allen,
like many other Americans who worried about our national
honor, became impatient with the president's policies.   Not
a jingoist, Allen was far from being a pacificist; indeed his

belligerent patriotism took a form in the next few years
something like the more mystical phase of Hitler's doctrine
of nationalism today, and one can fairly suspect that his reading of Nietzsche's superman may have contributed some
strength to his dogmatic belief in the virtue of the Anglo-
Saxon peoples. But from 1915 on Allen arbitrarily fixed a
gulf between Anglo-Saxon and Prussian blood. He had
never had a liking for Germany, or, speaking more strictly,
for Prussia; he abhorred what he understood to be Prussian
efficiency because it ran counter to his humanism and individualism; he disliked the military caste; he accepted without
question, as many of his fellow citizens did, the accounts of
German atrocities; and as the armies of the "blond beast"
trampled upon Belgium and swept on toward Paris, Paris
the seat of western civilization since the Renaissance, the
symbol of liberalism as set up against the mailed fist and its
thirst for iron and blood, he felt that watchful waiting was a
gesture of a cowardly weakling.

At first the war by mere accident was profitable for Allen:
it associated itself admirably with his fifteenth book and it
gave him a last opportunity to take a fall out of William Dean
Howells. He had intended to call his book *The Balancing of
the Clouds*, a phrase borrowed from Job 37:16, but the European appeal to arms suggested another title, so that from
November of 1914 to and including January of 1915 the story
appeared serially in the *Century* as "The Sword of Youth,"
dedicated, when published, in the American edition to George
Folsom Granberry and in the English to "the soldier youth
of England in this war of ours"—the pronoun showing Allen's disregard of the American proclamation of neutrality.
It is the first published volume in the mother-and-son trilogy.
Back we go to Kentucky, Kentucky in the midst of the Civil
War, where we meet in a farmhouse Mrs. Sumner, a large,
harsh, dominating woman whose husband has taken to the

army all of her sons but Joseph, the youngest. But Joseph, having now reached the age of seventeen, feels stirring within him "this great American inheritance of old dogged indomitable Anglo-Saxon traits"; heretofore he had been made aware of his mother's contempt because he of all her sons was small in size and delicate in sensibility; now he must show her that he is no unworthy child of such an Amazonian mother and of such a state as Kentucky. His mother's commands, her brutal pity for him, her pleadings only fortify his resolution—he will go to the Confederate forces. One other and stronger tie holds him to his home; nearby lives Lucy Morehead, a girl of his own age. His duty to his mother and the estate, his natural shrinking from bloodshed, and his adolescent liking for Lucy cause his resolution to waver, but for a short time only, and with his departure to don the gray uniform the first part comes to an end.

Here, wisely enough, Allen provided for an hiatus. He was no Kipling to describe heroic Tommies, he had not the talent of Stephen Crane for picturing battles he had never witnessed, and so he calmly opened Part Second with the announcement that two years had passed since Joseph left home, two years which had given firmness to the boy's character and converted his innocence into the experience of manhood, for war "often betters human nature by the exercise of the elements of its strength and by its struggle in some great cause, covering the welfare and the fate of a nation." We hear the roar of cannon off-stage only. But Joseph had to fight a battle even fiercer than those which left his comrades mangled by stump and stream, for he receives a letter from Lucy telling him of his mother's serious illness. He arranges to desert the field, he returns to Kentucky to find his mother dead and Lucy grown to womanhood. The war had brought maturity to her as to him, and at this point Allen became again emotional, so much so that in England *Great*

Thoughts reprinted his description under the title "Women in War-Time":

For are not the most beautiful generations of the women of any race produced during its long heroic wars? Is it not what women think of distant fighting-men that alone carries their natures to certain loftiest ranges of human expression? Not such beauty as comes to other women from thoughts of God—women whose brows, dedicated to heaven, have the pitifulness of blanched flowers; whose eyes are ever turned toward the dust as though the bold burning sun were too human a light, and these could be opened wide and unafraid only in dark places before the unsidereal radiance of silver lamps. But beauty which answers with frank and full understanding to all there is in the eyes of men, when these come home to them, as their saviors and lovers, from battle-plains where blood ran reddest and fiercest near the very wine-presses of death and the young vineyards of the slain. Is it nature's compensation to women for their passionate unfitness to carry on war that they can yet help to win its victories as the mates of warriors, who after the lapse of all Christian centuries are still to them the foremost and fullest of men?

The two most interesting facts that creep out from this rhetoric are Allen's unscientific belief in pre-natal influences and his indebtedness to Nietzsche's doctrines with respect to the missions of man and woman.

To Lucy's chagrin Joseph says nothing to her this time of love. He bears the weight, of course, of guilt before the opinion of the military, a weight which must be lifted by pardon or death. Back to the army he stoically goes, to find himself pardoned by the commander-in-chief, and then, with Appomattox over, he returns to Lucy and his inheritance. The youth has earned his golden spurs and justified the taking up of the sword.

Scarcely had the ink dried upon the book in February of 1915 before critics let Allen know that times had changed and that he might no longer consider himself the aristocrat of

American letters. The reviews were not many; most of them were perfunctory; and the intelligent ones found fault in a manner almost supercilious. The *Boston Transcript* grumbled with respect to his theme that "he must complicate it and overburden it with words, words, words," and the *Chicago Evening Post* alleged that it was blighted by "stump oratory." *The Nation*, still hot on Allen's scent, conceded that "despite its sentimentality, there is a Greek quality in this tale" but went on to say that "the reader might wish a slighter preoccupation with sex"—an unfair accusation if heedless reviewer ever made one, since no preoccupation with sex is to be discovered in the volume. It is the slightness of the novel that marks Allen's continued decline. Indeed "The Sword of Youth" is so attenuated in every respect that one feels that Allen was writing down to his public in retaliation for its failure to accept his best. The story is reminiscent of those tales which once appeared in *The Youth's Companion* inasmuch as it appropriately enough holds up heroism and gallantry as worthy of emulation but does not come near having significance, even in its praise of these qualities, for an adult mind. So reminiscent is Allen's story that it is not surprising to find him introducing near its close two scenes in which Joseph encounters Abraham Lincoln and Robert E. Lee—almost the unfailing prescription for a boy's story of Civil War days. As to the Greek quality, if "The Sword of Youth" has "austerity" it is the austerity of death. The tale was born dead, and only a Caesarian operation by the author brought it into the world. English opinion of the merits of the story was, because of its conservatism and its pleasure at finding Allen champion the cause of the Allies, much kinder than ours and remains so today.

The *Sword of Youth* was published as a book in February, 1915, and in the same month *The Bookman* contained Allen's last argument with Howells. The latter had declared in a press interview: "I have never believed that great events produced great literature. . . . War is an upheaval of civilization; it means death to all arts." Such a pacifistic position was quite untenable and Allen, who had never been touched by socialistic doctrines and who seems to have been oblivious to the career of Henry George, fell upon Howells with some glee. He pointed out in "War and Literature" that the *Iliad* and much of Greek sculpture had to do with martial exploits and warriors; so did the *Aeneid* and many Roman achievements in the arts; so did early Scandinavian literature, *Paradise Lost*, the Arthurian cycle; the poems and novels about Bruce and Wallace, Joan of Arc, Napoleon. War, he asserted roundly, is the greatest single motive in literature since "what the art of the world unerringly seeks and has always sought is the greatness of human nature; that is its theme, its vital, universal, deathless theme"—and to support his contention further might have mentioned our own contributions, such as Lincoln's address at Gettysburg, Whitman's "Drum-Taps," "The Battle Hymn of the Republic," and his fellow Kentuckian's "Bivouac of the Dead." He had no ear for whoever would speak of the horrors and barbarities of international strife; he was as strenuous as Nietzsche in upholding man's duty to purify himself by risking his property, his ease, and his life on the field of battle, and as the red laugh in France spread wider and wider and the Germans resorted to the use of poison-gas in savage attacks upon French Territorials and English and Canadian troops in the Ypres salient, as the Allied offensive on the western front broke down, and as the English found themselves blocked along the Dardanelles, Allen fumed and anathematized Wilson under his breath. Why couldn't the President see that it was our privilege to align ourselves beside the crusaders who were so intrepidly facing the Hun, the devastator of Belgium, the murderer of women and children, the menace to Anglo-Saxon culture and civilization?　He brooded bitterly over our inaction; it would have been better for him if he, like Henry James, could have thrown himself into some physical activity which would have afforded an outlet for his indignation, all the more likely to turn inward because of his loneliness and fatigue.　The thought of war did not upset him; he was no Romain Rolland.　It was the contemptible stand—as he maintained—of the United States before the conscience of the whole world that was too much for him to bear.　"He was never the same man after the war began," is Ellen Glasgow's recollection, and in the middle of June he wrote to George Folsom Granberry: "The war keeps me ill," and went on to deny that we should allow ourselves to be moved by Kuno Francke's plea for milk for starving Teutonic babies.　He stayed at Saratoga over the Fourth of July and two weeks later mailed with no little satisfaction a clipping to Mr. Granberry which observed that none of the famous German musicians had been Prussian. He was equally satisfied to inform his friend that *The Heroine in Bronze* was leading his books in sales—"All sales were small, but it led!"　Yet he betrayed no fear, no uncertainty as to the future.

Again in October he argued that war was an inspiration of literature, this time giving an interview to Joyce Kilmer. To the young poet he discoursed affably about the short story, denying that Poe had appreciably influenced the American writers of that type of fiction, thus making a judgment only partially correct, for Poe's theories and technique, if not his moods, dictated the form of the American "short-story" for almost a generation.　Instead of Poe Allen praised Balzac and Boccaccio and thought that the American tale had deteriorated in quality since 1895.　What would have been Allen's feelings could he have foreseen that the man to whom he was talking would within three years be killed in a war which was said to be a fountain for great art?

Nineteen-sixteen was unhappy and almost sterile for James Lane Allen. It began with a good omen when the Lexington chapter of the United Daughters of the Confederacy purchased Orlando Rouland's portrait of him and presented it to the Lexington Public Library on Washington's Birthday. Here was practical evidence that he had some honor in his own land and that a bit of immortality might be reserved for him. But he excused himself from attending the unveiling of the portrait, although he did send an address to be read on the occasion and he perused carefully the newspaper reports of what Dr. Thomas B. Macartney of the library Board of Trustees and Mayor James C. Rogers of the city said upon accepting the picture. Allen had at first liked the portrait; later upon talking it over with Annie he agreed that its counterfeit of his head and face was not too successful, but he was pleased that the library of his home town should hang on its wall this constant reminder that the Bluegrass had furnished one outstanding figure to American literature. From that time forth he felt more kindly toward the city that had resented *The Reign of Law*, mocked at the Christmas trilogy, and whispered that his vagaries could be explained only by his being a drug addict. Especially gratifying were the measures the superintendent of Lexington's schools—"good old Cassidy," Allen often called him—took to keep Allen's name green among school children by his speeches and by having the pupils honor Allen's birthday as a kind of holiday. Immediately after the 1916 celebration of his birth Allen sent to the *Lexington Herald* a dozen rules for young students who wished to write short stories. These rules, prefaced by a tribute to John Galsworthy because he could write with good manners of people who had bad manners, are so clear a disclosure of Allen's fealty to the

Genteel Tradition in the teeth of widespread contempt for it that they must be looked at:

1. You must shape your story wisely and well.
2. You must have color in the stories. (Here he recommended attention to Hawthorne).
3. You must inject good manners into it.
4. You must have good morals in it.
5. Write stories that are natural, not impossible.
6. Draw human beings naturally.
7. Have an important idea in it.
8. Choose a big emotion.
9. Make it a story of the actual.
10. Or make it a story of the ideal.
11. Write it with awe, as if before a big audience.
12. Write it with reverence to yourself, not vanity.

These precepts do not provide a coherent analysis of the art of short story writing but they are useful to beginners, even to those who have no use for either good manners or good morals. Noteworthy are the last two bits of advice, reminding us of Allen's dedication to literature and of the almost religious feeling with which Katherine Mansfield approached her work.

These dicta were laid down in December. Before his birthday in that month there had been weeks when he feared he would never see another natal anniversary, never write a short story again. Illness again struck him down, so severely this time that he was sent to Miss Patmore's sanitarium at 124 West Seventy-fifth Street, not far from where he had lived so handsomely in the days when his books were best sellers. For nearly three weeks he rested there, giving his weakening arteries a chance to recover some strength and listening to advice as to what diet would be beneficial to one suffering from nephritis. During this period of en forced absence from his desk he read what reviewers said of *A Cathedral Singer*, just published.

What they said did not hasten his convalescence. Those that were kind wrote nothing of moment. *The Nation* and the *Boston Transcript* hurt him deeply. The first, scoffing at his attempt to catch and translate the spirit of a place, remarked cruelly that "one rises from the perusal less impressed than the author hoped with the feeling that the cathedral possesses a significance too deep for tears." The second set forth in plain words the contemporary revolt against Allen and his kind:

We wonder if the author of such sentiments be supremely blind, supremely humorous, or simply successfully shrewd. But there is no doubt that the public likes them. This most recent effusion will be called "exquisite," "sweet," or "just lovely," according to the status of the commentator; for it combines an unhappy ending with that "glad," "bravery-in-misfortune" element so dear to the heart of the American people.

And the *London Times Literary Supplement* objected gently that "Mr. James Lane Allen is here, unfortunately, at his most solemn and most elaborate." Had he reached the end of his tether? Certainly he must, listening to the slow beating of his heart in half hours of keen misgiving, have come near thinking so. He was not keeping in step with the shifting times, he had fallen out of the line of march. He had lost the rhythm of success, of artistic success. Again came the haunting words: he was being judged by a generation that did not know him. This new world was rushing to buy books by Guy Empey and Private Peat. Only two things cheered him: Edward O'Brien praised *A Cathedral Singer* and Isaac F. Marcosson told how greatly James M. Barrie admired *A Kentucky Cardinal* and how H. G. Wells, whom Allen disliked as a pacifist, and John Galsworthy and Arnold Bennett were watching particularly the writing of Allen,

Dreiser, and David Graham Phillips. But he resigned himself to abandoning the mother-and-son trilogy as he had
given up the Christmas trilogy five years before. The last
volume was to have been called *The Little Third Person*
and was to tell of a woman with a great mother heart but
never given a child; on her honeymoon the bridegroom was
to cut a piece of meat for "the little third person" and on
their golden wedding anniversary he was to do the same.
Happily for Allen's reputation this story remained unwritten.

In that red paper-backed composition book in which Allen
had kept notes for *The Mettle of the Pasture* he had scrib-
bled this bit of characterization through an exclamation:
"Venerable!" she said. "And only seventy-six. What a
fool!" At the opening of 1917 the author of that stray bit
of characterization was sixty-seven, with nine years to go
before he dare think of calling himself venerable. And the
spirit of the lady who thus flaunted time was Allen's. He
was nearing seventy; his books were not selling well; his income, like the nation's at the beginning of the war, had
dwindled seriously; expenses had increased through medical
and hospital necessities, so that he was constrained to return
to magazine writing. But he was not through—he would
show them he was not through! He would make even this
generation respect him. He would let these young fellows
like Mencken, whom he thought too destructive, too unbal-
anced, and Dreiser, whom he thought unnecessarily drab
and unpleasant, know that there was good writing stuff left in
one of the older men. James was now dead—the war had
been too much with him—and Howells could do no better
than tell the awkward and unmotivated story of a man who
set up as God in Leatherwood, Ohio, but he, Allen, could still
break a lance for the outworn generation. For two or three
years he had been meditating, kneading, breathing upon a

plan to write not merely a good novel but a great one, something to stand out boldly on the shelf of his books, something to be his legacy to American literature. He had made
some starts upon it but had dropped his pen when sickness
intervened. In March of 1914 he wrote to Ellen Glasgow:
"Since you went away I have taken my future in my own
hands—at whatever cost—and in peace and quietness have
settled down to do one *great thing*—as the rest of my life's
work. Just to finish all the years of struggle and effort with
the greatest thing of all—greatest for me! So there I am,
and here I am! At work on a real novel, a long, very long
novel, of the first magnitude in every way—as magnitude
goes in American literature. This is a recital that will be
known to but few even as a plan. When you return, I shall
wish to tell you about it in some all-comprehending way.
It is to be dedicated to you if you will be able to say that you
so desire." A year later he was writing to Cassidy that he
was at work on a long novel which he hoped would advance
his position "far on ahead." But after four years he was
writing to the same friend: "I chafe, fret, worry, strain
against years and ill health, desperate with the realization
that I may never complete *one great book*."

What was this *magnum opus* which was forever to remain, unfortunately, only a plan? Nothing less than an ambitious historical or rather a chronicle novel which should
be a literary museum for the sorting and exhibiting of relics
of the past, remains of older sentiments and manners and
characters and events. He would return to the days and the
land of his youth and, summoning forth the precious images
that lay buried there, mount them on pedestals so that all
the world might wonder at their purity and beauty. He
meant first to call this novel *The Belfry of the Years;* later
he changed the tentative title to *Gather Ye Rosebuds* and
then to *A Pilgrim to His Youth* (had he read Leonard Mer-

rick's *Conrad in Quest of His Youth,* 1903?); and as yea
followed year without the consummation of his plan and a
his summoned memories became dearer to him than his ai.
ing body, the scheme grew under his hand until it reache
heroic proportions. In 1924 he was dictating a revised vei
sion of *A Pilgrim to His Youth* and describing the "pilgrim
in terms that fit himself most nicely:

He had reached that growth of years when the early pa
of his life, which had dropped nearly out of sight during middle
age, had begun to reappear, to glimmer here and there, to b
recognized, and to draw his gaze back to it with restored af
fection. This mystery of a late growth within him was not in re
sponse to any solicitation of his will. It is a phase of the myster
which is our life. We do not know what it means, this fidelity o
our souls, if we have souls, this readjustment of our bodies if w
are mere bodies. But whether the pity of the soul or the chem
istry of the body, this we know: that it is a high, a solemn,
consummate aspect of reality whose presence we cannot deny no
influence question. The wonder of it, the enchantment—tha
old things long forgotten begin to take on colors which turn ther
beautiful! We are aware that the change is wholly within our
selves yet we yield to the illusion that it is as a definite scene—th
land of memories. So that those wasted fields of reality are gree
again with spring, and all our senses travel to them and ente
again upon the quest of youth. The juices of their forbidden or
chards flow upon the tongue; a wild grape vine blooming some
where in those summer woods swells the nostril; the ear gather
up as music out of the silence the harsh noises of winter barns; for
gotten affections arise again within the heart for old comrade
Henceforth we live in two worlds: the unreal outer world o
every day fast perishing about us and that inner world wher
beckon undying memories.

Here is the fine rhythm of English prose in the classica
style, its pulse of emotion carefully restrained but throbbin
with blood. A pity that he did not always write as well eve

though such dignified cadences were as much out of fashion as the velvet and lace of the Age of Johnson.

But the "unreal outer world of every day" was not to be dismissed so lightly in 1917, and Allen's repose was not a little shaken when on the second of April in that year Woodrow Wilson stood before Congress and asked for a declaration of war upon Germany since God helping us we could do no other. Here was what Allen had been waiting for, yet what a barrier it was to be in the pathway of his plans, how it was to deflect his attention and weary and harass him. As the American people hurried to gird themselves for the crusade to which their leader had called them it seemed all at once to Allen as if the whole universe were being pulled down about his ears, so unsettled was everything, so distracted was everybody. Psychologically we had been made ready for war by "preparedness" campaigns and by the occupation of Vera Cruz, but from the angle of material readiness we were seen to be confused and short-handed. But not impotent. The nerves of the entire country quivered, leaped, tightened. George Creel waved the wand of propaganda and America rose to avenge Belgium's wrongs, to defend the rights of small nations, to make the world safe for democracy, to wage a war to end war. Thousands rushed to the colors. A draft law brought millions into service. Women joined the Red Cross, the Y. W. C. A., knitted socks and wristlets, prepared bandages, delivered speeches. The Liberty Bell went on a progress throughout the states to stimulate the sale of Liberty Bonds. Scientists bent over blueprints of submarines, hoping to find some way to destroy them easily, and concocted poisonous gases in their tubes. Experts disputed as to what kind of transport ship to build. Huge training camps sprang up magically; hundreds of thousands of young men learned to do squads right on drill grounds and to sing "Over There" in Y. M. C. A. huts.

Congress voted fabulous sums for expenditures and the president thrilled the world with pronouncements which future historians will see helped usher into being a new epoch in human affairs. The air crackled with electric flashes of enthusiasm, achievement, conquest. Our boys went to France, fought, died, triumphed. The United States became a world power, its chieftain the spokesman for world opinion.

Allen asked himself what his bit might be. He was almost sixty-eight and active service of any kind was out of the question. His contribution must perforce be small. To help conserve the paper supply he stopped unnecessary papers and magazines. He bought little silk French and American flags. He did without sugar and meat on the proper days. But the whole business distracted him; the general hysteria, the flood of hate loosed throughout our cities and towns, the din of accusation and denial, the tramp of the soldiery—all kept his nerves in a constant jangle. He was trying to complete another book but the god of war was staging so mighty a pageant that he could scarcely keep his eyes from it. To make matters worse what seemed to be a new and was certainly a deadly disease ravaged New York— the flu—and Allen, as fussy about his health now as Henry James ever was, crossed to Morristown, N. J., to escape the epidemic and to write for the *New York Times* his "Battle Hymn," which he entitled "Bywords of the War." In this verbose rhapsody he did little more than protest that the German people should be held responsible for the acts of the German government and that this war was one which would end all war. There was little more that he could do. Forced to be sedentary he tingled and stamped like an old war-horse who hears the call to charge. How stupidly bungling the administration was in its mobilization of our powers! Everywhere inefficiency, treachery, hesitancy, red tape, graft. He wrote out his anger at all the delay and looseness in *A Pil-*

grim to His Youth, in which the "war-sick, world-sick, life-sick" hero avers that "the whole nation began to groan and roar at the feeble, cramped, and crooked way in which the nation's strength stepped toward the desperate battlefields." Where were the great organizers and warriors such as we had once had, where the Washingtons and Grants and Lees and Jacksons?

The sixteenth book, with fewer than two hundred pages, was at last ready for the new publisher, Doubleday, Page and Company, and came out in January, 1918. It was almost ignored by the public prints; first, because of the storm and stress of international events, with which it had nothing to do, and second, because it was a book about a boy and for children, dedicated to "The Young Kentucky Forest-Lover." As a bit of literature *The Kentucky Warbler* might safely be ignored, but as a symptom of the workings of Allen's mind it asks a sympathetic examination. His writing of and for children is of instant significance as pointing to the unswerving movement of his disillusionment. He had reached that desolate windy plateau from which the eye can discover no green prospect, the mind no sense of pride in what has been done, and the will no intent to go further. There was so little left for James Lane Allen. Did anything remain but that easeful death of which his favorite poet had sung, death from which he shrank with natural compunction, but for which he sometimes unconsciously sighed as the final escape from futility? "Forget Me Death!—O Death, Forget Me Not!" he had written when youth and ambition had made the thought of our exit a grisly one, yet a consummation to be accepted by a melancholy philosopher. But then there had been the future, now there was so little except the past. "Grow old along with me"—what mockery! There was no one to grow old along with, his sister being more a burden than ever—he was even willing to say so openly in one let-

ter. Fame? He had tasted it, he knew how heady is its
wine, what a flush it brings to the cheeks, but it had lost its
flavor, had turned brackish. Keats, that marvelous boy, had
been right when in the grandest of English sonnets he had
stood on the wide world's shore and thought until love and
fame had sunk into nothingness. They were nothing. But
then Allen's puritanism came to the rescue: the one thing
left to do was to inspire youth, to beckon them upward.
Their elders were hopeless, mad, beyond assistance. But if
he could say one bright and cheering word to the newest
generation, could give them some encouragement whereby
they might be inspired to seek heights which their fathers
had failed to ascend, then he would have lived to some purpose and could die with some ease. When dead he could
live in them; he could still echo in their memories as the
voices of flute and violin. "You stand," he wrote in this
newest book, "beside some all but forgotten mound of human ashes; before you are arranged a band of youths, unconsciously holding in their hands the unlighted torches of
the future. You utter some word about the cold ashes and
silently one of them walks forward to the ashes, lights his
torch and goes his radiant way."

That was the purpose of *The Kentucky Warbler*—to help
some youth light his torch. The purpose was noble, the result a pathetic failure. "A pallid attempt at a reproduction
of the crystallizing point of adolescence," *The Dial* named
it, and pallid it seems today in contrast with novels of similar purpose—such as *Silberman*—or with a magnificent poem
like Whitman's "Out of the Cradle Endlessly Rocking,"
which, by a curious parallel, also introduces a bird as an important agent in a boy's awakening to the consciousness of
his powers. *The Kentucky Warbler* is not untrue in its psychology; it is inadequate rather than false; it does not take
us far enough, deep enough. But it was dedicated to children

and for them it gives enough of the truth, if not all that could be said. The hero's inferiority complex is sufficiently motivated; he is poor, he wears shabby clothes, he is sent to a public school while his sister Eleanor attends a private institution, he feels useless to his family and "roadless" to himself. His sleeping sex impulse is shown in his dreamy, hardly-felt interest in Jenny. That Allen was reading of psychoanalysis and was applying it to his fiction is made manifest by the way Daniel Webster's subconscious strength is reënforced in and by a dream and in his use of the word "forest" to express the dark growth and undergrowth of the subconscious mind. There were the customary touches of old-fashioned sentiment. After Webster announced his intention to go to a university and thus proved that he has set his feet upon a "road" the father "rudely with the back of his hand brushed away a tear that rolled down his cheek," while the mother stood beside Webster, "her hand on his head, her handkerchief pressed to her eyes." Later tears of happiness welled from the youth's eyes. Whimsical in part, simple in its portrayal of idyllic rural life in Kentucky, didactic in plan, *The Kentucky Warbler* is none the less moribund if not dead today. Not even its timid touches of satire, as when the father assures his son that the United States Senate held no member with a trace of resemblance to Daniel Webster, not even its speaking of the Germans as "the evil enemy," could endear it to a nation becoming aware of H. L. Mencken and given to the reading of newspaper headlines, editorials in sketchy paragraphs, and hymns of hate.

The war did more than raise a distracting clamor beneath Allen's ivory tower. It struck him a shrewd blow through his friendship with George Folsom Granberry, who was of course going to France. Not until then did Allen realize how much he relied upon the companionship of the younger man. Everything was falling to pieces, including civilization itself; everything was in a state of flux; in all about him he saw change, decay, irrationality, loss. He invited Granberry to a farewell dinner. Granberry, excited, hurried, recovering from illness, found time only for a refusal written on a postcard—a certain insult to the Kentuckian for whom circumstances could not modify manners. But for this once Allen's vexation could not last; the emergency did, after all, overrule etiquette. Wasn't the whole society he knew being blown to bits by gunpowder and might he not as well face the fact? He went to Granberry's office and found the musician out. "Ah," he remarked sadly to the secretary, "Mr. Granberry is just like that ray of sunshine coming between the shade and the windowsill—he is bright and cheering but you can't grasp him. Elusive." Pensively he stared out upon the restless crowds in the street below.

Perhaps it was then that he made the decisions by which he finally rejected the world. He would sell his furnishings; they were only so many impedimenta to a man who by this time was walking wearily down the road that led to the conviction that all is vanity. He would leave his dwindling estate to his sister for the duration of her natural life and after that it would go to erect in Lexington a fountain for children, a Fountain of Youth, he would have it called. Without remaining in New York to witness the selling of his effects at the Anderson Gallery he left with Annie for Charleston, South Carolina, and from there went to Asheville. It would seem that the loveliness of the Land of the Sky might have held them for the summer, but no; in July he was off to Saratoga Springs, and in the fall, returning to the metropolis, he was so dismayed by the inroads of flu that he went to the Beechwood Hotel in Summit, New Jersey, as though he were a refugee from a Florentine plague. "If I die Wilson will be partly responsible," he wrote, with what was not entirely humor. He had practically completed another book and he wished to live to see it in his hands. There was little else to live for. When in the middle of 1916 the doctor had handed him what he thought was his "death warrant" he said to himself that if he should be vouchsafed strength enough to write one more book it should be his gayest one, so that he might go down with colors flying. He would also by telling the story through Richardson's device of letters make an experiment in technique which he had never before tried.

Before this comedy in letters was published there came revolution in Germany, following hard upon British and American onslaughts which broke the Hindenburg line; the kaiser fled to Holland and New York City hysterically celebrated a false armistice before the real one was signed on the eleventh of November, 1918. To the Allies this termination brought peace with victory and the fateful problems of settlement, and to James Lane Allen it brought a relaxation of taut nerves which may have resulted in illness. At any rate, intestinal influenza sent him to the Roosevelt Hospital for over a week in February. Probably while recuperating he dreamed with hope of the success of his comedy in letters, but when it appeared a month later it brought with it no acclaim to renew his courage. The reviews were uniformly short and formal: the *Boston Transcript* was mocking; the *Providence Journal* tasted "sourness"; there was widespread complaint of "cloying manners." The *London Times Literary Supplement* waved it airily aside: "We really cannot take the slightest interest in the main thread of the tale." Allen's long nose for incense was offended but he made no complaint. Despite the fact that Ellen Glasgow designated it "delicious, perfect comedy," his equanimity was only partially restored and he knew again the bitterness of rejection by the public. "But who of us ever forgives the person that slights our best?" he queried in *The Emblems of Fidelity*, and America was consistently slighting his best. Could he win it back to him? He had closed this novel in an exalted mood:

My heart swells as one who feels himself climbing toward a height. There is kindled in me that strangest of all flames that burn in the human heart, the shining thought that my life is destined to be more than mine, that my work will make its way into other minds and mingle with the better, happier impulses of other lives.

This, it is true, was the cogitation of Beverley Sands but Beverley was the shadow of Allen. The question was, could he make himself again a part of American life, of American literature, or was he one of the cogs that might now be thrown away as useless?

The Emblems of Fidelity is not a comic masterpiece but it does contain some genuine humor, and after one has passed through ninety pages and has the situation well in hand he is in for an hour of enjoyment. I have read it several times, and each time I find myself laughing aloud at the correspondence of Clara Louise Chamberlain, who signs herself "proud daughter of the Southland," at the illiteracy of the Tennessee florists, Burns and Bruce, and at Beverley Sands's desperate efforts to untangle himself from the tendrils which so innocent a thing as a request for ferns threw around himself and his friends. The laughter, however, is not sustained; the bright sky is overclouded by clouds of cynicism that are small but black enough, so that the Spirit of Comedy can no longer shine through them. Strangely, it is the enlightened and liberated women, who Meredith insists are necessary for the presence of real comedy, that are responsible for the gloomy passages and the gloomy implications of the story.

The Emblems of Fidelity was the last of Allen's books for over four years. Its comparative failure shook him. In the meantime he must write for magazines, not so steadily as in the early days but at a pace sufficient to keep his name before editors and to earn him some money while he went on with his great work, the secret which he hugged to himself. He would call this long autobiographical and historical novel *The Days of Our Fathers: A Kentucky Novel of the Older America.* Memories glided into his mind like ghosts. He would recreate those years when the culture of the South, founded upon slavery, had given life a meaning and a richness that had been lost in the modern haste to use unwisely the tools science had placed in our hands. Great financial centralization had, after all, made us poorer than our ancestors. Ideas for short stories, essays, and verse swept him here and there. He would write *Tales of Europe,* a series of short stories about foreign cities, and he actually began one, "The Exiles of a Night, or The Bridge," in which two Neapolitans, Gasparo and Tito, became rivals for the love of Annette. He began a story to be named "A Flickering Candle," but the inspiration flickered and went out. He thought of stinging Wilson with an essay, "Socrates in the White House," but he could not distil the poison to his own satisfaction. Of *The Solid Ground,* which was to have been a novel, nothing is left save the title. He weighed the possibility of making money in the theater and labored over a comedy in four acts, *The Promoters,* which he speedily realized was too replete with long speeches and asides, too "talky" for the stage, and must be abandoned. To defend himself from the constantly recurring cry of sentimentality he composed a poem which he sent to *The Bookman;* then he went off to The Elms in Ridgefield, Connecticut, to criticize Wilson's dream of a League of Nations and to read Galsworthy's *Saint's Progress* with approval. There was a true writer and gentleman, he thought, one who had not sold out to the meretricious demand for sensationalism, who could write of adultery without being suspected of urging it upon his young readers.

The poem, "On The Mantlepiece," was printed in the September *Bookman.* It is at once defensive and offensive, *apologia* and attack, or perhaps it would be better to say that Allen, like any good strategist, seized an opportunity to advance instead of waiting to be annihilated and in doing so laid about him as lustily as he had done when *The Reign of Law* was being scourged in the pulpit. The reiterated accusation that he was wallowing in sentiment, that he could not or would not face life as it is, hoisted his patience at the moon and he set himself to administer to the young hard-boiled literati a punishing rebuke. His subtitle is indignant and supercilious: *Audi Alteram Partem.* To prove that he was not an old fogy and could meet them on their own ground he wrote in his first known trial of *vers libre,* employing eight stanzas varying in length from eight to thirty verses. As he charged upon his enemy he put Dickens forward as a shield:

> And all the literary offspring of Boz,
> Boz who despised your sentimentality
> But doted on his own sentimentality
> (As the rest of us)—
> All the literary offspring of Boz
> Who despise sentimentality about the toes of a cricket—
>
> *   *   *
>
> The twentieth-century Bozzers, green and leafy with genius
> And ready to exude poetic gum at the mere mention of the
>   natural
> And therefore never natural themselves
> Because no cult is natural
> But is only a saturated solution of self-consciousness,
> All the Neo-Bozzers must have wailed aloud
> At the sudden violent death
> Of the Cricket on the Hearth—

A natural thing making natural music,
Having been caught in an altogether unnatural place.

Read Keats, he commands the fault-finders, Keats

Who sang of the grasshopper
But who sang too of the Grecian urn on the mantelpiece
(Or some equivalent of the mantelpiece)
Sang of the sentimental, artificial urn on the mantelpiece—

Finally he assures himself and his critics that there is left a man here and there who does not look upon literature as the entrance to a dissecting room or a cemetery for ghoulish depredations but to whom poems or stories are, as they were to Keats,

—little pictures
To bring him near the beauty that is far away or beyond him.

That key of "beauty that is far away" is the one in which many of Allen's latter pieces are played.

In Connecticut he toyed with dreams of old Kentucky and his great American novel. He visualized heroes who in middle or old age longed to return to Lexington in order to escape the unkindness and heartlessness of the eastern cities. One novel would have presented a Kentucky husband who invited as a visitor to his house an old flame, only to have his wife reciprocate by summoning as her guest a former suitor of hers, now a famous but stricken author, and it is a pity this novel perished in its inception; its opening paragraphs are most promising. Little waves of nostalgia swept over him but broke upon the rocks of his pride. He told his acquaintances that he meant to go back to Kentucky, purchase a farm, and die on his own soil, but in his heart he knew that it was too late to escape into the primitive—that *ignis fatuus* of all wearied artists—and that his exile would not end as long as he breathed. He yearned for a taste of Bluegrass honey and M. A. Cassidy sent him a jar of the amber sweet. Another kind of sweet was supplied by Hugh Walpole's statement to New York interviewers that there were "six of your novelists who I personally think merit the attention of British book-readers: Hergesheimer, Poole, and Mrs. Wharton, James Lane Allen, Ellen Glasgow, Willa Sibert Cather, and Katherine Fullerton Gerould."[3] This was in 1919, and gave Allen the consolation of reflecting that to some cultivated Englishmen, at least, he had stood in the front rank of American writers for well-nigh a third of a century.

Chill winds and snow again drove him and his sister south, to Augusta, Georgia, this time, but with the blooming of laurel they felt the irresistible call of Asheville and its environs. From there he wrote querulously about his mail, blaming Postmaster-General Burleson for its tardy and uncertain delivery. Somewhat querulous, also, was the only thing he wrote for publication in 1920, a trialogue with the reminiscent title of "Heaven's Little Ironies" in which he smiled with unconcealed mockery at publishers, critics, and novelists. The conversation is in dramatic form, the scene is Heaven. Two spirits are bored by a sorrowing third who confides to them that indigestion cut short his days just before he was to indite the Great American Novel. After he flies off disconsolately the remaining spirits confess their identities and compare their lots.

FIRST SPIRIT. Once to have been a publisher who was not an angel; now to be an angel who is not a publisher! I am not dissatisfied. But it was a pleasant thing—*that:* being lord of creation.

SECOND SPIRIT. To have had one quill and no wings; to have had a pair of wings and no quill! I do not complain that here there is nothing to complain of. But as you say—it was a pleasant thing—*that:* being judge of all the earth.

---

[3] That Mrs. Gerould is named seventh in a list of "six" suggests that Mr. Walpole was thinking of her as a short story writer.

But if the perfections of Heaven stopped the mouth of the critic the check of *The Bookman* did not prevent Allen from complaining that he was poorly paid for his contribution, and he wrote for it no more. Walking about in the pleasant grounds of the Grove Park Inn he thought long and deeply over the future and how he should confront it. He had no wish to cease writing; there was never a time when stories did not jostle each other in the avenues of his brain; but he preferred to write at long leisure and to write of such things as he pleased. It was now all too obvious that he must again write for magazines, for this business of going south, north, or west in quest of health for his sister or himself was proving costly in all ways; his recent books had been selling cheaply at a dollar or a dollar and a quarter and they had not been selling well. Some of his investments had not been wise and both the income from his railroad bonds and the value of those bonds had been sharply reduced. He would write magazine stories, go on with his long novel, and recoup his losses. But it was hard to write these days, hard to force thoughts which longed for some cushion of ease to attend to the concentrated business of creation and assembly; hard, too, to send them out to a world which would probably receive them coolly if not scornfully. To conceive a story was not difficult but to shape it in words was irksome. The pathos of his own case, the pathos of his sister's incapacity and disfigurement were worth a sigh, and truly nothing is more maddening than to know you could do something well if you had the needed physical strength; yet he allowed little of self-pity to escape in his letters. Now and then the sigh became audible, pardonably so.

To his great credit he made no surrender of his literary standards in order to convert popularity into coin. He would make no recovery in that fashion. Rather, he raised those standards, resolving that if he must write stories for mag-

azines they should at least not be magazine stories. He set
before himself as a new but not too-distant goal the telling
of stories based upon broad human themes, having their
setting in Kentucky, perhaps, but deriving their truth from
universal experience. He drew a distinction between what
he called the Opera House story and the Carnegie Hall
story; the former was closely allied to a nation or a community: operas in French about Frenchmen; operas in German about places in Germany, operas in Italian about Italians
in Italy. So we had stories, especially in American literature,
which were fastened to the soil of New England or Virginia
or the Middle West, and most of our fiction had grown from
the sense of locality. It was time, he believed, for the short
story to transcend such limitations and to take on the nature
of a concert at Carnegie Hall, where one hears symphonies
that speak everlastingly to the whole civilized world. "The
higher we rise, the broader we are, the more civilized, cosmopolitan, the fainter the background becomes, the farther
away," he was to write in an unfinished introduction to his
last volume. This, then, was what he would do: he would
separate soil from human nature in his retorts and test-tubes
and extract the essence of human nature to make fragrant
those few stories which he knew he might still have time to
write.

And so we have the inspiring spectacle of a seventy-two-
year-old gentleman, regarded by his young compeers as *passé*
and outmoded, cast out into outer darkness as Howells and
James had been in their closing days, as out of place in a society of rugged individualists as Henry Adams had been,
suddenly raising his head in defiance and pride, refusing to
remain in *terra incognita* or to be regarded politely as fit to be
set aside in some well-placed niche, and proving that he
could, at his years and with a record of failure behind him
since 1912, hold his own with all but the best. His recovery

from decline was remarkable. In the next four years he was to produce very sparingly, to be sure—five stories in the four years—but each narrative was to have some of the qualities of enduring literature, and we must believe that only his waning strength kept him from giving us more than five. He explained the shortness of these stories by pleading his health and resignedly wrote that he hoped his work, the great novel he had planned, would be carried on by some other writer, someone superior to himself. He knew that the embers of his genius were dying but patiently and hopefully he blew upon them until the flame rose high again, then sank forever. The five stories are "The Ash-Can" (*Century,* September, 1921), "Miss Locke" (*Century,* March, 1922), "The Alabaster Box" (*Harper's,* August, 1923), "The Violet" (*Harper's,* June, 1924), and "The Landmark" (1925), left in an incomplete form at his death but published posthumously along with "The Ash-Can," "Miss Locke," and "The Violet" in *The Landmark* (1925). This last of Allen's books is rounded out with "La Tendresse," a dialogue which shall be described in its place.

Just what Allen meant by calling "The Ash-Can" "a most daring and difficult study" it is hard to say. Did he think it daring because it was an appeal to break the Volstead Act— which, in a way, it was—or because it pleaded for a confessional, such as that of the Catholic Church? Or because, which is more likely, the story about an ash-can was actually his own ash-can? Certainly there is no difficulty about the theme, which is that of the value of releasing to another person the pent-up emotions which grind and tear within the breast of him who tries to imprison them. The ash-can is for the unnamed doctor in the story a symbol for the receptacle into which we pour our woes and vexations and defeats in order to be rid of them. The doctor condemns as selfish the person who makes an ash-can of another, often the one near and dear to him, but his friend the bishop defends the practice and points out the utility of the receptacle. "I have never warmed," he says, "toward the man who would tell nothing," thus putting his approval not only upon the receiver but also the giver of repressed confidence. Then wine is served while the doctor beams and quotes Keats's undying lines about the blushful Hippocrene. The draught of wine transforms him:

He, holding a wine-glass, became a gentleman of the ages, enjoying the liberty of golden, cloud-capped, gracious things, manners, ceremonies, pageants, which one by one were dropping from the human scene. Some day, he said, the tapestries also will go, ruled out by "righteousness," and bare bagging be demanded in the name of God.

These were outspoken words for a *passé* gentleman in 1921! Under the influence of the wine the doctor, who resembles Allen in his emphasis upon self-containment, draws his chair close to the bishop's, and with a suddenness which gives the narrative an O. Henry twist, confides in one outburst the thing which he would under all other circumstances have kept locked in his bosom. What he said was so much what Allen would have said that its summary must be quoted:

Ghastly pantomime of baffled power, strength that could not be put forth as strength; picture of action that should be action but could not be action; the foul thing in life that attacks the thing which is fair; something low that gets the upper hand of what is above it; something crooked that treads down in the road of life what walks straight. He did not withhold, he did not cease, till he was disburdened, emptied.

When the doctor has finished the bishop cries, "Why did you not tell me of this long ago?" and proceeds to match the confession of his guest. Unable to console his friend, the doctor lays his hands upon the bishop's head, they stand up recover their usual manner of discourse and bearing, and part for the evening.

"The Ash-Can" is a grave story gravely told, with undertones of sadness that are easily caught. As pure narration it has almost no value. But neither do most of Chekhov's stories. What makes it an artistic success is that it accomplished exactly what its author meant it to: a digging into the ground of life until one of the twisted roots of experience is separated from the others and held in the hand for all to see. "The Ash-Can" reflects, as Allen intended it to reflect, a universal truth and does so with a tiny mirror and the utmost economy of effort.

In "Miss Locke" he also probed his own mind and experience, but not, this time, to illustrate a principle of Freudian psychology. Here is one of the best stories Allen wrote. Its main defect is that it is extended past the place where it should have stopped—as usual, he did not know where or when to end for the best effect—that the point of the story is dragged out and exhibited to us as though we could not be trusted to find it. The reason for this parade is doubtless that the whole story, like three others of these last tales, was torn bodily and with pain from Allen's heart. Whether or not he knew a Miss Locke is immaterial; certainly he had treasured the memory of an ideal—one founded, probably upon no real woman—and certainly he had lived to regret that by shunning the obtainable because it lacked perfection he had made the mixture of life, as he wrote, not "drinkable," and he was so anxious for other idealists to benefit from his mistake and to learn to mingle the ideal and the actual that he posted his text on a billboard. At the outset of "Miss Locke" Allen, for the first and only time, contrived a pleasant mystification for his readers, and the mystery is maintained with honest cleverness until the story is near its end—until, in other words, the paragraph with which it should have closed. Has Miss Locke been deliberately imitating another woman and will Gridley manage to find the unknown prototype, are questions which, by virtue of their peculiar surrounding factors, hold attention close to the pages. Why does Miss Locke make movements to put back from her forehead a lock of hair that is not there? Has Gridley known or only created in fancy a woman who made the same graceful gesture? Why does Miss Locke tap impatiently on the floor a foot obviously not made for dancing? How can she, against all her nature, dress so becomingly, use a certain perfume, read a certain book, play the piano in a kind of dumb show, repeat some pungent phrases, unless she is imitating some perfect Unknown, whose dimly sensed mind and body captivate Gridley as they must have fascinated the go-between through whom he saw them? To learn the whereabouts and the identity of that Unknown, Gridley does the most unchivalrous thing done by any of Allen's heroes in begging Miss Locke, who he can see loves him, to tell him the name of the girl she has been understudying. There is where the story should stop. But Allen has Miss Locke give an answer which can surprise only the naïve, and on that level of anticlimax, so common in his stories, "Miss Locke" goes on to its ineffectual conclusion. Even a mediocre writer would have deleted the last eight words, which are titles that he had at different times applied tentatively but rejected.

Objection must also be made to some of the phrasing. Some of it is unpardonably lacking in vividness, especially if it is intended to describe interiors; Allen's eye was always sharper for outdoor settings than for those indoors, and when he writes of Gridley's "turning the pages of a sumptuous volume of etching prints in the rich, deep, quiet library," of his living in "carelessly splendid bachelor rooms," and of his listening to "soft, ravishing music," we fail to see and hear what we are supposed to experience and we almost feel that we are hearkening to Pomona as she reads aloud her cheap romances to the eavesdroppers on Rudder Grange. Allen made a curiously awkward and inane transition in one place, too, for to use as a paragraph "The luxurious bachelor rooms were very quiet; moments passed" is to betray a lack of sureness in making time pass. But these are only minor flaws, and the cumulative effect of the whole story is one of dignity and truth, an effect which leaves vibrations in one's mind long after the story has been read and understood. To leave those vibrations is to write with art.

"I never put myself into my stories, any of them," Allen informed Lucille Naff of Lexington in December of 1923. Yet he was then or shortly after working upon one of the most subjective of all his tales. In fact, "The Alabaster Box" is perhaps the most self-revealing thing he wrote. He liked the sound of the words in that title, and the scriptural account of the woman who broke her precious box in order to anoint the feet and head of Jesus had long fascinated him; he had even used the words, "the alabaster box," in *The Reign of Law.* How rarely was an alabaster box broken nowadays and how starved we all were for a little kindness— that had been his conviction thirty-five years ago when he had moved Edmund Gosse with "Always Bussing His Friends" and it was the conviction which he wrote into this new story revolving about the burial of a man regretted by his family only because his demise upset domestic routine. Bitterly, contemptuously, Allen describes their grief:

Yet the affliction of the wife would depict itself to him as no other than if she found herself on the floor of her bedroom by the breakdown of a long-used couch; the loss of their father distressed the daughters as much as if they had, as usual, come downstairs to enjoy the front porch and had found the front porch gone. Mother and children looked upon mortality in this instance as a sweeping miscarriage of the reliable; they would cheerfully wear mourning as a tribute to themselves.

A new minister in the town (Lexington) who has been secured to preach the sermon is puzzled by the indifference of the relatives and friends. He glosses over his ignorance of the dead man's obvious failure by choosing to talk of the alabaster box and to exhort his audience "not to withhold the expression of our love from the living."

On the way to the cemetery Allen takes us inside various conveyances and lets us overhear the conversations about the sermon and the dead man, and shortly we realize that we are reading one of the most profoundly sad and most profoundly disillusioned things we have read in so small a compass. I do not, indeed, know of anything sadder in American literature. "The Alabaster Box" chants a dirge for passing, well-intentioned, futile humanity which is often defeated by the very innocence of its desires and the strength of its aspirations. Listen to the child rebuke its mother unwittingly and then ask the disturbing question: "Mamma, where do they keep alabaster boxes?" Listen to the frankly cynical conclusions of the four ladies, the heartbreaking worldliness of the four children, the angry cry of the gentleman who wanted to know: "Could they not have shown the decency to stay away and let him be borne through the town as neglected as he lived?" and who goes on to philosophize that if we do someone a kind act once he is thankful but that if we go on doing kindnesses to him he comes to look upon it as the performance of a duty. Ponder the town minister's reply to the charge that the dead man was a hypocrite: "No man dare practice with his fellow men the whole of the virtue that is in him." Finally two older men give us Allen's comment upon the indifference felt for the dead man: he had belonged to an age which knew and practised kindness but he had outlived that age and was being mocked by people of a new order, even though they had accepted his assistance. "You and I know," exclaims one, "that once there did exist such a virtue in the American people—American kindness!" That had been the trouble with Robert: he "came too late to be understood. The southerners are not the people they were." To which the other replies drearily: "Yes, too late. The Americans are not the people they were."

The dead man was, of course, not Robert but James Lane Allen. There can be no doubt that he was here projecting himself into the future, dramatizing his exit from life, and conjuring up comments which he anticipated might be made over his coffin. The revulsion against being stared at when dead was his own. When he dictated the last sentence: "His patient, his old-time Southerner, his old-stock American, had found and had finished his journey on the ancient ascending road" he knew that he had been writing if not of himself then of a phantom that walked pretty close to his side. "The Alabaster Box" he made to end in courageous vein, with a plea that all of us give the best not only to ourselves but also to our fellow travelers and that the descendants of the "old stock" of Americans should unite solidly to preserve the institutions of our country, but no brave twist at the end could conceal the dejection which inspired most of the pages. That dejection originated in Allen's knowledge, slowly and painfully acquired, that the crowd is not even conscious of the principles by which a gentleman lives and that because of its ignorance it can do nothing else than misunderstand the man to whom those principles are more than bread and meat.

The author of "The Alabaster Box" did not realize how prophetically he had written; the attractive purple-and-silver-bound copy of the story was the last of his books that he held in his hand. He saw one more of his stories in black and white. "The Violet" holds another unique place in Allen's history inasmuch as it was the only one of his printed works— if we except the letters from England which appear in *The Emblems of Fidelity*—that laid its scene in whole or in part

on foreign soil. It begins badly. The rise of the Bolsheviks
and the formation of the Union of Soviet Republics had sent
Allen to the reading of Russian history and there he had
come upon what Henry James would have called the "wind-
blown grain of sand," but because he was unsure of his scene
he selected descriptive details clumsily and with a too apparent effort to wash in a background, thereby giving an
amateurish effect to his attempt to set the stage for his sentry
who was to guard for the Empress Catherine the first violet
of spring. Allen did not know Russia, and no mention of
the size of the Imperial Palace, of Catherine's morals, or of
kvas, meod, caviar, and *klouvka* could hide his ignorance;
rather it called attention to his setting up of cardboard props.
In the first draft of the story he did make a tired effort at a
word-picture of the sentry's life on his father's farm, but this
was fortunately cut from the manuscript sent to the editor of
Harper's. As the tale progresses it improves vastly; the
passion of the two chief actors comes as a surprise, and the
grim background of forest, absolute power and absolute obe-
dience, and of the innocent little Grand Duchesses seems
like a Greek chorus to comment upon the darkly inevitable
action of the plot. Because the ending is inevitable it is easily
foreseen and correctly placed, and if we could but believe in
Leon and his sweetheart "The Violet" would be one of
Allen's triumphs. But they overstrain credulity. The wanton coquetry, the wanton jealousy, and the wanton cruelty
of Kyra can be readily accepted, as can the fear and courage
and fatalism of Leon, but otherwise both are represented as
too high-minded and too quick in conversation for people of
their class. Had the guardsman been a bit more stolid and
considerably less gifted with insight, had the serving-maid
been a bit less shrewd and somewhat more commonplace
each would have contributed a missing reality to the clash
between Slav steadfastness and gypsy caprice. Nevertheless

Harper's thought well enough of "The Violet" to give it a place of honor and a handsome colored plate after a painting by Sigismond de Ivanowski.

On the fifth of September, 1924, President George Brett of the Macmillan Company wrote to Allen, apropos the publication of a volume of short stories which was to be *The Landmark,* that he thought the Kentuckian's "the best work that has been offered to the American public, being, in fact, the only American work of classic value which is offered to the American public in these days." Moved by this tribute and by a surmise of the shortness of life left him, Allen decided to have Macmillan publish a volume comprising the stories we have just discussed (without, of course, *The Alabaster Box,* which had already been published by Harper) and two more, which had not yet been given to a printer. The hope for the great novel was thus tacitly abandoned. That hope he had finally put into an outline which he set down in his own hand:

A Pilgrim to His Youth
And Other Stories

———

Part First
A Pilgrim to His Youth
A Pilgrim to the Frontier (A Family
    Episode in the Days of Our Fathers)
Part Second
The Little Third Person
The Ashcan
Miss Locke
Part Third
An Irony of Heaven
A White House Ghost
La Tendresse

Of these stories "The Ash-Can" and "Miss Locke" had been printed under those titles; "An Irony of Heaven" was probably "Heaven's Little Ironies"; "La Tendresse" was in manuscript, awaiting publication; and "A Pilgrim to the Frontier" doubtless became "The Landmark," the title which was given to the first story in the last volume; "A White House Ghost" may have been the unfinished "Socrates in the White House." The remaining tales were never written.

"The Landmark" is a combination of the old and the new Allen. Its theme is akin to that of *The Mettle of the Pasture*. Indeed, the two titles meant to Allen the same thing: the mystic seal, the stamp of character set upon the Kentuckian, dweller in "the most beautiful pastures of the new world." This is their landmark—*The Passion of the Pastures and Their Story*—that is, the fortitude and suffering of Kentucky settlers who were made men by that which they had to endure and face. It is that mark which Thomas Worthington tries to define and describe to his ne'er-do-well son as he sends him west to redeem himself from the newly-risen vices in Lexington. "Every man of them," he says inflexibly, alluding to the pioneers, "stood on his own feet, stood by his own guns, cut his own path, sinned his own sins, cursed no other man for his failure." Side by side with this admiration for individualism is Allen's expression of the idea that Nature is salutary in its manifestations and that only man is vile; here, too, is the phrase about "the pariahs of the public road" to apply to the women of the town, and the clause "one who walked the earth in purity" to apply to the virtuous mother; finally there is the remark that "when manners begin to leave a man, something of what was best in his character has already left him." These are echoes of things we have heard in earlier books. The detailed and leisurely telling of the story also recalls the earlier Allen, and the account of a household divided against itself might have been written at the time of *The Bride of the Mistletoe*. The air of "The Landmark" is one of Georgian stateliness and elegance covering disunion, shame, and outraged parenthood; that, too, is Allen of old. But the note of disenchantment and dejection belongs to the new Allen. "Tragedy in one guise or another," he writes, "stalks unhindered past every well-set barrier and enters and stands beside us at the hearthstones of our felicity ere we have begun to smile." No other sentence declares so decisively the distance he had traveled since the time when in the last century he had held that life was "neither agnostic nor pessimistic."

"La Tendresse" fitly rounds out *The Landmark* and brings an end to Allen's writing. No one who knows his history can read it without a quiver of sadness, for nothing is sadder than the restrained pining of a brave man who has been hurt beyond healing. Old and lonely and all but defeated, with the end of his life and the end of his money all too visible, he groped his way back to the time when he had been victorious in a world of youth and sunshine and flowers—he returned to the girl-wife of Adam Moss. She had died in 1895, twenty-nine years before, and it is of unquestioned significance that now as he heard the approaching footsteps of the inevitable Visitor he should have brought Georgiana back with his pen. Was it because she was his favorite among his heroines? Or was he trying to touch the "mystic chords of memory" and remind an indifferent public of what he had once done? Or because there was a real Georgiana whom he had never forgotten, to whom he had clung tenaciously in a world of shadows? Perhaps all of these questions should be answered affirmatively; certainly the first one can, but only James Lane Allen could have replied authoritatively to the third. Georgiana became to him, at any rate, the symbol of lost loveliness; as such he recalled her, and in this last of his stories folded her and Adam Moss to his heart. They were two who would never offend him, never cool toward him, never disappoint him. "La Tendresse" is the briefest of epilogues for a long literary career. In two short scenes Georgiana begs Charon for news of her husband: does he work in the garden now? she wants to know. Not now, Charon tells her. Then surely he walks in the fields he loved—the autumn fields? And Charon's reply is: "He walks in the fields, thinking, remembering, hoping." And so was Allen walking in the fields of his labors, walking and thinking and remembering and hoping—hoping for reunion with someone, with his Georgiana? Was the thrilling cry which brings "La Tendresse" to an end the greeting which he hoped presently to hear? We shall never know. A few rare people do cherish such secrets.

It must not be supposed that during these lean years James Lane Allen presented a funereal face to the world, that he made overt efforts to obtain sympathy, or that any one looking at him would have thought of him as pathetic. He was as erect and dignified as ever. His eye could still control discourtesy or hostility, and his last photograph shows a face as stern and military as that of a Prussian field-marshall. He was careful with his money, it is true, but he had never been prodigal; had, in fact, been credited by many as being a bit discouraging as a lender or giver. And so no one outside his bank knew that his capital had shrunken to little more than ten thousand dollars and that by 1924 he was obliged to borrow money on his securities. For the most part he went on living as before, quiet and apart, not suffering from the lack of any material comfort but denied the assurance that his name had not been writ in water; a man who did not blink the fact that in some way he had always been estranged from the world. His self-imposed isolation did not spring from a reluctance to endure morons gladly Like the idealist Plato described he had long felt that th

wisest course for him was to crouch, as it were, behind a stone
wall and let the loud resistless wind, which he could not stop
or moderate, blow overhead. This attitude, so characteristic
of him, was not a matter of priggishness. "We do not yet
see that virtue is Height," wrote Emerson in "Self-Reliance,"
and what the world has also not yet learned is that men who
like Allen covet the noblest virtue sometimes take on a lofti-
ness which is no proclamation of superiority but which arises
quite naturally from their residence on the Height. The instinct of the uncomprehending is always to sneer at these
dwellers upon the Height. The crowd never understands—
if, indeed, it ever reads—the lines which Lionel Johnson
wrote of Pater but which might as well have been written for
Allen:

> Oh, golden patience of the travailing soul
>> So hungered for the goal,
> And vowed to keep, through subtly vigilant pain,
>> From pastime on the plain,
> Enamoured of the difficult mountain air
>> Up Beauty's Hill of Prayer!
> Stern is the faith of art, right stern, and he
>> Loved her severity.

He did not always breathe the rarefied air of Olympus.
There were occasions when he shared rather surprisingly the
emotions of the man in the street. This was true throughout
the war with the Central Powers. It was true in 1921 when
Georges Carpentier invaded the United States with the hope
of carrying to France the heavyweight championship of the
world, for Allen, along with most newspaper readers, wel-
comed the invader, finding in him, as they thought, an intelligence and a grace which they wished to see succeed over the
ignorance and brute strength of the Manassa Mauler, who
was, moreover, condemned for alleged shirking during the
war. Allen was one of the many disappointed when Jack

Dempsey disposed quite easily of the opponent who angered him by one hard blow; it looked as though the lower type was forever destined to triumph over the higher. Also in 1921 he was as much delighted with Centre College's defeat of Harvard as he was with the request of the Sorbonne for a set of his works; the victory of the little Kentucky college, gladdening all Kentuckians, came as a kind of long-postponed overthrow of the boastful Yankee and the 6-0 score became a posthumous offering to the gray-clad men who had died for the Lost Cause. Another common touch is supplied by his faith in the now-forgotten philosopher Coué, who in 1923 was instructing Americans to believe themselves getting better and better every day and in every way. More stimulating than the Gallic visitor was Allen's knowledge that he had outlived James and Howells, that old as he was he still had no difficulty in getting his stories accepted and published. The old masters, he complacently reminded a few of his friends, had not been so fortunate; they had been left behind more decisively than he. But this cause for self-gratulation could not bridge the chasm of the future. His sister and he could no longer live on his investments and he knew, hard as it was to face the fact, that his day of great earning was over. Not many months away stood the ghosts of humilia-tion and want. How many months away, was the question. How long would he be compelled to accept the issue of making ends meet? He worried silently, lost sleep, then developed chronic insomnia.

One evening he had a terrifying experience. Walking along the street he suddenly realized that all noise had ceased. There was the constant stream of traffic—trolley cars, automobiles, mortorcycles, a constant shuffling procession of human beings. But he heard no bells, no escape from ex-haust pipes, no murmur and mutter and roar, no horns and shouts. Hastily he stepped into a Childs restaurant and seated himself at a table; the place was crowded and he should have heard the normal sounds of conversation and laughter and clinking dishes. But his ears were sealed. Presently they opened and his hearing was as it should have been. Shaken, he consulted his physician, who knew that a small clot had temporarily formed in his patient's brain and who prescribed complete rest. And so just a few days before his birthday and before Christmas in 1924 Allen went to the Roosevelt Hospital. He was listless about Christmas. The sight of gifts and letters pleased him, but he toyed nervelessly with unopened packages and had little curiosity about the contents of the missives. What was Christmas now to him— that season which had inspired the writing of his much-censured trilogy? The doctors agreed that he had no specific illness unless a state of general collapse could be called specific. The body had served the mind as long as it was able. Now it was, said one doctor, like the filament of an electric light globe that slowly cools and darkens.

As the brain became starved for lack of blood because of impeded circulation his thoughts began to arrange themselves incoherently. Sometimes he seemed to hear such music as John Gray had heard while he lay convalescing from illness. Once he said to Mr. Granberry: "The wonders of scientific development are amazing! How is it music can be made to come from behind that picture? Sometimes it comes from the bureau—and it is of such lovely quality! I had to get up and examine that picture to see if any mechanism had been installed behind it, but the music evidently does not depend on any special installation. I wonder if all the rooms of the hospital have the same arrangement." At another time he told his friend that he had been deceived for a few minutes into believing that musicians were concealed behind the screen in his room, but had found upon examination that he had been listening to the same marvelous contrivance. Again, he reported that the authorities had had the great kindness to arrange for his sister to speak to him in the same way, and her voice had come to him distinctly and naturally. He now and then spoke, in these moments of hallucination, of historical events as though they were taking place before his eyes and once or twice he felt that he was responsible for some of the action. Social affairs, the episodes of his life, purely personal matters, the achievements of literature lost all chronology and perspective during these irrational intervals, which were interrupted by long periods when he was wholly normal. Twice he spoke of plans for his funeral as though he were already dead, and he commanded that his face should be covered and not seen after he had left the land of living men. Contrary to a previously settled agreement he now urged Mr. Granberry to take Annie back to Lexington, where she might end her days among her people. No matter how confused he otherwise was he remained clear upon one point: his body was to be taken back to Lexington and placed in the cemetery chapel with no lying in state, no opening of the casket, no display of any kind, and with no one to accompany it but this man whom he had chosen as his literary executor and who remained with him to the last. Music, Annie, the code of the gentleman—these hovered about his deathbed. But his sister was present only as the music was present, for she was herself so seriously ill that she survived him only twelve days and died without knowing her brother had preceded her into whatever lies beyond.

On the fifteenth of February James Lane Allen passed into a coma which ended in his death three days later. George Folsom Granberry closed his eyes and drew the sheet over the white face. His body was brought to Lexington and there on a stormy Saturday morning, the twenty-first of February, 1925, it was interred beside his parents and his uncl John Allen.

Naturally, his passing made no such stir as it would have made in 1905 or even 1915. Leading newspapers carried stories of his career and made polite comments upon his writings. John Finley wrote a fine and sympathetic tribute for the *New York Times* which moved Joseph Gilder, who long ago had angered Allen by criticizing *The Choir Invisible*, to write a letter to the same paper, touching upon the time of Allen's introduction to the New York public through the columns of *The Critic*. The passage in "A Cathedral Singer" which prophesies the growth of the Cathedral of St. John the Divine was given to the air over Station WJZ. The *Boston Transcript* dealt kindly with the posthumous "The Landmark." And then the ripples made by his personality widened and widened until they reached the distant shore of history.

Perhaps James Lane Allen would have liked best of all to have had quoted over his grave those words from *Hamlet* of which he was so fond, that mournful valedictory of Horatio over the dead Prince of Denmark:

Goodnight, sweet prince,
And flights of angels sing thee to thy rest!

CHAPTER VII

THE LANDMARK

It would be folly to try to stretch James Lane Allen into the stature of a giant or to claim for him a seat among the mighty. It would be equally foolish to insist that his laurels, faded since the turn of the century, can by any magic of literary horticulture be restored to their early freshness. But it would also be unwise or dishonest for an historian of our literature to fail to record that those laurels once sat securely upon his head and that their greenness gave no augury of a change to the sere and yellow. Though the historian may be confident that Allen will never again be considered first-rate he must nevertheless realize that this minor novelist must be examined by anyone who wishes to understand our national taste in letters during the period extending from 1890 to 1914. As a differentiated member of the local color group, as a writer of short stories that are still included in anthologies, as a channel through which certain foreign impulses toward realism found their way into our literature, as a one-time very popular novelist, as a man who battled with courage and sometimes with single hand against the adversities of this world and an almost complete change in his country's mores, and, finally, as an outstanding champion of what is now alluded to with deprecation as the Genteel Tradition, James Lane Allen deserves and will repay close study and sympathetic interpretation. And the end of such an examination will lead the impartial reader to see that if Allen was overpraised in the nineties, and unfortunately so, since it delayed for long his emancipation from writing too localized and too sentimental, he is underpraised by the present, whose dogmatic young critics unwillingly lay a wreath upon the tombs of the recently dead. To be impatient with the near-past is the first law of a young prophet.

The preceding chapters have made clear the respect in which Allen's work was held for two decades. Over and over it was said by reviewers good, bad, and indifferent that he was to be ranked next to Hawthorne, that he was the aristocrat of living American writers, that his style was the purest and most distinguished to be found among his contemporaries. Nor were these opinions affected to any considerable extent by the mercantile success of Allen's books; the tributes are almost invariably given to the care with which Allen went over the battlefields on which are fought the struggles of the soul and to the manner in which he reported his observations and deductions, the manner especially in which he pictured a mystic union between the terrain of that battlefield and the issues thereupon to be decided. If the critics of that day had praised merely the best-selling books they would have given their most glowing adjectives to *In His Steps*. Allen was rarely complimented upon his purely narrative ability. Nobody proclaimed that his characters resembled those met in barber shops or canebrakes or that he was able to maintain that suspense which keeps the reader on the edge of a chair, or that the conversations he set down were such as one might overhear on Fifth Avenue or Broadway or even on Main Street in Lexington. It will be seen upon examination, therefore, that the qualities for which he was once most commended are the very ones for which he is nowadays most heartily condemned, for recent chroniclers of American literature are prone to dismiss Allen lightly with unfavorable mention of his sentimentality in registering the manners of a bygone day, of the unreality with which he invested the people in his books. Because he made the public shed tears over Mrs. Falconer's renunciation or Georgiana's death he is today called maudlin and neurotic, and because he introduced into his pages some men and women who lived and had their beings on a lofty plane of honor he is today called unfailingly romantic. The fate which he foresaw has overtaken him as it overtakes—and this should give pause even to cocksure critics—all writers except the very greatest: he was of one generation but is sentenced by another. It is our duty as we take our place on the judgment seat to listen to the testimony presented by each generation, to ponder the worth of this testimony, and to speculate upon the possibility of a higher court's reversal of our decision.

The first accusation to be weighed—because it resounds so loudly in our courtroom—is that of sentimentality; that is, an overemphasis upon the emotional, a susceptibility to feelings which are given an exaggerated value.   Allen, it is charged, endowed his heroes and heroines with this vice, deliberately appealed to its presence among his readers in the hope of gaining their approval, and made his style the engine of his intent.   It was even said by younger men that his state of mind was effeminate, that he was personally effeminate; that he had a fondness for scenes and speeches of unnecessary tenderness; that he was partial to melancholy partings and deathbeds.   His best-known heroes and heroines, they point out, came to tragic ends: Father Palemon died because his soul was tortured beyond endurance; the same was true of Sister Dolorosa; John Gray and Mrs. Falconer never confessed their love because she was married to an other; Georgiana died after childbirth; Rowan Meredith died in expiation of a heedless sin; Ashby Truesdale was killed by an automobile; Doctor Birney's son died that his parents might be brought together.   All his fiction, more over, is in a minor key; everywhere we hear the note of sad ness, the plaintive airs of flute and violin.   Even *The Em blems of Fidelity* leaves one with the doleful feeling that hu man affections are transient and often the sport of irrelevant forces. As for *The Last Christmas Tree* and *The Alabaster Box*—they are of the most desperate things written by our countrymen.

Now for a writer to make use of death and defeat is not to brand himself a sentimentalist unless we change our definition of sentimentality. No one has indicted Sophocles or Aeschylus or Shakespeare or Thomas Hardy on the grounds of sentimentality. On the other hand, death as found in *The Old Curiosity Shop* or *East Lynne* is certainly made the basis for calling Dickens and Mrs. Henry Wood sentimental, and it is our business to decide whether when Allen brings about the downfall of his protagonists he is more like the first-mentioned writers or more like the remaining two. What is precisely the distinction, so far as literary standards go, between the death of Tess of the D'Urbervilles, which is a moving scene, and the death of Little Nell, which is also a moving scene? The brief answer is that the execution of Tess gives us that catharsis of pity and terror which tragedy always supplies and that the passing of Little Nell leaves us only an impermanent grief, like the brief perfume of a flower, because one so young and sweet should thus be cut off. If we are parents we are especially stirred, apprehensive lest our children be taken from us. We may even as we read wipe our eyes or cheeks furtively with our handkerchiefs, for to be seen weeping would be acknowledgment that *we* are sentimental. It is quite probable that Thackeray wept as he read of Little Nell's demise—he was not ashamed of his emotions. It is quite probable that Dickens wept as he wrote the scene with the memory of Mary Hogarth to inspire him, and that he enjoyed weeping. It would not be surprising to learn that he hoped we would enjoy weeping over the deathbed, and that in order to heighten our enjoyment of our tears and to give a full outlet to his grief he elected to write in dithyrambics that today sound perilously like burlesque. There is, of course, no pensive necrophilia in *Tess*. The last of the D'Urbervilles is no fair-haired and innocent child snatched from our midst by the Grim Reaper so that we may water her grave with tears out of which "some good is born, some gentler nature comes." She is instead the symbol of man's eternal struggle to be virtuous and of man's eternal and inevitable overthrow in that struggle by forces over which neither he nor anyone else has any authority, by a relentless Chance which rules all things by the simple expedient of neglecting to rule them. Hardy does not lay hold upon our hearts with determined hands as Tess is led to the gallows; he assumes no lyrical prose to arouse our lamentations for a girl who never meant to do ill; he mentions with a dreadful austerity the flying of a black flag and leaves us stunned, shuddering at the impotence of the human race in the face of "the President of the Immortals." Here is grandeur which no one could be irreverent enough to parody.

If we ask ourselves, then, which of these writers Allen resembles the more closely the answer is that he mingled the tragic with the merely pathetic, that he sometimes gathered into his characters that brave and long-enduring suffering in the eyes of destiny, that assertion of human arrogance even as the lightning flashes, that makes for tragic situation, but that sometimes he surrendered to the fashion and wrote only to make our eyes grow moist. Father Palemon and Sister Dolorosa had a passion for God and had sworn vows to him; they also knew passion and longing for human beings of the opposite sex; and because they were caught in that trap of conflict between two of the fiercest of human aspirations they stand before us today as truly tragic figures. The sentry in "The Violet" is likewise the victim of the war between duty and love, and his fate acquires some of this grandeur by the very triviality which brings it about. The two sets of families in the Christmas triology are dimly tragic because the are entangled in a net which they helped to weave and from which they are powerless to escape. John Gray and Mrs. Falconer are faintly tragic because they were parted by a code which made it impossible for either to speak of the heart's desire. The dead man in "The Alabaster Box" was the last advocate of an old order and thus genuinely tragic.

On the other hand, the death of David in *Flute and Violin* fails to touch us because there was nothing in the story to make such an end unavoidable and we know that it came only to set fire to our sympathies, not to satisfy our logic. The decline of Georgiana is pathetic and handled with a restraint that forbids us to cry out on its sentimentality; Rowan Meredith's punishment might have been tragic were it not that we also refuse to believe in its inevitability—it is contributed, we see, to afford another object lesson in virtue and morality; the Birney child is likewise carried off by the author's providence rather than by nature; and the running down of Ashby Truesdale is, in spite of its attempt to sharpen another of life's little ironies, sheer melodrama.

It is obvious, then, that at least half of Allen's climaxes are sentimental, and that others come close to the border between what is in a twilight mood and what is tragic. Often the style by its raising or lowering of effects serves to plunge the scene into the first or elevate it into the second. The sentimentalist always gives himself away by his style, because in it he doth protest too much either for sweetness and light or for the cult of the hard-boiled, and Allen showed from *Flute and Violin* to *The Landmark* a censurable tendency to stick sable plumes upon his phrases or to bedeck them with chaplets of daisies. It was his style, as we have seen, modelled upon English classics and therefore graceful, unhurried, elegant, fastidious. If we selected a color to describe it that color would be lavender; if we compared it to a material texture we should call it brocaded tapestry; if we likened it to music, as Allen might have wished, we should say that it never sounded a shrill note, that it occasionally had the exquisite mournfulness of Chopin's piano, sometimes the majestic diapason of Tchaikowsky's orchestra. Almost never does Allen give the impression of having written spontaneously and easily. The reason is that he did not write spontaneously and easily; each turn of clause, each disposition of phrase was the result of a labored process of selection and rejection, of weighing and almost tasting and smelling words. Very much like his spine Allen's written pages are inflexible; there was a correct way to do a thing and there was a precise way to write of a thing, and any deviation in either instance was an immorality. The classicist's passion for perfection had been supplemented by Flaubert's philosophy of *le mot juste*, and Allen felt the impact of both teachings. Once he jotted down some memoranda on the demands upon a stylist who, he thought, should have:

1. Enormous and ever ready vocabulary of classic English words.
2. Ear for music.
3. Sincerity of nature; love of truth.
4. Clarity of intellectual process—logic.

The significance of the demand for "classic English words" is self-evident, and with respect to readiness of vocabulary Allen boasted that in all his writing he never used a dictionary.

For over a decade this conscientious classicism in style covered a multitude of sins in sentiment; indeed, the sentimental dressing added to the pleasures of Allen's earlier readers. In those days if one failed to be carried on by Allen's recital of events he could at least delight in the swing of his cadences and the sheen of his diction. The English public especially found a reminiscent joy in his writing, and they have kept that joy longer than we have, although not every American, fortunately, has succumbed to the lure of these syncopated styles which seek an affinity with jazz. In 1907 *The Academy* in a three-and-a-half-page analysis of Allen's place voiced contemporary English opinion by stating that "irrespective of the scenes among which his novels are planned, which are not germane to the literary effect, he possesses exactly the daintiness of prose which promised well in Mr. Le Gallienne, rendered, however, permanent and homogeneous by a virility and purpose for which we may search the work of the latter author in vain." And also: "The very first impression gained by a discriminating reader of his books, we imagine, would be one of dignity and purity in the language." In 1912 Brentano's *Book Chat* was willing to say that "his style is so distinguished for its urbanity and dignity, that the man possessing it could have lived nowhere else than with the gentlemen of letters," and while this is too vague to be of importance as a critical statement it does deliver to us a useful word—gentlemanly. Allen's style was gentlemanly. It was well-bred, decorous, shapely. It was studiously correct. It was sometimes too serious. But it was never vulgar, flashy, or cheap. He did not stuff our mouths with rose petals. He did not indulge in too much imagery, and he avoided that supreme fault of the stylist who has little to say, that of substituting epithets and appositives for ideas. Nor did he abuse our hearing by the firing of conversational cartridges like Meredith's.

Today Allen's style is condemned. It is called ornate, sentimental, artificial. It is alleged that he was in bondage to rhetoric; that he confused the life that he should have reported with the making of phrases by which he sought to report it; that, in short, he gave us not literature but belles-lettres. In answer to these accusations Allen's advocate can do nothing else than throw his client upon the mercy of the

254 JAMES LANE ALLEN

court. Too often Allen piled up his adjectives; too often he told his stories in words whose gravity and chastity displease present readers. Not always so, however: *Summer in Arcady* is sparely and energetically written, and *The Reign of Law* and *The Mettle of the Pasture* move forward with spirit, albeit the momentum fails somewhat toward the close of the last volume. *A Kentucky Cardinal* sparkles with vitality. But let us admit that the other books are guilty in one way or another of the stylistic faults preferred against them; they do offer an elegance that sometimes becomes a little wearisome and they have a tendency to break out of bounds and become sentimental in diction. *The Bookman* in 1930 said of these stories that they dripped "saccharine sweetness," and when one finds Allen describing a blind man in *The Heroine in Bronze* as "a stranger smitten with eyes of perpetual night" he has simply found a characteristic touch which persuades him that he cannot acquit Allen of this much-pressed indictment. One such descriptive touch is almost enough to brand an author.

Nevertheless, it must always be remembered that we do not judge Allen fairly unless we become his contemporaries, unless we realize that he was writing in a tradition and for a public that can today scarcely be said to exist. It is best to write for the future—great masters do—but it is no sin to write for one's own time. American literature inevitably changes its manners as and when the American people change theirs, and we dare not forget that Allen wrote for people more leisurely, more demonstrative of their feelings, more devoted to politeness than we are. English and American writers of the eighteenth and nineteenth centuries addressed themselves on the whole to cultivated readers, but in the twentieth century, thanks to rapid presses, cheap paper, and universal education, writers must keep in mind that their audience, whatever its schooling or numbers, is made up of a few cultured people and a great mass of uneducated or half-educated individuals who do not know what elegance is and who will tolerate no measure of its display. Especially do we lack what is conveniently called the education of the heart. We crave the sensational not only in incident but also in language; we feed upon the raucous, the jazzy, the gruesome, the baroque, irreverent, and profane. We become easily fatigued in trying to follow Meredith or James—or Allen—because we have allowed our minds to stay shallow. We demand snappy tabloid stories retailed in snappy tabloid conversation and action. The precision, the expertness, the power with which an old-fashioned writer could marshal his words strike us as being histrionic, affected, and dull. "Why doesn't he say right out what he is trying to say?" we cry vexedly. We object that he is giving marble from an Attic quarry when we asked for a sandwich from a filling-station. We turn to a William Faulkner with the conviction that we are passing from a language so unfamiliar that it scarcely seems English to a vocabulary which, if not entirely ours, is patently contemporary and lifted from some cross-section of our country. But all we have done is to acknowledge again that other times bring other manners. Elliptical, breathless, crackling, demoralized styles are completely justified in the 1920's and 1930's, but why do we not add, not only that Allen's style was completely justified by *his* time but also that it remains to be proved that recent writing is any better; that is, clearer, more vivid, *more successful in accomplishing its ends?* Young novelists derive their styles from the tempo of a bewildered and chaotic age. Allen's style flowed calmly from a fountain of eighteenth-century rationalism which identified whatever was with what was right. That is the heart of the distinction between them.

The same defense can and must be advanced for Allen's characterizations. They are called unreal, exaggerated, such ladies and gentlemen as never lived on land or sea. They are snubbed as sentimental. Always this contempt for sentimentality! It needs examination, for it is symptomatic of changed tastes. Allen's men and women conceive of love as a divine rapture that might very well last forever, that is chiefly spiritual in quality; they are loyal to themselves and each other; they weep when they feel like weeping and they laugh when they are happy; they believe that they are small by contrast with what were called the eternal verities, that truth and honor and chastity were paramount to the desires of the individual. And for this they are derided as sentimental and unreal. This question of characterization is so closely allied to the entire matter of the Genteel Tradition that we shall postpone further discussion for a few pages, but let us note that late in his life, while he was working upon *A Pilgrim to His Youth,* Allen denied that he had idealized the aristocrats of the old order. "It has become," he wrote, "the duty of the American historian to insist that they are not among the romances of memory; they were a reality of their day." Nor is he unsupported in throwing out this challenge. He is backed up, of course, by many romantic novels and tales of ante-bellum days, and even if we reject these fictions as too highly tinted we should set down in their favor that they are singularly unanimous in their point of view with respect to the old gentility and that where there is so much smoke there is likely to be some flame. Histories, memoirs, biographies, letters corroborate Allen's statement. The reason so many of his men and women seem to us nothing but the adumbrations of an old, lonely, and sentimental gentleman is that the types he pictured are now nearly extinct.

An impartial opinion, indeed, must give Allen some credit instead of all blame for creating these characters and for writing of them as he did. If he wrote sentimentally it was because he was sentimental—what healthy, normal person is not?—and not because he pretended to be. If his people are easily stirred, if they shed tears over situations which we of today with inverted sentimentality face with a cynical laugh, if they are emotional, generous, high-minded—if they are all these things and more, just wherein did Allen err or wherefore is he to be condemned? Read the histories. The generations he wrote about were sentimental and quickly moved, and many representatives of them were high-minded to a degree which is to their descendants amusingly innocent. The gallery of daguerreotypes which Allen exhibited constitutes, even though the features are touched up, an addition to social history; we get arresting details of dress and gesture and lineament. What Harry A. Toulmin called Allen's "noble delineations of a noble race, his touching revelations of unknown phases of Kentucky life and manners" must be examined by anyone who wishes to write a history of the South or to understand that the spirit of the Bluegrass was not so violent as publicity often made it. Nor does that element of its spirit which we are now inspecting deserve mockery. Every human being has also his inalienable right to mood and temperament. We do not cavil when Dostoevsky's or Chekhov's protagonists weep over small misadventures or brood upon their souls. We excuse them because they are Slavs and we feel comfortably superior inasmuch as we can resent tearfulness on the part of the Anglo-Saxon. Yet if the southerner of Allen's day took less pains to conceal his feelings than we do—and history proves that to be true—then was Allen not as justified in making them sentimental or introspective? To give literary treatment to his section he had to do just that. And it is to be added that not all of his men and women were perfect in behavior and character; he did not violate too far the modesties of nature.

Nothing gave Allen more trouble than the construction

of plots that would be ingenious, interesting, and persuasive, and in nothing else is his lack of mastery more apparent. Most of his fiction evolved like Hawthorne's from a moral concept or the posing of a moral problem, and Allen's difficulty lay in transferring that morality from the realm of speculation to the purlieus of action. He could plan the course of action in a general way, fit the characters and words to it, foresee the outcome, but he had little facility in the invention of incident, and so he was obliged to rely heavily upon the escape *motif* or the test *motif*. Since the world in those days might be well lost for love, that passion was the one that set most of his plots in motion; man and woman must be drawn to each other, but not blindly, for a recognized question of ethics is almost always entangled with their attachment to complicate it. Love, obstacle (rarely more than one), solution (happy or unhappy)—this was his formula, but it left large gaps which had to be filled in the event the narrative was to be a novel. The beloved was to be won and held only if the male proved worthy and the proof were established through a test. Will Father Palemon remain true to his vows as a monk? Will Hillary betray the trust Daphne has in him? Will David conform by adopting a religion in which he no longer believes? Can Rowan Meredith atone for a sin of the flesh? Should Professor Ousley pretend a domesticity he no longer feels? Can Donald Clough resist his sweetheart's interference with his career? Such are the fulcra upon which his plots turn, but they do not swing far in any direction. The constant recurrence of the test *motif* demonstrates a narrowness of experience, an absence of originality, and the longer his books become the more obvious are the limitations, the thinner the story. The number of his words has little or nothing to do with his effect upon our imagination, and we can remember Miss Locke much more readily than we can any of the young ladies of *The Mettle c the Pasture.* Characters he did not repeat as he did the favorite crux of his plots but he displayed no wide range of characterization.

Because of the slackness of his power to contrive incident and to create a variety of characters he was more at ease in the short story than in the novel, and there is accidental but gratifying justice in the fact that his career began with *Flute and Violin* and ended with *The Landmark,* as there is justice in the fact that anthologies still include something from his group of early short fiction and that magazines still reprint them; justice, too, in the view of Henry van Dyke, privately expressed in 1930, that "I still regard him as one of the most distinguished American writers in the art of the short story." Professor Fred Lewis Pattee wrote in *The Development of the American Short Story:* "He [Allen] studied the art of fiction as the musician studies the organ. . . . He sought to deepen the channel of the short story, and he sought also to give to the form the literary distinction it had in the days of Irving and Hawthorne. The promise of his first volume impressed all who reviewed it." Unfortunately, Professor Pattee's book was published before Allen returned to the short story, so that our authority on that type of fiction had been led to believe Allen's career as finished so far as the short story went. Something must therefore be added to what Mr. Pattee said in 1915.

The short story may very loosely be said to fall into three classes. The first is literature in its most primitive sense; that is, it is concerned mainly with the relation of a happening; its business is to interest us by the play of action and by our doubt as to the successful outcome of the hero's enterprises. To this class belong all the thousand and one varieties of the tale of mystery and adventure which regales our lighter moments of escape from a workaday world. The second class has something to say; it was not written to entertain, to enthrall, or to excite by the use of physical conflict but rather to interpret some aspect of life in general, to throw some light upon the dark places of the human soul, to multiply our personalities by adding to them the vicarious experiences of others who have fought some inward battle. To this class belong, for example, the magnificent stories of Anton Chekhov, which sometimes seem to have almost no action at all but which do capture and hold up to our scrutiny significant moments in the history of some being, unimportant though he may have been. The third class combines the first two, giving us at once colorful action and a comment upon the mysteries of the world in which we live, and of this type are the equally magnificent "Heart of Darkness" and "Youth" of Joseph Conrad.

Without exception Allen's short stories fall into the second class, which is one reason they have survived. For the ensnaring of a significant moment in human experience he possessed a quick eye, nimble fingers, and that refinement of feeling and imagination which we sometimes call intuition. In the short story he had much less difficulty in securing and maintaining his point of view; his humor was more pliable, more easily adjusted to the length of the narrative; his sentimentality less likely to offend; his carefulness less likely to become too apparent. He was happiest in the short story. The very conscientiousness with which he wrote made the composition of a novel an irksome strain, especially since he had a tendency to verbiage and irrelevancy. For reasons doubtless connected with the limits of his nervous endurance he preferred the novelette form. His papers show how meticulously he worked. Did he write about birds he first read up in ornithology, and similarly he would prepare himself on trees, the past of the Hudson valley, the essential geographical, social, and historical data necessary to the presentation of any locality, even that of Lexington. To be sure the labor to which he addressed himself was no more than has been done by many scrupulous writers; indeed, it was much less than that performed by, say, Hervey Allen for the sending into the world of *Anthony Adverse;* but his patience and sincerity were not too frequently found in his contemporaries of the nineties. James Lane Allen was almost forty-two when his first book was published; life had been fairly hard and lonely; some of the spark had been dulled within him, and he wrote thenceforward because he was determined to push to the head of the crowd, because he loved literature, because he wished to leave behind something memorable, and not because he was driven by surplus energy and passion to create the beautiful. Physically as well as mentally he could best support the short story. Only four of his books— *The Choir Invisible, The Reign of Law, The Mettle of the Pasture,* and *The Heroine in Bronze*—are of substantial bulk, and we should infer, even if we did not have his word for it, that for reasons of physical limitations and artistic satisfaction he knew himself most full of wit when brief. To know Allen at his best, therefore, is to be acquainted with "The White Cowl," "Sister Dolorosa," "Two Gentlemen of Kentucky," "King Solomon of Kentucky," *A Kentucky Cardinal, Summer in Arcady, The Bride of the Mistletoe, The Last Christmas Tree, The Alabaster Box,* "Miss Locke," "The Ash-can," and "The Violet." Reading them in that order is like sitting in a concert hall and hearing an orchestral series of tone poems. One catches first the woodland notes of flute and violin and oboe, with playful arpeggios and sunny melodies and now and then a sombre undertone from the cellos; then the brasses burst forth, drowning the flutes with a sinister suggestion of the evil in nature; then the tone deepens with a movement for strings only in the bleak and wintry Christmas theme; then the drums and trumpets announce a short funeral march plangent with manly despair;

finally the full orchestra is heard in a song of serene acceptance of the fortunes of existence, not untouched by the strains of melancholy long drawn out.

That melancholy which, to change the figure, runs like a vein of black marble throughout his work was noted and commented upon from the first. It is easily accounted for. He came from the Allens of the Bluegrass of Kentucky, and the aristocratic families of that plateau, no matter what the state's neutrality, were likely to be of the South southern during the Civil War. Allen expressed it because he felt the pathos and tragedy of the Lost Cause with its attendant bereavements, impoverishment, humiliation in a defeat in arms. The melancholy of southern literature after the war was no mere lagging imitation of a romantic mood; it was the direct utterance of pride brought to its fall, of political oppression endured at best with resignation. The landscape, too, that Allen knew as a boy and youth determined to some extent the shape of his passions—"no ruggedness, no wildness, no savagery"—and the evenness of natural architecture directed him toward a monotony of mood that could easily become melancholy, all the more easily since he shut himself off from active participation in sport or politics and grew to have that saddest of all feelings, that one is alien and perhaps unwelcome to his kind. This was the chief reason for his melancholy. When he came to learn that the honesty which he brought to society would be met by quibbling or outright dishonesty, that refinement and modesty and honor did not equip one to meet his fellows on common ground, that good taste was a liability rather than an asset, that truth was always elusive, and that the meaning and purpose of life were not to be found—then his reaction was a profound disappointment which lasted throughout his maturity. How often did he repeat the story of one who brought his most precious gift to another only to have it rejected.

The writings of James Lane Allen in chronological order epitomize almost the whole literary era in which he lived. From *Flute and Violin* to *The Reign of Law,* then to the Christmas triology, then to *The Landmark* he was moving with the cycle of American literature which went from romance to realism, then to symbolism, and then back to realism. Perhaps we are now completing the cycle by entering a decade during which romance will dominate the lists of best sellers. Allen escaped from ending where he began only by virtue of the white-lipped gravity and the universality of the stories which came latest from his pen. The realism of his last days was not the realism found in Dreiser or Sherwood Anderson, Floyd Dell or Eugene O'Neill or Edgar Lee Masters. Against whatever was, in its ultimate effect or even in its temporary impression, impure or sordid, against a surrender to animalism or futility or any doctrine which counseled forgiveness for man's misdeeds because of his driven will, against any suggestion to condescend to newer and more vulgar manners or to put aside the Ten Commandments as outworn, he set his face implacably. Like Harold at Hastings he fought for what he regarded as Anglo-Saxon supremacy threatened by foreign invasion. Like Harold he fell on the field, defeated but not dishonored. He was the last champion of the Genteel Tradition.

What was this Genteel Tradition, this doctrine and discipline which once rallied beneath its banner so many shining ones and which is now mentioned only with scorn? Its banner was, of course, the banner of the Tories in 1900, for those who clung to older regulations for behavior and who believed that there were boundaries over which no gentleman passed in conversation, thought, deed, or writing. It held aloft a standard of manners; indeed, it came to be practically nothing but a manner, a mode of conduct exemplified

in literature. How absurd was the manner and how far did
it tend to emasculate those who subscribed to its fashion?
Some future historian will do American letters a service by
answering those queries at length and with complete candor.
He will be a critic; that is, a man in search of the absolute.
He will be balanced, impartial, judicious, and cultivated.

No one has more aptly defined the spirit of the Genteel
Tradition than did James Lane Allen when he proposed in
The Emblems of Fidelity that the "highest law" of a "glo-
riously endowed nature" was *le génie oblige,* to be translated
to mean that "he who has genius, no matter what the world
may do to him, no matter what ruin Nature may work in him,
is under obligations so long as he lives to do nothing mean
and to do nothing meanly." *To do nothing mean and to do
nothing meanly*—that was the device of the Great Tradition.
The central problem of life is what to do with it. Allen had
his answer to the problem and stated it in the above words.
Today we have no answer, and so we deride the men of his
type as inhibited and afraid of life; we laugh at their ivory
towers and chaste epitaphs. We say that their innocence was
a mask that covered a longing to do evil, that they were
ignorant of the ways of the world and therefore ineffectual
in their interpretations of those ways, that they were stiff of
neck and stiff of shirt and altogether priggish and unsexed.
Well, let us see.

Upholders of the Genteel Tradition were at once classicists, romanticists, and humanists. They proved themselves
classicists by their desire for perfection of form and for objectivity of treatment, by their longing for a union of dignity
and beauty, and by their conception that a writer has an obligation to improve the taste and morals of the people of his
time. Some of its roots strike down into that rationalistic
philosophy of the eighteenth century which held that order,
even though postulated upon injustice, is better than dis

order, even though springing from the administration of justice; the complacent doctrine that whatever is is right, and that any needed changes should be effected through a slow reform making use of satire and education. That our genteel writers like Longfellow, Lowell, and Aldrich, James, Howells, and Allen, labored to achieve perfection in style and in form is a fact so obvious as to require no demonstration beyond what has already been made by critics and biographers. That these writers held it their duty to be censors rather than agitators is no less apparent. As far as social problems were concerned none of them could possibly be suspected of radicalism. Longfellow, for example, was lukewarm in the composition of anti-slavery poems, but he did dedicate a long life to the dissemination of foreign culture; James wished to soften and brighten the harsher outlines of Yankee society while he pointed out to Europeans that Yankee puritanism had its merits, but he wished above all things to preserve the balance of a civilization founded upon the amenities and to allow improvement to come through the patient infiltration of ideas; and Howells, who came nearest having unorthodox political views, stopped short of socialism because of a persistent skepticism as to the righteousness of mass rule—at least in his lifetime. Whether internationalists like James or nationalists like Allen these writers showed no desire for revolution of any kind; James was the only one who even hinted in a novel of the chance of a violent class warfare. As a group they respected the gospel of laissez-faire and (with the mentioned exception of Howells) kept their coats quite free from stains of liberalism. Howells alone showed anything like concern for the lot of the working man. The others accepted democracy but like Lowell or Allen found in its practice certain ills which might become a fatal disease to the body politic, and they tacitly agreed that society as then organized was too satisfactory to justify much tinkering with its machinery. At least it was satisfactory to them. It had rewarded them, and it is no easy thing to find fault with a society that has permitted one to win that kind of success he most craves.

The genteel writer had no more intention to disrupt the course of literature than he had to disorganize society. He was not only genteel but also a traditionalist. All those writers were students of literature; several of them had taught it in colleges; and their historical sense persuaded them of the existence of a few fundamentals that distinguished great and lasting literature from the merely popular and passing. The qualities which made a novel great for today were identical with those observances of form and spirit and style which had made literature great in the past. New themes, of course, would arise with the increasing complications which man must face; new conditions would warrant characters whose superficial natures, at least, would seem different from those found in Greek or Elizabethan drama; new words and new outlets for human vitality might call for variations in phraseology; but the fundamentals, they felt, would remain unchanged and experiments must be entered into with proper caution. Great literature must be addressed to the conscience of the reader. It must have as profound an ethical import as the author can contrive. Here again they found themselves in harmony with eighteenth-century English writers, who had been so attentive to questions of morals and manners. Literature, to the mind of a novelist who wrote in the Genteel Tradition, had no business to present a cross-section of life for the sake of the cross-section only; it had no justification in registering the malodorous thoughts that might run through a woman's brain for the sole reason of observing a turbid stream of consciousness. Literature and the author of that literature owed a duty to the human race, and that duty was to strive through teaching more or less artfully concealed to lead man onward in his rather pathetic struggle to crawl out of the cave and the jungle. It is at this point that the dialectical materialist and the advocate of realism for realism's sake scoff the loudest in discrediting the writers thus described. Here is where they raise their voices to cry out that such novelists as James and Howells and Allen were lacking in masculine vigor, terror-stricken before the aspects of reality, neurotically anxious to be stainless in person and in writing. They quote Arthur Symons's definition of art as beginning when a man wishes to immortalize the most vivid moment he has ever lived and they demand to be told what were the "vivid moments" of James and Howells and Allen. How could men who did not burn with a hard gem-like flame hope to share the pain and beauty and ugliness of man's associations with his fellows and to reproduce those things in their fiction? Did they not insist upon ethical values simply because they were ignorant, fearful, and cloistered?

Now a gentleman is not necessarily a fool or a poltroon. Howells, James, Allen and their kind knew of the existence of such things as murder, arson, rape, adultery, suicide, embezzlement, and all the other crimes and perversions which make up the calendar of sin, together with the details which give to such things their lurid attractions. But they chose to refrain from using them or to use them very sparingly, and some of them abstained from using the violent or criminal at all. Why? To answer that query correctly is to get at the very heart of the Genteel Tradition. Mr. V. F. Calverton argues in *The Liberation of American Literature* that the code of the genteel writers was the product of an economic condition; that in the Gilded Age, when capital was girding itself to seize all the rich plunder that the continent afforded, the foremost necessity of the business man was to obtain credit and that the indispensable requirement for the securing of credit was respectability. Bourgeois ideology (is there a more tiresome phrase?) was so colored with this expedient respectability that literature and literary persons were unavoidably governed by it, and, in short, Longfellow wrote very proper poetry because he was bourgeois and therefore obliged to keep in good standing with his bankers, and Whittier wrote fiery abolition poetry, it would follow, for the same reason. The argument is an interesting one, with, doubtless, some relation to the truth, but it is too simple and too convenient to Mr. Calverton's purpose to be entirely satisfying. Nor does one need to carry it to a *reductio ad absurdum* in order to establish its fallacy. When American gentility in letters was at its height the most capitalistic, the most bourgeois nation in Europe was France, and if the demand for credit to support an economic structure accounts for a prim literature, why, we should like to ask, was the literature of France anything but prim in the closing decades of the nineteenth century? Or, to bring the question back to ourselves, why did our literature from 1900 on grow ever more non-respectable from the point of view of bourgeois morality at the very time when our credit was expanding in a grandiose fashion that presently brought on an inevitable débâcle? English puritanism of the time of Oliver Cromwell assuredly began as a revolutionary force to be wielded against an aristocracy, but its piety, its morality, were protests against the popular idea of court vice, not against the social pattern which called forth that aristocracy. The psalm of the Roundhead was sung in opposition to the rousing tune of the Cavalier as the middle class took arms against the upper class; literary fashions—like styles in dress —were inextricably interwoven with political opinions, but the relations of cause and effect are not and were not so easily ascertained as Mr. Calverton thinks. Historical materialism does not tell the whole story.

Were our writers, then, genteel because of a personal timidity or a lack of masculine vigor—because they were, as Henry James called Emerson, unsexed women? Here is a query much more difficult to answer inasmuch as it involves a knowledge of personalities that is quite beyond anyone's power to acquire, even though he be an enterprising psychoanalyst. How is masculinity to be measured or determined? Simply by a man's attitude toward sex, which should, I suppose, be spelled with a capital letter? A young man came into my office this morning and told me that he thought the genteel writers were eunuchs, an opinion which may be taken as being fairly prevalent among the more advanced college students. Mr. Ludwig Lewisohn in *Expression in America* blames them for not having been frank enough in describing the sex histories of their characters and says by and by that they neglected sex because they thought too much about it. If this singular reasoning be trustworthy then Eugene O'Neill and Robinson Jeffers and Theodore Dreiser and Erskine Caldwell and Tiffany Thayer and a multitude of living dramatists, poets, and novelists must think entirely too little about sex and Mr. Lewisohn should scold them for their innocence, if not, indeed, for their impotence. I know nothing of the genes which may have fixed the destinies of James, Howells, Aldrich, Higginson, Stoddard, Cable, Gilder, van Dyke, Allen, and others of their school. Neither does anyone else. I know nothing of their blood counts, and to try to prove that they were capable of leading the life of a drunkard or a wastrel would be useless folly. Some of them did not marry; none of them confronted his fellows with loud drum beats, but these facts convict no man of a deficiency in mental, moral, or physical stamina. I do not know that it would be of any avail to remind the young critic that these effete gentlemen could climb mountains, walk through Europe, hunt and fish. One enlightening thing we can do: contrast the ages of these "emasculated" writers with those of some of the less genteel writers and artists of the same period. Aubrey Beardsley, Ernest Dowson, Lionel Johnson, Hubert Crackanthorpe, Stephen Crane, and Frank Norris did not live to be forty. Oscar Wilde died at forty-four, Francis Thompson at forty-eight. The average age of the Americans first named was at death seventy-eight. This contrast, to be sure, is of little value but it is of some relevance. Men who live to be seventy-eight can scarcely have been decent only because they were too soft and wan, and if anything else were to be said in their favor we might examine the weight and bulk of their literary output and realize that no inconsiderable robustness was requisite for its production. Perhaps instead of reasoning that they were abnormal physically because they were decent it would be more logical to believe that they were decent because they were normal.

No, the reasons these genteel writers resolved to do nothing mean and to do nothing meanly were the obvious and therefore the often overlooked ones. They imitated English authors. They inherited a puritan tradition. They were men of culture, a quality which brings us back to the starting point of the influence of classicism upon their point of view. American poets followed in Tennyson's steps not because they were in fear of their bankers but because they thought Tennyson a good poet; even Poe placed him in the front rank, and it has never been charged that Poe succumbed to bourgeois seductions. American novelists respected Scott because he was courageous, manly, and honorable—qualities which are as valuable to an aristocracy as to a government of the bourgeoisie; they admired Sir Walter's novels because they were solid achievements in the presentment of historical fiction and not because they had regulated either their criticism or their ethics to suit the holder of a mortgage. As inheritors of a puritan tradition they had received a sense of obligation to do their best to make their neighbors perfect, and to this tradition was added the lesson taught by a ripened culture which included familiarity with Plato, Aristotle, and Horace's *Ars Poetica*.

Consider how much and in what manner they differed from novelists of a present popular school of fiction. Allen's *The Doctor's Christmas Eve* is a story of domestic infelicity, of a physician in love with his best friend's wife, of that wife's neglect by her husband, of the things that have made the doctor what he is, of the meeting of the children of both families, of the death of the Birney boy and the drawing together of father and mother. Suppose the material had been handled by one of our newer novelists. The scene would have been placed farther south, say in Mississippi or Georgia. We might first discover Dr. Birney, a decayed scion of a decaying aristocratic family, fleeing from bloodhounds that are pursuing him through a pine forest. Exhausted, he would stop at a negro's cabin, and while drinking from a gourd he would review his past life in such a way that we would understand why he had lost the right woman and married the wrong one. After he disappeared into the wood a mob would reach the cabin and explain that the fugitive had cut his wife's throat. Then again we would follow the doctor's thoughts while he runs terror-stricken from the shouts closing in upon him; by means of this review we would learn that he has seduced Mrs. Ousley because, being half black, he had always hated her husband, who was pure white. By this time Dr. Birney would have circled back to his house, which he would set on fire in order to destroy his two sleeping children. When the mob captures him he will be first hanged and then burned, while an idiot boy explains to a black prostitute how well the punishment fits the crime. The negress will then reveal that

Dr. Birney is her grandson and the mob will caper with joy upon being told that it has lynched a part negro.

Stories of this penny-dreadful type—and the synopsis was not a great exaggeration—have to the sophisticated man no significance, no meaning whatever. They may be excellent reporting of dialect, appearances, actions, and scenes, they may exhibit more latent power than Allen ever showed, but because their authors bring little to their material they leave little there but that material. Graphic representation alone does not make a great painting, as Andrea del Sarto lamented in Browning's famous monologue. The painter of a great painting must be a great man. The writer of a great novel must be a great man. Dostoevsky also introduces us to sordid people, but they teach us something of the meaning or the lack of meaning in existence; they were not created just to shock us or to minister to our prurience. Chekhov in "The Shooting Party" portrayed as psychopathic a murderer as any later novelist could wish but he did not think it necessary to saturate his pages with profanity and incest. Now Mr. Faulkner has as much right to give us Popeye and Mr. Caldwell to give us the unholy families of Ty Ty and of Jeeter Lester as Anthony Trollope had to concentrate upon the clerics of Barchester. Literature is a boundless realm. But the genteel writers were also within their prerogatives when they moved in a polite and distinguished society. There are drawing-rooms and garden houses in the world as well as mill towns, speakeasies, and tumble-down cabins. An author's taste guides him in his choice of milieu. What several critics should allow is that a genteel novelist had as much right to his taste as Mr. Faulkner has to his. Intolerance is the vice of these critics; they condemn all that is genteel because gentility offends them, associates itself in their minds with an economic order with which they are in active disagreement; but they give us no rationale of criticism, they do not explain why "a slice of life" is inevitably superior fiction, why Edith Wharton is ridiculously futile and Mr. Faulkner the hope of American literature; they instead laugh so loudly or damn so bitterly that we are fearful of differing with them. The taste of the genteel writer may or may not have been better than the taste of the hard-boiled writer but he must not be penalized for having had that taste until someone demonstrates that it unfitted him to be a good novelist. Or that "good" taste is bad in itself. Perhaps that can be done.

Upholders of the Genteel Tradition were romantic in attributing to man qualities which lifted him above the animalistic, and romantic in their love of nature; they were humanistic in their respect for discipline and in their emphasis upon the value of the individual. To be sure they did not agree unanimously upon all of these points. Henry James, for example, came to believe that life should be an occasion for living instead of a spectacle to be observed. But on the whole, the heroes and heroines invented by these writers were people of high breeding, high courage. In this there was not so much the following of Scott as there was the taking, consciously or unwittingly, of a refuge from a mechanistic interpretation of life which the doctrine of evolution had spread, and sometimes, it must be conceded, this flight looks much like a burying of heads in the sand. All of the genteel writers had had their thought heavily conditioned by science, which spread like a roc's wing over the Victorian era. All of them balked at following to logical conclusions the findings of science with respect to man. They refused to see him as an animal dependent upon respiration and alimentation, having within him no spark of divinity and therefore no destiny. They did not fear life, but they did fear grossness, animality, and if it was pointed out to them that vulgarity was a large part of the existence of *homo sapiens* their answer was that the will could limit the amount of vulgarity which one would permit himself to practice or to see. They preferred—again a matter of taste—to introduce characters in whom the public could find a hope of escape from a philosophy of futility and determinism, characters who overrode circumstance, who could be honest, even pure; human beings instead of brutes. To some readers of today this innocence and purity are amusing. To others it is not entirely unwise —it might even be proved that feminine chastity has had something to do with the health and happiness of the race— and the novels are not wholly comic. One function of literature is undoubtedly to present men and women as they are, but another one is to present them as in their more aspiring moments they would like to be. There is nothing immature or cowardly about this second function. It may be, indeed, the strict result of a scientific attitude, for if science teaches us that man's body has evolved from a low form does it not also hold that his mind is capable of development, that his moral sense can be sharpened and his conduct made more social? We do not laugh at the man who tries to improve a machine. Why should we mock the man who tries, no matter how clumsily, to improve a human being?

The genteel writers (almost always realistic in technique) were romantic in purpose because they exaggerated the noble qualities of their protagonists. They were not unaware of the strength that lay within the naturalistic novel. They were not unacquainted with French symbolism. But they knew that modern naturalism and symbolism sprang from the jaded taste of the nineties and that these trends would unless modified, end by defeating themselves. Decadence is its own avenger. Sensationalism wears itself out. We share a profound and almost instinctive desire to grow in decency and the genteel writer told himself that it were better to err on the side of that decency rather than on the other side. Too often he did err in exaggeration of one kind or another, for romantic writing is likely to end in art for art's sake, and often, especially in Allen, we are conscious that his error led him into a vacuum.

For this romantic optimism presented to Allen a problem almost peculiar to him. Naturally he was romantic, but naturally he was also melancholy, and his growth in knowledge and experience presently took away from him all but the shell of romance. He had, as he wrote in *The Last Christmas Tree*, no solution for the universe, yet hoped for the best and lived for it. There might be no reward for doing nothing mean and nothing meanly, but he and the other genteel writers continued on the whole to picture heroines as good, beautiful, and true, and their heroes as worthy of the heroines. And so Allen's idealism became closely tied up with his Americanism: a nationalistic spirit akin to Theodore Roosevelt's and in some respects not dissimilar to Nazi race prejudice. It was, thought Allen, the old stock of Americans that had made our nation great; it was their virtues that we were losing, and we must fight to recover and retain them if we intend to continue a great people. The Anglo-Saxon pioneer remained in his mind the highest type of man, and those passages in *The Bride of the Mistletoe* which describe the descent of family traits through generations of those old-time Americans should be read in the light of his prejudices. He deplored immigration because it diluted the old blood. In *A Pilgrim to His Youth* he exclaimed: "Might that never be—the United States of the foreigners," and in 1924 he wrote to Cassidy that our Revolution had to be fought over again by the Revolutionary stock, which must take up arms against the countless denizens of alien race. But again, in this bit of "idealism," we find his characteristic mixture of belief and disbelief; he romanticized what he thought were Anglo-Saxon traits but he distrusted the rule of the people, especially when the people were no longer "pure" Anglo-Saxon. His faith in democracy, which came from his ink bottle when it came at all, evaporated once he walked the sidewalks of New York. He could not believe that a formal process of naturalization converted a foreigner into an American. Nor had he more than the mildest interest in the laborer. He had no patience with equalitarian doctrine. "Only now," he said in *A Pilgrim to His Youth,* "have we begun to realize that, shout democracy till we die, enforce it by law as we may, cajole it by institutions as we will, straight through the theory and the idea and the laws and the institution there runs the same hard and fast stratification of human beings that was the work of measureless ages and cannot be undone in an age—that stratification of racial castes which exhibits an upper and a middle and a lower class. So that if we could remove the upper and the middle—as we sometimes try—at once the lower reforms out of itself as best it can the upper and the middle: for when man ceases to look up to a god and will no longer look up to man, civilization ends."

As we read these words (probably inspired by the Russian experiment) we at once perceive that Allen unintentionally revealed the weakness of the position held by the genteel writers, a weakness already mentioned: they were not merely genteel, they were also traditionalists. The wit and charm and grace of the society to which they were partial depended, they believed, upon a maintenance of the *status quo,* and they wished that society preserved because they believed it the best, because it suited their taste, because they would not or could not write of another. James was as frank as Meredith in stating that his art relied upon the existence of a *civilized* society, and the genteel writers as a class knew or divined vaguely that they must support a social organization which, with all its faults, was, because of its order, its stratification, their proper milieu. I have not, it must be remembered, denied the tremendous influence exerted upon literature by economic compulsives; I have simply denied the thesis that the Genteel Tradition had economic motives only. I think that the genteel writer could more easily have supported the loss of his fortune through a revolution than he could have faced the destruction of good taste, for he sensed that the overthrow or modification of the social organism he knew would let ugly forces loose; that urbanity would be dispossessed by violence; that the polished speech of the man of the world or the rougher dialect of an honest rustic like David Harum would be supplanted by conversation which would shriek in his ears. It was taste which commanded him to avert his eyes from the doings of nine-tenths of our population and to look fondly upon the small minority which understood, even if it did not always manifest, reason and the will of God. We can admire his respect for exquisite diction, we can praise his objectivity, we can sympathize with his wish to improve standards of feeling and action, we can understand his craving for a cultivated society, but nothing can atone for the fact that the cumulative effect of these ideals was to cause him to ignore too much of the storm and stress which made life excitingly sweet and bitter, painful and delightful. The genteel writers preferred the lighter comedy, the nuances, the shift and play, the opiate dreams and diversions of a well-mannered society; they exalted its manners to a Manner. But they did so to their lasting peril, since they failed to record for the future anything save a partial history of their times, a history which should have set down with no shrinking and no apology the crudities, the uncontrollable passions, the warfare of titanic economic forces, the urge and fling and swing which boiled over all around them. We were becoming a world power to the accompaniment of brazen imperialism and public and private rapacity while the genteel writers led us to tea-tables and walked with us through rose gardens. They chose tradition rather than actuality and so became the creatures of that tradition; they were, indeed, the finest flower of the tradition which asks that the pen should be a golden spur.   That tradition is dead, and only a bold prophet would be willing to say that it can be resurrected.   Manners may, it is conceivable, return to the conventions of the Victorian; speech and dress may become staid; the present romantic fashion for experiment in literature and conduct may languish; but it is unlikely that writers will ever again set up a tradition whereby they turn their backs upon the unpleasant facts of existence and muzzle themselves for the sake of taste.   Truth was once forced to wed Taste, but the marriage was not made in heaven.

NOTES ON SOURCES

CHAPTER I

For the picture of Lexington and the Bluegrass I am indebted to "Lexington: A Cultural Center in the Eighteenth Century West" (1928), an unpublished Master's dissertation at the University of Kentucky by Harriet B. Glascock, and to Lewis Collins's *Historical Sketches of Kentucky* (Cincinnati, 1847). The genealogy of the Allen family was prepared by Allen himself; additional and confirmatory material is found in F. A. Vickers, *The Abridged Compendium of American Genealogy* (Chicago, 1925), p. 404. "The Payne Family" is the title of a typewritten MS. left by Allen; it contains the story of Col. Devall Payne's assault upon George Washington, a story mentioned by Lewis and Richard Collins, *History of Kentucky* (Louisville, 1924), II, 577 and alluded to by Allen in his *The Blue-Grass Region of Kentucky* (New York, 1892), pp. 37-38. George W. Ranck, *The Travelling Church* (c. 1910), presents the history of the immigration of the congregation with which came Allen's direct ancestry. Mrs. Frank Gentry, until her death last year the closest relative of James Lane Allen, was authority for the material relating to Helen Foster Allen and for many other statements about the Allen family. Details of Allen's schooling and teaching were taken from a conversation with Walter K. Patterson, his first important schoolmaster; a letter from James H. Stover, his companion in preparatory school days; a letter from Dr. William B. Smith, his closest friend in college; conversations with several of his pupils; the registration books of Kentucky University (not the University of Kentucky) and catalogues of the same institution; the catalogue of Bethany College for 1881-82; traditions at Bethany; and a letter from President Cloyd Goodnight of Bethany College to J. H. Nelson, dated Dec. 6, 1926.

CHAPTER II

Files of *Harper's New Monthly Magazine*, *The Century Magazine*, *Lippincott's Magazine*, *The Critic*, *The Manhattan*,

The Continent, and *The Atlantic Monthly* were read for the period 1878-1898 (if publication extended throughout) to discover not only Allen's contributions but also the things he was reading and the general literary background. For interest in localities, directly connected with the local color movement, see A. Van Cleef, "The Hot Springs of Arkansas," *Harper's New Monthly Magazine,* LVI (January, 1878), 193-210; F. E. Fryatt, "The Navesink Highlands," *Harper's New Monthly Magazine,* LIX (September, 1879), 541-553; "Gold-Mining in Georgia," *Harper's New Monthly Magazine,* LIX (September, 1879), 509-519; Frank Taylor, "Through Texas," *Harper's New Monthly Magazine,* LIX (October, 1879), 703-718; A. A. Hayes, "Grub-Stakes and Millions," *Harper's New Monthly Magazine,* LX (February, 1880), 380-397; C. C. Coffin, "Dakota Wheat Fields," *Harper's New Monthly Magazine,* LX (March, 1880), 529-535. Allen's account of his first selling of a MS. to *The Critic,* his visit to Cincinnati, and his calling upon Alden in New York is found in his "Henry Mills Alden," *The Bookman,* L (November, 1919), 330-336. Henry James's essay on Alphonse Daudet is in *The Century Magazine,* XXVI (August, 1883), 498-509. According to Nancy H. Banks, "James Lane Allen," *The Bookman,* I (June, 1895), 303, Allen went to New York with "a few dollars" in his pocket; the sum is made $100 by "Novelist James Lane Allen," *Kansas City Times,* May 23, 1897, and $50 by Edwin Carlile Litsey, "James Lane Allen, Biographical Facts and Comments," *Book News,* XXIV (July, 1906), 753. Allen reports his travel into the Cumberland Mountains in *The Blue-Grass Region of Kentucky* (New York, 1892), pp. 232-322. The narrative of Annie Allen's marriage is taken from conversations with Mrs. Frank Gentry and Mrs. W. T. Lafferty, of Lexington. Charles C. Moore's *Behind the Bars: 31498* was published in Lexington in 1899; his complaint against Allen is found on pp. 30-31. Joseph B. Gilder gave me copies of Edmund Gosse's letter to him relative to Allen's "Always Bussing His Friends," and of Allen's reply to Gilder. Jessie B. Rittenhouse, "Memories of Madison Cawein," *The Bookman,* LVI (November, 1922), 305-312, is authority for the account of Allen's visit to Cawein. The notice of the death of Helen Foster Allen is taken from *The Lexington Transcript*, June 7, 1899. For details of Allen's life in Cincinnati I am indebted to Mr. George Fox, who also secured for me copies of Allen's letters to Miss Hollingshed, dated July 8, 1890, and December 29, 1890.

Chapter III

Every issue of *The Literary Digest* from 1884 to 1926 was scanned for evidence of literary trends and popular tastes; the other periodicals mentioned in the references for Chapter II were likewise used continually. That American publishers were issuing more books by American than by European authors is proved by figures taken from Brander Matthews, "The Literary Independence of the United States," *The Cosmopolitan Magazine*, XIII (July, 1892), 343-50. C. D. Warner's protest against unhealthy fiction is found in his "The Novel and the Common School," *The Atlantic Monthly*, LXV (June, 1890), 721-731. The symposium on whether an author should weep before trying to bring tears to his readers is in *The Critic* for March 24, 1886. The 1891 criticism of American authors by *The Edinburgh Review* is in CLXXVIII (January, 1891), 32. Allen states in the preface to the 1900 edition of *Flute and Violin* that "King Solomon of Kentucky" and "Two Gentlemen of Kentucky" were founded upon real people and events. The harsh criticism of *Flute and Violin* is found in *The Athenaeum* for July 23, 1892. All of Allen's acquaintances agree that he always felt that Catholics were prejudiced against him; the story of the real or fancied insult to him in Cincinnati came from George Folsom Granberry. The anecdote of the Trappist monk in the Campagna was printed in the *New York Sun*, April 19, 1905. The quotation from Isaac F. Marcosson is from a letter to me dated November 15, 1929. Allen's defense of Kentucky tempers is found in "County Court Day in Kentucky," *The Blue-Grass Region of Kentucky* (New York, 1892), pp. 111-112. Page's praise of Allen is expressed in "Literature in the South Since the War," *Lippincott's Magazine* for November, 1891. Henry M. Alden's comment on

A Kentucky Cardinal is taken from a review of that novel in the *Cincinnati Times-Star*, May 1, 1894. Lucy L. Hazard calls Allen neurasthenic in *The Frontier in American Literature* (New York, 1927), pp. 75-76. Favorite novels in the United States in 1894 are listed in "Literary Notes," *The Literary Digest*, VIII (February 15, 1894), 376; F. Marion Crawford's popularity is attested in "Literary Notes," *The Literary Digest*, VIII (March 15, 1894), 494. H. W. Mabie's opinion of *A Kentucky Cardinal* is given in "James Lane Allen" (with portrait), *The Outlook*, LVI (June 5, 1897), 357-360. For other reviews of that novel see bibliography for 1894. The third edition of Cherbuliez's *Le Secret du précepteur* was published by Librairie Hachette et Cie, Paris. The few details of Allen's first trip to Europe are gathered from a letter of I. F. Marcosson to me dated November 15, 1929, from a short article on bicycling Allen wrote to *The Critic* for October 12, 1895, from a copy of the *Hampstead and Highgate Express* for July 17, 1894, and from Allen's "A Sunday Bird Market in London," in the *New York Tribune*, March 15, 1895, and "English Wood-Notes (With Kentucky Echoes)," *The Southern Magazine* for February, 1895. The titles of Allen's favorite novels at this time are included in Weldon Fawcett's "A Blue-Grass Novelist," *Peterson's Magazine* for April, 1896. Lewis Collins's account of a Lexington schoolmaster's battle with a cougar is found in his *Historical Sketches of Kentucky* (Cincinnati, 1847), p. 295; he here gives the schoolmaster's name as McKinley. Joseph Gilder's criticism of *The Choir Invisible* is printed in *The Critic*, XXX (May 29, 1897), 368. See bibliography for 1897 for other reviews. The most popular novels in the United States in 1897 were named in *The Bookman*, IV (February, 1897); "Chronicle and Comment" of *The Bookman*, XXXIV (January, 1912), 465, puts *The Choir Invisible* at the head of best sellers for 1897; Mark Sullivan records its popularity in *Our Times: The Turn of the Century* (New York, 1926), p. 210; see also Radclyffe Hall, "American Literature in England," *The Bookman*, LXV (May, 1927), 312. Allen's objection to a dramatization of *The Choir Invisible* is made clear in his letter to John Wilson Townsend dated March

14, 1913. William H. Townsend, then City Attorney of Lexington, gave me a transcript of the agreement, dated November 26, 1929, between that city and Curtis Brown, Ltd., for a London dramatization and presentation of *The Choir Invisible*. Allen's verdict upon his "feminine" fiction is set forth in his preface to the 1900 edition of *Flute and Violin*.

CHAPTER IV

Charles Hemstreet's book is *Literary New York: Its Landmarks and Associations* (New York, 1903). Henry van Dyke's statement about Allen is from his letter to me dated January 11, 1930; Arthur B. Maurice's from a letter to me dated November 14, 1929. The manner of New York publication of *Sapho* is described in *The Critic* for October 27, 1888. Joshua Caldwell's lament over the erotic novel is in his "Our Unclean Fiction," *The New England Magazine*, III (December, 1890), 434-439. Carl Van Doren's favorable opinion of *Summer in Arcady* is presented in *Contemporary American Novelists* (New York, 1922), p. 27. The English objection to Nature in *Summer in Arcady* is found in "Summer in Arcady: A Tale of Nature," *The Saturday Review*, LXXXIII (February 20, 1897), 204-205. H. W. Mabie's praise of *Summer in Arcady* is written in "James Lane Allen," *The Outlook*, LVI (June 5, 1897), 357-360. See bibliography under 1896 and 1897 for further criticisms of *Summer in Arcady*. Allen's "King Solomon of Kentucky: An Address" was printed in *The Outlook*, XC (December 19, 1908), 884-886. Dr. William B. Smith in a letter to me dated March 15, 1928, declared: "Many years later in New York City he [Allen] told me that 'David' in *The Reign of Law* was a reproduction of me." Arthur B. Maurice wrote of the first sales of *The Reign of Law* in "James Lane Allen's Country," *The Bookman*, XII (October, 1900), 154-162. President McGarvey's sermon against *The Reign of Law* is found in *The Lexington Leader*, October 8, 1900; Allen's reply is in the same paper, November 11, 1900. Dr. Chadwick's tribute to *The Reign of Law* is taken from *The Literary Digest*, XXII (February 16, 1901), 198-199. Best ellers just before *The Reign of Law* are listed in *The Bookman,*

XXXIV (January, 1912), 465. *The Literary Digest* tells of the popularity of *The Reign of Law* in England in XXI (November 3, 1900), 524. (The American title was mentioned, not the title of the English edition). Allen contributed to the symposium "Will the Novel Disappear?" *The North American Review*, CLXXV (September, 1902), 290-292. For Allen's plan for *The Mettle of the Pasture* see "Chronicle and Comment," *The Bookman*, VII (July, 1898), 373. The title of this novel is taken from Shakespeare's *King Henry V*, Act III, Scene 1, line 27. *The Nation*, in its obituary paragraph on Allen, CXX (March 4, 1925), 229, accused him of being melodramatic. Allen's letter to a Lexington student, Lucille Naff (Clay), denying that he ever projected himself into his fiction, is dated December 23, 1923. The English critic of Mrs. Conyers (of *The Mettle of the Pasture*) wrote in *The Athenaeum* for September 5, 1903. *The Outlook* reviewer was A. E. Hancock (see bibliography for 1903). Henry van Dyke's letter to me was dated January 11, 1930. The quotations from Sue Porter Heatwole are from a letter to me dated May 18, 1930.

CHAPTER V

The description of Allen is lifted from Edwin C. Litsey, "James Lane Allen: Biographical Facts and Comments," *Book News*, XXIV (July, 1906), 753. Allen's "fretful" letter to M. A. Cassidy was dated January 26, 1923. Richard Burton's "Of Those Who Walk Alone" was printed in *The Century Magazine*, LXXVIII (May, 1909), 53. The letter from T. S. Jones to me was dated May 27, 1929. The description of Allen's rooms and attire was gathered from conversations with several of his visitors and from a catalogue of his effects offered for sale by the Anderson Galleries, March 9, 1918. The second quotation from T. S. Jones is from a letter to me dated June 12, 1929. For reviews of *The Bride of the Mistletoe* see bibliography for 1909. The *New York Times* announced Allen's departure for Europe in the issue of July 3, 1909. Sir Edmund Gosse's letter to me was dated May 18, 1927. Allen's letter to John Wilson Townsend was dated September 21, 1909; Allen had therefore been abroad less than three months. William Winter's denunciation of Ibsen and Maeterlinck is in the *New York Tribune* for January 27, 1904. The bill for Allen's purchase of Hovey's translation of Maeterlinck was left among his papers. See bibliography for 1910 for reviews of *The Doctor's Christmas Eve.* See John Wilson Townsend's *James Lane Allen: A Personal Note* (Louisville, 1928), p. 94, for Allen's statement that he would wait perhaps ten years before publishing the third volume of the Christmas trilogy. R. Dalverny, manager of the Hotel Frascati, Le Havre, wrote me in a letter dated May 27, 1930, that all records pertaining to the hotel had been destroyed during the war. George F. Granberry took my query about Allen's use of drugs to Dr. Rolfe Floyd, who replied to Granberry in a letter dated October 11, 1927. Sue Porter Heatwole told me of her correspondent's condemnation of the Christmas trilogy in a letter dated May 18, 1930. Elizabeth Madox Roberts told me in conversation that she considered *The Bride of the Mistletoe* Allen's best work.

Chapter VI

Most of the information given in this chapter was gathered from conversations with George Folsom Granberry, Cale Young Rice, Alice Hegan Rice, John Wilson Townsend, M. A. Cassidy, and from Allen's letters to Ellen Glasgow, Cassidy, and Townsend. Dr. Rolfe Floyd's allusion to Allen and Catholicism is from a letter to me dated July 21, 1930. Richard Burton wrote of his visit to Allen in a letter to me dated May 17 [1930]. "As a painter of love scenes he [Allen] would not easily find his master," appears in a review of *The Choir Invisible* in *The Saturday Review,* LXXXIV (July 3, 1897), 19. *The Nation* regretted the decay of literary allusion in Volume LXIX (November 16, 1899), 36. A letter from The Macmillan Company, dated October 7, 1912, and addressed to Allen at the Majestic Hotel, Philadelphia, mentioned $3,000 as being due on the delivery of the manuscript of *The Heroine in Bronze.* The bill for Allen's purchase of Nietzsche from The Macmillan Company was found among his papers. Best sellers in 1912 are listed in "Chronicle and Comment," *The Bookman,* XXXVI (June, 1913). See bib-

liographies for reviews of books mentioned in this chapter. I am
not at liberty to reveal the line of R. W. Gilder's verse which
offended Allen. Allen's choice of "the best short story in English" is found in a symposium printed in the *New York Times,*
January 25, 1915. Hardy's sonnet is given the date 1866 in *Collected Poems of Thomas Hardy* (New York, 1926), p. 7.
Allen's "Rules for Short Story Writing for Beginners" was
printed in the *Lexington Herald* (December 24, 1916). The
interest of leading English novelists in Allen's works is revealed
in Joyce Kilmer's interview with I. F. Marcosson, *New York
Times Magazine Section,* November 12, 1916. The theme of
The Little Third Person was communicated to me by George Fol-
som Granberry. All Allen's projected works mentioned were
found in fragmentary form among his papers, as were two small
silk French and British flags. Hugh Walpole's appraisal of
American novelists is given in an interview printed in the *New
York Evening Globe,* October 6, 1919. A letter from Eden
Phillpotts to Allen dated April 15, 1919 suggests strongly that
Phillpotts was the original of Edward Blackthorne in *Emblems of
Fidelity.* That Allen always had more stories in mind than he
could write is his declaration in a preface to *The Landmark;*
his broad classification of stories is made in an introduction to the
same volume. Allen called "The Ash-Can" "a most daring and
difficult study" in a letter to M. A. Cassidy dated January 26,
1922. The plan of the first draft of "The Violet" was told me
by Mr. Granberry, who is also authority for the statement that
Allen originally intended to end the story by having a second violet
grow in the place of the stolen one—an ending, it seems to me,
more dramatic than the one finally written. Evidence that Allen
was borrowing, with stocks and bonds as collateral, was found
among his papers.

CHAPTER VII

Allen's memoranda on style were found among his literary
remains. The charge of "saccharine sweetness" was brough
against Allen by Eudora Ramsay Richardson, "The South Grow
Up," *The Bookman,* LXX (January, 1930), 545. Allen'
phrase which I have used to define the Genteel Tradition is foun

on p. 32 of *The Emblems of Fidelity*. For V. F. Calverton's opinion of the genteel writers read *The Liberation of American Literature* (New York, 1932), Chapter V; for Ludwig Lewisohn's read *Expression in America* (New York, 1932), pp. 238-241. The parody of the "hard-boiled" novel, inspired, of course, by the better known writings of William Faulkner and Erskine Caldwell, was directly motivated by reading Faulkner's "Wash," *Harper's Magazine*, CLXVIII (February, 1934), 258-266.

BIBLIOGRAPHY

A chronological list of the writings of James Lane Allen, together with the most significant contemporary reviews of them and the more recent critical appraisals of the man and his work.

1883

"On the First Page of *The Portrait of a Lady*," *The Critic*, III (January 27, 1883), 27-28.

"Henry James and Alphonse Daudet," *The Critic*, III (August 11, 1883), 327.

"Anonymity: The Breadwinners," *The Critic*, III (December 22, 1883), 517-18.

1884

Letter to *The Critic*, IV (January 5, 1884), 10.

"Night Shadows in Poe's Poetry," *The Continent*, V (January 23, 1884), 102-04.

"Keats and His Critics," *The Critic*, IV (February 23, 1884), 85.

"Midwinter" (poem), *Harper's New Monthly Magazine*, LXVIII (March, 1884), 531.

"Henry James on American Traits," *The Continent*, V (March 19, 1884), 361-63.

"Pepys' Appetite," *The Critic*, IV (May 31, 1884), 253.

"A Word about Heine," *The Critic*, V (July 26, 1884), 37.

"The Rifled Hive" (poem), *Lippincott's Magazine*, XXXIV (September, 1884), 247-48.

"Balzac and the Literary Circles of His Time," *Manhattan Magazine*, IV (September, 1884), 308-19.

"Mary Reynolds and *Archibald Malmaison*," *The Critic*, V (September 20, 1884), 133-34.

1885

"Too Much Momentum," *Harper's New Monthly Magazine*, LXX (April, 1885), 701-10.

"The Old Kentucky Home," *New York Evening Post*, July 14, 1885.

"Kentucky Home Speech," *New York Evening Post*, July 27, 1885.

"Beneath the Veil" (poem), *Atlantic Monthly*, LVI (September, 1885), 398-99.

1886

"Local Color," *The Critic*, VIII (January 9, 1886), 13.

"The Blue-Grass Region of Kentucky," *Harper's New Monthly Magazine*, LXXII (February, 1886), 365-82.

"Through Cumberland Gap on Horseback," *Harper's New Monthly Magazine*, LXXIII (June, 1886), 50-66.

"Dr. Jekyll and Dr. Grimshawe," *The Critic*, IX (July 10, 1886), 17.

"Realism and Romance," *New York Evening Post*, July 31, 1886.

1887

"Should Critics Be Gentlemen?" *The Critic*, X (January 15, 1887), 25.

"Part of an Old Story: the Story of Angelo and Francesca," *Century Magazine*, XXXIII (February, 1887), 507-14.

"Mrs. Stowe's Uncle Tom at Home in Kentucky," *Century Magazine*, XXXIV (October, 1887), 853-67.

"Caterpillar Critics," *The Forum*, IV (November, 1887), 332-41.

1888

"Always Bussing His Friends," *The Critic*, XII (March 3, 1888), 99-100.

"Two Kentucky Gentlemen of the Old School," *Century Magazine*, XXXV (April, 1888), 945-57.

"Parturiunt Montes," *The Critic*, XIII (July 21, 1888), 25.

"A Home of the Silent Brotherhood," *Century Magazine*, XXXVI (August, 1888), 483-96.

"The White Cowl," *Century Magazine*, XXXVI (September, 1888), 684-97.

"James Lane Allen, of Chicago," *The Critic*, XIII (September 29, 1888), 155.

1889

"A New-Year Act for the Benefit of Authors," *The Critic*, XIV January 12, 1889), 13-14.

"1819 James Russell Lowell 1889" (letter to *The Critic*), *The Critic*, XIV (February 23, 1889), 95.

"King Solomon of Kentucky," *Century Magazine*, XXXVIII (June, 1889), 244-54.

"County Court Day in Kentucky," *Harper's New Monthly Magazine*, LXXIX (August, 1889), 383-97.

"Kentucky Fairs," *Harper's New Monthly Magazine*, LXXIX (September, 1889), 553-68.

1890

"Posthumous Fame," *Century Magazine*, XXXIX (March, 1890), 671-79.

"Mountain Passes of the Cumberland," *Harper's New Monthly Magazine*, LXXXI (September, 1890), 561-76.

"Taylor's 'Origin of the Aryans' " (unsigned), *The Critic*, XVII (September 6, 1890), 115.

"*The Origin of the Aryans*, Again" (letter signed, The Reviewer), *The Critic*, XVII (November 1, 1890), 224.

"Flute and Violin," *Harper's New Monthly Magazine*, LXXXII (December, 1890), 58-80.

"Sister Dolorosa," *Century Magazine*, LXI (December, 1890), 265-74; (January, 1891), 432-43; (February, 1891), 580-92.

1891

Flute and Violin and Other Kentucky Tales and Romances. New York, Harper & Brothers.

"Certain Criticisms of Certain Tales," *Century Magazine*, XLII (May, 1891), 153-54.

"On Novelties in Pathos," *The Critic*, XIX (October 31, 1891) 233-34.

REVIEWS AND OTHER COMMENTS

Fox, John, Jr. *The Writer*, V (July, 1891), 135.

Page, Thomas Nelson. "Literature in the South Since the War," *Lippincott's Magazine*, XLVIII (November, 1891), 740.

L. H. "A Roman Catholic's View of 'Sister Dolorosa'," *Century Magazine*, XLIII (November, 1891), 157-58.

1892

Flute and Violin and Other Kentucky Tales. Edinburgh, David Douglas.

Sister Dolorosa and Posthumous Fame. Edinburgh, David Douglas.

The Blue-Grass Region of Kentucky and Other Kentucky Articles. New York, Harper & Brothers.

"Homesteads of the Blue-Grass," *Century Magazine*, XLIV (May, 1892), 51-63.

"John Gray," *Lippincott's Magazine*, XLIX (June, 1892), 643.

"In Looking on the Happy Autumn Fields" and "Beneath the Veil" (poems), *Blades o' Bluegrass* (ed. by Fanny P. Dickey). Louisville, Morton.

1893

John Gray: A Kentucky Tale of the Olden Time. Philadelphia, J. B. Lippincott Company.

REVIEWS AND OTHER COMMENTS

"James Lane Allen," *Book News*, XI (May, 1893), 380.

1894

"A Kentucky Cardinal," *Harper's New Monthly Magazine*, LXXXVIII (May, 1894), 926-40, LXXXIX (June, 1894), 20-33.

A Kentucky Cardinal: A Story. New York, Harper & Brothers.

1895

Aftermath. New York, Harper & Brothers.

"English Wood-Notes (with Kentucky Echoes)," *The Southern Magazine*, V (February, 1895), 419-32.

"A Sunday Bird Market in London," *New York Tribune*, March 15, 1895.

"Butterflies: A Tale of Nature," *Cosmopolitan Magazine*, XX (December, 1895), 158-68; (January, 1896), 269-79; (February, 1896), 389-401; (March, 1896), 533-44.

REVIEWS AND OTHER COMMENTS

Banks, Nancy H. "James Lane Allen," *The Bookman*, I (June, 1895), 303-05.

"A Sketch of James Lane Allen" (condensed from the above), *The Literary Digest*, XI (July 6, 1895), 10.

"James Lane Allen of Kentucky," *St. Louis Republic*, July 14, 1895.

1896

Summer in Arcady: A Tale of Nature. New York and London, The Macmillan Company.

A Kentucky Cardinal. London, Osgood, McIlvaine.

"The Gentleman in American Fiction," *The Bookman*, IV (October, 1896), 118-21. This essay was condensed in *The Literary Digest*, XIV (November 14, 1896), 45.

Selection from *Summer in Arcady;* also "Old King Solomon's Coronation," *Library of the World's Best Literature* (ed. by C. D. Warner). New York, Peale and Hill. I, 409-27.

REVIEWS AND OTHER COMMENTS

MacArthur, James. "A Modern Arcadian Idyll," *The Bookman*, III (June, 1896), 347-49.

Fawcett, Waldon. "A Blue-Grass Novelist," *Peterson's Magazine*, n.s. VI (April, 1896), 424-27.

"Force of James Lane Allen's Literary Works," *The Literary Digest*, XII (January 11, 1896), 11-12.

1897

The Choir Invisible. New York and London, The Macmillan Company.

"Two Principles in Recent American Fiction," *Atlantic Monthly*, LXXX (October, 1897), 433-41. This essay was condensed in *The Literary Digest*, XV (October 9, 1897), 701-02.

"Forget Me Death!—O Death, Forget Me Not" (poem), *The Bookman*, VI (December, 1897), 291.

REVIEWS AND OTHER COMMENTS

Mr. James Lane Allen and His Books (pamphlet). New York, The Macmillan Company.

"A Summer in Arcady," *Saturday Review*, LXXXIII (February 20, 1897), 204-05.

"Novelist James Lane Allen," *Kansas City Times*, May 23, 1897.

Gilder, Joseph B. Review of *The Choir Invisible*, *The Critic*, XXX (May 29, 1897), 368.

"Two Opinions of *The Choir Invisible*," *The Literary Digest*, XV (June 19, 1897), 219-20.

MacArthur, James. "A Note on Mr. James Lane Allen," *The Bookman*, V (June, 1897), 288-90.

Mabie, Hamilton Wright. "James Lane Allen," *The Outlook*, LVI (June 5, 1897), 357.

Scudder, H. E. "Mr. Allen's *The Choir Invisible*," *Atlantic Monthly*, LXXX (July, 1897), 143-44.

See also reviews in *Vogue*, IX (February 25, 1897), 126; *The Nation*, LXV (July 1, 1897), 17; *Saturday Review*, LXXXIV (July 3, 1897), 19.

1898

A Kentucky Cardinal. Toronto, Morang.

1899

Two Gentlemen of Kentucky. New York and London, Harper & Brothers.

1900

The Reign of Law: A Tale of the Kentucky Hemp Fields. New York, The Macmillan Company.

A Kentucky Cardinal, The Blue-Grass Region of Kentucky, Flute and Violin, 3 vols. London, The Macmillan Company.

A Kentucky Cardinal and Aftermath. Revised edition with preface. New York and London, The Macmillan Company. Also a tall autographed edition limited to 100 copies. New York, The Macmillan Company.

Chimney Corner Graduates. Springfield, Mass., Home Correspondence School.

"Hemp" (chapter from *The Reign of Law*), *Current Literature,* XXIX (August, 1900), 152-53.

The Choir Invisible, dramatized by Frances Hastings. New York, Liebler & Company.

The Increasing Purpose (English title for *The Reign of Law*). London, The Macmillan Company.

REVIEWS AND OTHER COMMENTS

Mr. James Lane Allen's "The Reign of Law": A Controversy and Some Opinions Concerning It (pamphlet). New York, The Macmillan Company.

Payne, Leonidas W. "The Stories of James Lane Allen," *Sewanee Review,* VIII (January, 1900), 45.

Sherman, Ellen Burns. "The Works of James Lane Allen," *The Book Buyer,* XX (June, 1900), 374-77.

"James Lane Allen: An Inquiry," *The Academy,* LIX (July 14, 1900), 35-36.

LeGallienne, Richard. Article in *Boston Evening Transcript,* August 11, 1900.

Giltner, Leigh Gordon. "James Lane Allen—A Study," *Modern Culture,* XII (December, 1900), 347-52.

Tyler, Joseph Z. "The Historical Background of Allen's *The Reign of Law,*" *Modern Culture,* XII (December, 1900), 352-54.

See also reviews in *The Dial,* XXIX (July 1, 1900), 21-22; *The Athenaeum,* No. 3794 (July 14, 1900), 53; *The Church Standard,* LXXIX (July, 1900), 377; *Catholic News,* XIV (August 18, 1900), 1, 20; *London Times,* September 15, 1900.

1901

"Has the Philippine War Hurt Our Literature?" *St. Louis Republic,* February 10, 1901.

REVIEWS AND OTHER COMMENTS

"Is Mr. Allen's *The Reign of Law* an Infidel Work?" *The Literary Digest,* XXII (February 16, 1901), 198-99.

Bennett, Arnold. *Fame and Fiction*. London, G. Richards. Pp. 169-81.

1902

Strænge Love. Translation of *The Reign of Law*, by J. Christian Bay. Aarhus, Denmark, Aarhus amts Folkeblad's Bogtrykkeri.

"A New Poet" (review of E. A. Valentine's *The Ship of Silence*), *The Outlook*, LXXI (August 9, 1902), 935-38.

"Will the Novel Disappear?" *North American Review*, CLXXV (September, 1902), 290-91.

REVIEWS AND OTHER COMMENTS

Findlater, Jane. "On Religious Novels," *The National Review*, XXXIX (March, 1902), 88-98.

1903

The Mettle of the Pasture. New York and London, The Macmillan Company.

Interview in *The Lamp*, XXVII (September, 1903), 117.

REVIEWS AND OTHER COMMENTS

Carman, Bliss. "Mr. Allen's New Idyll," *New York Times Review of Books and Art*, July 18, 1903.

Hancock, Albert E. "The Art of James Lane Allen," *The Outlook*, LXXIV (August 15, 1903), 953-55.

See also review in *The Athenaeum*, No. 3958 (September 5, 1903), 309-10.

1905

"American Fiction" (review of E. A. Valentine's *Hecla Sandwith*), *New York Times*, April 15, 1905.

Interview in *New York Times*, April 19, 1905.

1906

Burnett, Vivian. "David in *The Reign of Law*," *Book News*, XXIV (July, 1906), 766-67.

Litsey, Edwin C. "James Lane Allen: Biographical Facts and Comments," *Book News*, XXIV (July, 1906), 753.

Rogers, Joseph M. "Lexington in Literature," *Book News,* XXIV (July, 1906), 758-59.
Rutherford, Mildred L. *The South in History and Literature.* Atlanta, Georgia, Franklin-Turner Company. Pp. 586-89.

1907

"Two Gentlemen of Kentucky," *Library of Southern Literature.* Atlanta, Georgia, Martin and Hoyt Company. I, 41-85. Biographical sketch by Isaac F. Marcosson.

1908

"The Last Christmas Tree," *Saturday Evening Post,* CLXXXI (December 5, 1908), 3.
"King Solomon of Kentucky: An Address," *The Outlook,* XC (December 19, 1908), 884-86.

1909

The Bride of the Mistletoe. New York and London, The Macmillan Company.

REVIEWS AND OTHER COMMENTS

"James Lane Allen," *The Academy,* LXXVI (February 20, 1909), 800-03.
"James Lane Allen," *Living Age,* XLIII (7th series) (June 12, 1909), 689-96. Reprinted from the article in *The Academy.*
Burton, Richard. "James Lane Allen's New Story," *The Bellman,* VII (August 28, 1909), 1029.
Mabie, Hamilton Wright. "Summer Novels Worth Reading," *Ladies' Home Journal,* XXVI (August, 1909), 32.
See also the following reviews:
  Bradley, William. *Boston Herald,* July 2, 1909.
  Bradford, John A. *The Bellman,* VII (August 21, 1909), 999-1000.
  Hawthorne, Hildegarde. *The Bookman,* XXIX (July, 1909), 539-41.
  Boston Transcript, June 30, 1909; *The Nation,* LXXXIX (July 1, 1909), 16; *Chicago Evening Post,* July 2, 1909; *New York Times,* July 3, 1909; *Philadelphia*

Press, July 31, 1909; *The Athenaeum,* No. 4265 (July 24, 1909), 91; *The Congregationalist,* XCIV (July 24, 1909), 117; *The Bookman,* XXIX (August, 1909), 578; *Saturday Review,* CVIII (August 21, 1909), 232-33; *Current Literature,* XLVII (September, 1909), 337-38; *The Literary Digest,* XXXIX (September 4, 1909), 349.

1910

The Doctor's Christmas Eve. New York and London, The Macmillan Company.

"The Gentleman in American Fiction" (reprint), *The Bookman,* XXXII (November, 1910), 309.

"James Lane Allen of the Future Christmas" (interview), *New York Times,* December 25, 1910.

REVIEWS AND OTHER COMMENTS

James Lane Allen—A Sketch of the Author of "The Doctor's Christmas Eve" (pamphlet). New York, The Macmillan Company.

Marcosson, Isaac F. "The South in Fiction," *The Bookman,* XXXII (December, 1909), 360-70.

See also reviews in *The Outlook,* XCVI (December 10, 1910), 811-12; *Lexington Herald,* December 18, 1910; *The Literary Digest,* XLI (December 24, 1910), 1205; *The Athenaeum,* No. 4339 (December 24, 1910), 790; *Boston Transcript,* December 24, 1910; *New York Evening Post,* December 31, 1910.

1911

L'Invisible Chœur. Translation of *The Choir Invisible* by A. Bohn. Paris, Fischbacher.

"The National Spirit of Thanksgiving," *Munsey's Magazine,* XLVI (November, 1911), 159-67.

"Song of the Hemp" (poem from The Reign of Law), and "Beneath the Veil" (poem), *The Pathfinder,* V (November, 1911), 8-10.

REVIEWS AND OTHER COMMENTS

Bradley, William A. "James Lane Allen's *The Doctor's Christmas Eve,*" *The Bookman,* XXXII (February, 1911), 640-42.

Jones, T. S., Jr. "On the Fly Leaf of *The Choir Invisible*" (sonnet), *Boston Transcript,* July 7, 1911.

Toulmin, Harry A. *Social Historians.* Boston, Badger. Pp. 101-130.

See also reviews of *The Doctor's Christmas Eve* in *The Nation,* XCII (January 5, 1911), 13; *New York Times,* January 7, 1911.

1912

The Heroine in Bronze, or A Portrait of a Girl. New York and London, The Macmillan Company.

REVIEWS AND OTHER COMMENTS

Bennett, Arnold. "The Future of the American Novel," *North American Review,* CXCV (January, 1912), 76-83.

Markham, Edwin. "Romances in New York's Streets," *Chicago Examiner,* December 28, 1912.

See also *St. Louis Mirror,* November 14, 1912; *The Outlook,* CII (November 23, 1912), 650-51; *Manchester Guardian,* November 27, 1912; *New York Tribune,* December 21, 1912; *Brentano's Book Chat,* December, 1912.

1913

Interview given to James E. King for *Boston Transcript,* August 9, 1912.

REVIEWS AND OTHER COMMENTS

Cooper, Frederick T. "The Magnitude of Themes—Some Recent Novels," *The Bookman,* XXXVI (January, 1913), 558-66.

"Heroine in Bronze," *Review of Reviews,* XLVII (February, 1913), 240.

Mabie, Hamilton Wright. "American Novelists," *The Mentor,* I (August 4, 1913), 1-11.

1914

The Last Christmas Tree: An Idyl of Immortality. Portland, Maine, Thomas B. Mosher. Limited to 1000 copies, 50 on Japan vellum.

Introduction to John Wilson Townsend's *Kentucky in American Letters.* Cedar Rapids, Iowa, Torch Press.

"What is the Best Short Story in English?" (contribution to a symposium), *New York Times,* January 25, 1914.

"On Favorite Shakespeare Quotations," *New York Times,* April 19, 1914.

"A Cathedral Singer," *Century Magazine,* LXXXVIII (May, 1914), 1-26.

"The Sword of Youth," *Century Magazine,* LXXXIX (November, 1914), 1-28; (December, 1914), 209-21; (January, 1915), 442-59.

1915

The Sword of Youth. New York, The Century Company.

Foreword to T. S. Jones's *The Voice in the Silence.* Portland, Maine, Thomas B. Mosher.

Letter from Allen quoted in *Who's Cobb and Why.* New York, Doran.

"War and Literature," *The Bookman,* XL (February, 1915), 648-52.

Message to the Kentucky Educational Association, April 21.

"Great Victorians," *New York Times,* September 5, 1915.

"Short Story Has Deteriorated Since 1895" (interview given to Joyce Kilmer), *New York Times,* October 10, 1915.

REVIEWS AND OTHER COMMENTS

Pattee, Fred Lewis. *History of American Literature Since 1870.* New York, The Century Company. Pp. 365-72.

See also reviews in *Boston Transcript,* February 24; *Philadelphia Public Ledger,* February 27, 1915; *The Nation,* C (March 4, 1915), 250; *New York Evening Post,* March 11, 1915; *Chicago Evening Post,* April 16, 1915; *Pittsburgh Post,* April 17, 1915.

1916

A Cathedral Singer. New York, The Century Company.

Statement on typical American novel, *New York Times,* March 16, 1916.

"Rules for Short Story Writing for Beginners," *Lexington Herald,* December 24, 1916.

REVIEWS AND OTHER COMMENTS

Cassidy, M. A. "James Lane Allen Day in Lexington Schools," *Journal of Education,* LXXXIII (January 13, 1916), 46-47.

Farquhar, E. F. "James Lane Allen: An Inquiry," *Lexington Herald,* December 24, 1916.

See also reviews in *Boston Transcript,* March 18, 1916; *New York Times,* March 19, 1916; *London Times,* April 13, 1916; *The Nation,* CIII (July 13, 1916), 38-39; *Life,* LXVIII (July 20, 1916), 118.

1917

"Tribute to William Dean Howells on His Eightieth Birthday," *New York Times,* March 25, 1917.

"Bywords of the War," *New York Times,* May 5, 1917.

Letters on the Teuton nations' replies to the Pope on the question of peace, *New York Times,* September 24, 1917.

"The German Fox," *New York Times,* December 29, 1917.

REVIEWS AND OTHER COMMENTS

Pattee, Fred Lewis. "The Short Story," *Cambridge History of American Literature.* New York, G. P. Putnam's Sons. II, 388, 390.

Cook, E. A. "James Lane Allen," *The Bellman,* XXIII (October 6, 1917), 378-80.

1918

The Kentucky Warbler. Garden City, Doubleday Page; London, Cassell.

REVIEWS AND OTHER COMMENTS

Review in *The Dial,* LXIV (March 14, 1918), 248.

1919

The Emblems of Fidelity: A Comedy in Letters. Garden City, Doubleday, Page.

"On the Mantelpiece: Audi Alteram Partem" (poem), *The Bookman*, L (September, 1919), 91-94.

"Henry Mills Alden," *The Bookman*, L (November, 1919), 330-36.

REVIEWS AND OTHER COMMENTS

Grozier, Edwin A. *One Hundred Best Novels Condensed.* New York, Harper and Brothers. P. 110.

Marcosson, Isaac F. "Some Literary Friendships," *Saturday Evening Post*, CXCII (August 16, 1919), 8-9, 104, 107, 110.

Walpole, Hugh. Interview in *New York Evening Globe*, October 6, 1919.

See also reviews in *New York Times*, March 9, 1919; *Providence Journal*, April 20, 1919; *Springfield Republican*, April 28, 1919; *Boston Transcript*, April 30, 1919; *The Nation*, CVIII (May 3, 1919), 699-700; *London Times*, November 13, 1919.

1920

"Heaven's Little Ironies," *The Bookman*, LI (August, 1920), 616-19.

"Old Mill on the Elkhorn," *The Miller's Holiday: Short Stories from "The Northwestern Miller"* (Minneapolis, Miller Publishing Company), pp. 133-91.

REVIEWS AND OTHER COMMENTS

Marcosson, Isaac F. *Adventures in Interviewing.* London, Lane. Pp. 24-27, 36, 228-32, 243, 255, 259, 260, 271, 298.

1921

"The Ash-Can," *Century Magazine*, CII (September, 1921), 657-67.

REVIEWS AND OTHER COMMENTS

Van Doren, Carl. *The American Novel.* New York, The Macmillan Company. Pp. 248, 258.

1922

"Miss Locke," *Century Magazine,* CIII (March, 1922), 676-98.

Reviews and Other Comments

Van Doren, Carl. *Contemporary Novelists, 1900-1920.* New York, The Macmillan Company. Pp. 24-27.

1923

"The Alabaster Box," *Harper's Magazine,* CXLVII (August, 1923), 338-50.
The Alabaster Box. New York, Harper & Brothers.
Flute and Violin and Other Stories. Edinburgh, Foulis.

Reviews and Other Comments

Pattee, Fred Lewis. *The Development of the American Short Story.* New York, Harper and Brothers. Pp. 312-13.
Cassidy, M. A. "Dr. James Lane Allen," *Journal of Education,* XCIII (October 18, 1923), 378-79.

1924

"The Violet," *Harper's Magazine,* CXLIX (June, 1924), 41-56.
"A Message," *The Transylvanian,* XXXIII (June, 1924), 1.
A Kentucky Cardinal and Aftermath (edited for school use by Jane C. Tunnell). New York, The Macmillan Company.

1925

The Landmark (published posthumously). New York, The Macmillan Company.
"King Solomon of Kentucky," *Great Short Stories of the World* (edited by B. H. Clark and Maxim Lieber). New York, R. M. McBride and Company. Pp. 984-1001.
"King Solomon of Kentucky," *The Golden Book,* I (May, 1925), 692-702.

Obituary Notices

New York Times, February 19 and 20, 1925; *New York World,* February 19, 1925; *New York Evening Post,* February 20, 1925; *Lexington Herald,* February 21, 1925; *Lexingto*

Leader, February 21, 1925; John H. Finley in *New York Times Book Review,* March 1, 1925; Joseph B. Gilder in letter to *New York Times,* March 7, 1925; *The Nation* CXX (March 4, 1925), 229; *The Outlook,* CXXXIX (March 4, 1925), 330.

1926

A Kentucky Cardinal and Aftermath (in Modern Readers' Series, ed. by Jane C. Tunnell). New York, The Macmillan Company.

1927

"A Kentucky Cardinal," *The Golden Book,* V (February, 1927), 202-20; (March, 1927), 402-09: (April, 1927), 527-37.

REVIEWS AND OTHER COMMENTS

Hazard, Lucy Lockwood. *The Frontier in American Literature.* New York, Thomas Y. Crowell Company. Pp. 75-77.
Smith, C. Alphonso. *Southern Literary Studies.* Chapel Hill, N. C., The University of North Carolina Press. P. 67.
Townsend, John Wilson. *James Lane Allen: A Personal Note.* Louisville, Courier-Journal Job Printing Company.

1928

Knight, Grant C. "Allen's Christmas Trilogy and Its Meaning," *The Bookman,* LXVIII (December, 1928), 411-15.
———. "James Lane Allen and Fayette County," *Lexington Herald,* June 27.
Nelson, John H. Article in *Dictionary of American Biography.* New York, Charles Scribner's Sons. I, 195-97.

1929

"Aftermath," *The Golden Book,* X (July, 1929), 94-105; (August, 1929), 94-105; (September, 1929), 93-107.
"Two Gentlemen of Kentucky," *The Literature of America* (ed. by Quinn, Baugh, and Howe). New York, Charles Scribner's Sons. Pp. 1131-1143.

1934

"King Solomon of Kentucky," *A Book of the Short Story* (ed. by
E. A. Cross). New York, American Book Company. Pp.
414-30.

PROJECTED AND UNPUBLISHED WORKS

"The Novelist" (long essay).

"The Days of Our Fathers: A Kentucky Novel of the Older
America" (novel, possibly a trilogy).

"Autobiography."

"The Exiles of a Night, or The Bridge" (short story).

"A Pilgrim to His Youth" (novel).

"A Flickering Candle" (short story).

"The Belfry of the Years" (also "Gather Ye Rosebuds" novel).

"The Promoters" (drama).

"The Solid Ground" (novel).

"Socrates at the White House" (dialogue).

"In Praise of Light" (also "In Praise of Candles," essay).

"The Hidden Life" (essay).

"Fiction in Letter Form" (essay).

INDEX